DATABASE & DATA WAREHOUSING TECHNOLOGIES

Database & Data Warehousing Technologies

Editor:

Dr. Jovan Pehcevski, Ph.D.

ArclerPress

www.arclerpress.com

Database & Data Warehousing Technologies
Editor: Dr. Jovan Pehcevski, Ph.D.

708 3rd Avenue, 6th Floor
New York
NY 10017
United States of America
www.arclerpress.com

ISBN: 978-1-68094-464-8

Library of Congress Control Number: 2016951157

Arcler Press LLC publishes wide variety of books and eBooks. For more information about Arcler Press and its products, visit our website at www.arclerpress.com

About the Editor

Dr. Jovan Pehcevski, Ph.D.

Jovan obtained his PhD in Computer Science from RMIT University in Melbourne, Australia in 2007. His research interests include big data, business intelligence and predictive analytics, data and information science, information retrieval, XML, web services and service-oriented architectures, and relational and NoSQL database systems. He has published over 30 journal and conference papers and he also serves as a journal and conference reviewer. He is currently working as a Dean and Associate Professor at European University in Skopje, Macedonia.

Contents

List of Contributors

Palllavi Kalokhe
Department of Information Technology, Gharda Institute of Technology, Lavel, Khed, Maharashtra, India

Kranti Gajmal
Department of Information Technology, Gharda Institute of Technology, Lavel, Khed, Maharashtra, India

Rasim Alguliev
Institute of Information Technology of ANAS, Baku, Azerbaijan

Rena Gasimova
Institute of Information Technology of ANAS, Baku, Azerbaijan

Rajni Jindal
Dept. of Computer Engineering, Delhi Technological University Formerly Delhi College of Engineering (DCE), Bawana Road, Delhi-42

Shweta Taneja
Dept. of Computer Engineering, Delhi Technological University Formerly Delhi College of Engineering (DCE), Bawana Road, Delhi-42

Azwa Abdul Aziz
Faculty of Informatics, Department of Computer Science, University Sultan Zainal Abidin (UniSZA), 21030, Gong Badak, Terengganu Malaysia

Md Yazid Mohd Saman
Faculty of Informatics, Department of Computer Science, University Sultan Zainal Abidin (UniSZA), 21030, Gong Badak, Terengganu Malaysia

Mohd Pouzi Hamzah
Faculty of Informatics, Department of Computer Science, University Sultan Zainal Abidin (UniSZA), 21030, Gong Badak, Terengganu Malaysia

Erappa G.
HMS institute of Technology, Tumkur

Dr. K. Krishnamoorthy
Sudharsan Engineering College, Pudukkottai, Tamilnadu

Thippaswamy G.
Bangalore Technological Institute, Bangalore

G.Satyanarayana Reddy
CMR College of Information Technology, Hyderabad, India

Rallabandi Srinivasu
St. Mary's Group of Institutions, Hyderabad, India

M. Poorna Chander Rao
MCA Dept. St.Mary's College of Engg. & Technology, Hyderabad, India

Srikanth Reddy Rikkula
MCA Dept. St.Mary's College of Engg. & Technology, Hyderabad, India

Cornelia Kraus
Teradata Corporation, Augsburg, Germany

Raul Valverde
Department of Supply Chain Management and Technology Management, Concordia University, Montreal, Canada

M. Victoria Hebseeba
Department of Computer Science, Rayalaseema University, Andhra Pradesh

Dr. T. Bhasakara Reddy
Department of Computer Science, S.K University, Andhra Pradesh

Prof. B. Lakshma Reddy
Director, Garden City College, Bangalore, Karnataka

Dr. T. Venkateswarulu
Department of Computer Science, Gate College, Tirupathi

Alexandre Borba Salvador
Faculty of Management, Economics and Accounting, University of São Paulo, São Paulo, Brazil

Ana Akemi Ikeda
Faculty of Management, Economics and Accounting, University of São Paulo, São Paulo, Brazil

Dr.Osama E.Sheta
Department of Mathematics Faculty of Science, Zagazig University, Zagazig, Elsharkia, Egypt.

Ahmed Nour Eldeen
Department of Mathematics Faculty of Science, Zagazig University, Zagazig, Elsharkia, Egypt.

Qiang Wang
Orthopedic Surgery, Changshu Hospital Affiliated to Nanjing University of Chinese Medicine, Changshu, China

Yingchao Shen
Orthopedic Surgery, Changshu Hospital Affiliated to Nanjing University of Chinese Medicine, Changshu, China

Francesco Pessina
Department of Electronics and Information, Politecnico di Milano, Milan, Italy

Marco Masseroli
Department of Electronics and Information, Politecnico di Milano, Milan, Italy

Arif Canakoglu
Department of Electronics and Information, Politecnico di Milano, Milan, Italy

Kolja Henckel
Bioinformatics Resource Facility, Center for Biotechnology, Bielefeld University, Bielefeld, Germany
International Graduate School in Bioinformatics and Genome Research, Bielefeld University, Bielefeld, Germany
Technical Faculty, Bielefeld University, Bielefeld, Germany
Computational Genomics, Center for Biotechnology, Bielefeld University, Bielefeld, Germany
Faculty for Biology and Genetics, Bielefeld University, Bielefeld, Germany

Kai J Runte
Bioinformatics Resource Facility, Center for Biotechnology, Bielefeld University, Bielefeld, Germany
Computational Genomics, Center for Biotechnology, Bielefeld University, Bielefeld, Germany
Faculty for Biology and Genetics, Bielefeld University, Bielefeld, Germany

Thomas Bekel
Bioinformatics Resource Facility, Center for Biotechnology, Bielefeld University, Bielefeld, Germany
Computational Genomics, Center for Biotechnology, Bielefeld University, Bielefeld, Germany
Faculty for Biology and Genetics, Bielefeld University, Bielefeld, Germany

Michael Dondrup
Bioinformatics Resource Facility, Center for Biotechnology, Bielefeld University, Bielefeld, Germany
Computational Genomics, Center for Biotechnology, Bielefeld University, Bielefeld, Germany
Faculty for Biology and Genetics, Bielefeld University, Bielefeld, Germany

Tobias Jakobi
Bioinformatics Resource Facility, Center for Biotechnology, Bielefeld University, Bielefeld, Germany
Technical Faculty, Bielefeld University, Bielefeld, Germany
Faculty for Biology and Genetics, Bielefeld University, Bielefeld, Germany

Helge Küster
International Graduate School in Bioinformatics and Genome Research, Bielefeld University, Bielefeld, Germany
Faculty for Biology and Genetics, Bielefeld University, Bielefeld, Germany
Genomics of Legume Plants, Institute for Genome Research and Systems Biology, Center for Biotechnology, Bielefeld University, Bielefeld, Germany
Institute for Plant Genetics, Leibniz Universität Hannover, Germany

Alexander Goesmann
Bioinformatics Resource Facility, Center for Biotechnology, Bielefeld University, Bielefeld, Germany

Computational Genomics, Center for Biotechnology, Bielefeld University, Bielefeld, Germany
Faculty for Biology and Genetics, Bielefeld University, Bielefeld, Germany

Assia Rharbi
AMIPS Mohammadia School of Engineers, University Mohammed V, Agdal, Rabat, Morocco

Khadija Amine
Laboratory GAIA Spectroscopy Faculty of Science Ain Chock - University Hassan II, Casablanca, Morocco
Search Laboratory Lipoprotein and Atherosclerosis Research Unit Associated with CNRS-34-URAC, Faculty of Sciences Ben Msik-Casablanca, Hassan II Mohammedia University, Morocco

Zohra Bakkoury
AMIPS Mohammadia School of Engineers, University Mohammed V, Agdal, Rabat, Morocco

Afaf Mikou
Laboratory GAIA Spectroscopy Faculty of Science Ain Chock - University Hassan II, Casablanc, Morocco

Anass Kettani
Search Laboratory Lipoprotein and Atherosclerosis Research Unit Associated with CNRS-34-URAC, Faculty of Sciences Ben Msik-Casablanca, Hassan II Mohammedia University, Morocco

Abdelkader Betari
ENSA Oujda, Université Mohammed Premier Oujda, Morocco

Habiba Mejhed
Cadi Ayyad University, Marrakech Computer Engineering Department, Micro Computer Lab on Chip Embedded Systems. National School of Applied Sciences, Morocco
Cadi Ayyad University, Marrakech Laboratory of Ecology and Environment, Faculty of Science Semlalia, Morocco

Samia Boussaa
University Louis Pasteur Strasbourg I, Laboratory of Parasitology, Faculty of Pharmacy, France

Nour El Houda Mejhed
University Sidi Mohammed Ben Abdellah, Fes Computer Engineering Department, National School of Applied Sciences in Fes, Morocco

Xuanzi Hu
Dongguan College, China

Benjapuk Jongmuenwai
Informatics Program. Nakhon Ratchasima Rajabhat University, 340 Suranarai road. Tumbon Naimaung. Maung District. Nakhon Ratchasima 30000, Thailand

Parinya Chinjoho
Informatics Program. Nakhon Ratchasima Rajabhat University, 340 Suranarai road. Tumbon Naimaung. Maung District. Nakhon Ratchasima 30000, Thailand

Sangpetch Prachai
Informatics Program. Nakhon Ratchasima Rajabhat University, 340 Suranarai road. Tumbon Naimaung. Maung District. Nakhon Ratchasima 30000, Thailand

Pelin Vardarlıer
School of Business and Management Science, Istanbul Medipol University, Beykoz, İstanbul, 34810, Turkey

Gökhan Silahtaroğlu
School of Business and Management Science, Istanbul Medipol University, Beykoz, İstanbul, 34810, Turkey

Preface

Data Warehouse is a type of data organization on which decision-making systems are based. The data storage in a data warehouse system typically needs to fully cover one or more business areas (e.g., procurement, sales), and the data in the data warehouse needs to be comprehensive, meaning that it should be fully integrated with the internal data organization. These data records must include a longer period of time (five, ten or more years) because this longer time periodical analysis is very significant for every business. Smaller data warehouses that include data from only one business area are called sectorial warehouses, or data marts.

The data warehouse is designed for managers, but also for everyone performing various analytical tasks, such as monitoring and reporting operations based on different business rules and carried out by placing directed queries and analysis of the results obtained; analysis and diagnosis jobs based on skills, performing an iterative analysis and discovery of the information needed; and planning and simulation operations based on knowledge, performing modeling and execution of a drafted model. The usual system design splits the database and the data warehouse, where the database is concerned with transactions and queries, while the warehouse enables analytical reports and a decision support system. Since the data warehouse is oriented towards business analysis, its storage does not need to be promptly updated as is the case with the data in the associated relational database. Today, with hardware advancements and the advanced design of database management systems, the database and the data warehouse can be stored on the same data server (in the same data center). Such database management systems can separately handle the transactions and the analytical reports. The main users of data warehouse systems are big businesses (banks, telecoms, big retailers, e-commerce portals) and their potential use cases include consumers' behavior prediction, product recommendations, fraud detection, future trends envisioning etc. Data warehouses are also used in medical/genomic research studies, since biomedical questions are usually complex, and numerous valuables and heterogeneous data are increasingly available to answer these questions. Data warehouses have also been applied to public institutions that offer e-government services, processing spatial data mostly collected from Geographical Information Systems (GIS). This edition covers topics from data warehouse technology aspects, as well as applications of data warehouses in the business sector, bio-medical domain and the public sector. Section 1 focuses on data warehouse technology, describing data warehouse design using process-oriented requirement analysis, data registration of domain names in the data warehouse construction task, comparative study of data warehouse design approaches, base analysis techniques in data qualities framework for data warehouses, and critical factors influencing the adoptions of a data warehouse. Section 2 focuses on data warehouse applications in the business sector, describing essential elements to support decision-making process in industries, data warehouse design for the detection of fraud in the supply chain, data load manifestation in process chains in SAP business warehouse, and big data usage in the marketing information system. Section 3 focuses on data warehouse applications in the bio-medical domain, describing building a health care data warehouse for cancer diseases, building an osteoporosis data warehouse in the osteoporosis community, complex queries on an integrative genomic and proteomic data warehouse, Truncatulix – a data warehouse for the legume community, and approaches to access biological data sources. Section 4 focuses on data warehouse applications in the public sector, describing data warehouse for leishmaniosis in Marrakech City, data warehouse technology and application in data center design for e-government, data warehouse use of geographic information system for ornamentals, and gossip management at universities using the big data warehouse model.

Editor

Dr. Jovan Pehcevski, Ph.D.

INTRODUCTION

A database is a collection of information that is organized so that it can easily be accessed, managed, and updated. In one view, databases can be classified according to types of content: bibliographic, full-text, numeric, and images.

In computing, databases are sometimes classified according to their organizational approach. The most prevalent approach is the relational database, a tabular database in which data is defined so that it can be reorganized and accessed in a number of different ways. A distributed database is one that can be dispersed or replicated among different points in a network. An object-oriented programming database is one that is congruent with the data defined in object classes and subclasses.

Computer databases typically contain aggregations of data records or files, such as sales transactions, product catalogs and inventories, and customer profiles. Typically, a database manager provides users the capabilities of controlling read/write access, specifying report generation, and analyzing usage. Databases and database managers are prevalent in large mainframe systems, but are also present in smaller distributed workstation and mid-range systems such as the AS/400 and on personal computers. SQL (Structured Query Language) is a standard language for making interactive queries from and updating a database such as IBM's DB2, Microsoft's SQL Server, and database products from Oracle, Sybase, and Computer Associates.

Data warehousing combines data from multiple, usually varied, sources into one comprehensive and easily manipulated database. Different methods can then be used by a company or organization to access this data for a wide range of purposes. Analysis can be performed to determine trends over time and to create plans based on this information. Smaller companies often use more limited formats to analyze more precise or smaller data sets, though warehousing can also utilize these methods

Accessing Data through Warehousing

Common methods for accessing systems of data warehousing include queries, reporting, and analysis. Because warehousing creates one database, the number of sources can be nearly limitless, provided the system can handle the volume. The final result, however, is homogeneous data, which can be more easily manipulated. System queries are used to gain information from a warehouse and this creates a report for analysis.

Uses for Data Warehouses

Companies commonly use data warehousing to analyze trends over time. They might use it to view day-to-day operations, but its primary function is often strategic planning based on long-term data overviews. From such reports, companies make business models, forecasts, and other projections. Routinely, because the data stored in data warehouses is intended to provide more overview-like reporting, the data is read-only.

This does not mean that data warehousing involves information that is never updated. On the contrary, the data stored in warehouses is updated all the time. It is the reporting and the analysis that take more of a long-term view.

Limitations on Warehousing

Data warehousing is not always the best method for storing all of a company's data. Companies often use it to house the necessary information for specific analysis. More comprehensive data storage requires different capacities that are more static and less easily manipulated than those used for warehousing. This can include internal servers or data storage terminals meant to be accessed and used by various individuals within a business.

Smaller Solutions for Data Storage

While larger companies typically use data warehousing to analyze big sets of information for enterprise purposes, smaller companies wishing to review just one subject often utilize "data marts." These are much more specific and targeted in their storage and reporting. Data warehousing can include smaller amounts of data grouped into "marts," which are then connected together as part of the larger system. In this way, a major company might use both warehousing and data marts, letting users choose the best source and functionality depending on their current needs.

What is the Difference between Data Warehousing and Business Intelligence?

Data warehousing and business intelligence are two terms that are a common source of confusion, both inside and outside of the information technology (IT) industry. Usually, data warehousing refers to the technology used to actually create a repository of data. Business intelligence refers to the tools and applications used in the analysis and interpretation of data. These two elements have grown substantially and are forecast to experience continued growth into the future.

Data warehousing is comprised of two primary tools: databases and hardware. In a data warehouse, there are multiple databases and data tables used to store information. These tables are related to each other through the use of common information or keys. The size of a data warehouse is limited by the storage capacity of the hardware.

The hardware required for a data warehouse includes a server, hard drives, and processors. In most organizations, the data is accessible via the shared network or Intranet. A data architect usually is responsible for setting up the database structure and managing the process for the updating of data from the original sources.

Business intelligence is a term used to describe analytical software. Data warehousing and business intelligence solutions can work together to provide and support a user dashboard that offers customized information to the user. The software provided in a business intelligence solution usually includes the ability to manage large data sets, create queries, and generate reports. An important aspect of any business intelligence solution is the usability.

The primary distinction between these solutions is their purpose. A data warehouse is designed to hold and support the transactional data, while the business intelligence solution is used to access and review the data. These terms often are used interchangeably, but mean very different things.

Staff members who work with data warehousing and business intelligence tools typically must have a combination of information technology skills. They must be able to manage and support the technology, from both a hardware and software perspective. Additional skills for data warehousing staff usually include relational database management and creation of database structures. Business intelligence staff usually must have training in statistics and mathematics, as well as programming logic.

The growth in these two solutions is due to the maturity of business technology. As organizations accumulated more transactional data, they needed a way to access that data in a meaningful way. These tools are used to create reports that can identify trends and help to inform sound business decisions.

What is Data Warehouse Architecture?

Data warehouse architecture is a design that encapsulates all the facets of data warehousing for an enterprise environment. Data warehousing is the creation of a central domain to store complex, decentralized enterprise data in a logical unit that enables data mining, business intelligence, and overall access to all relevant data within an organization. Data warehouse architecture is inclusive of all reporting requirements, data management, security requirements, band width requirements, and storage requirements.

When creating a data warehouse architecture, it is important to break the architecture into specific domains that are joined into a holistic final design. This design should be considered the blue print for the enterprise data architecture. In particular, several primary areas should be developed when considering data warehouse architecture. These areas are source system access, staging area process, data enrichment process, data architecture, business intelligence process, and storage requirements.

Data warehousing requires source data to be transferred from a transactional or database of record into the data warehouse. This process is simplified into the term Extract Transform and Load (ETL), which basically encapsulates the areas of source system access, data enrichment, and data architecture. For the sake of clarity, it is better to design these architectural areas in detail, which outlines how the ETL process will be achieved. While some data is required from the source systems, all data is not desirable as it would overburden the enterprise warehouse. The primary areas of concern when addressing the source system layer are data access methodologies, data required from the source system, and refresh requirements.

The next data warehousing architectural layer to consider is the staging area process. As most data from source systems will require validation and data cleansing, it is important to create a landing zone for source data to reside prior to loading into the business rules layer of the data warehouse. The staging area maintains raw data feeds from source systems that are typically time stamped to ensure the recentness of data.

The data enrichment or business rules process is where data is cleaned to meet the desired outcome of the data warehouse. A good example of this cleansing approach is using address cleansing tools; in the event the source system has incorrect data, the data enrichment process will run the address from the raw data set into a business rule system that would correct invalid addresses. This is also the time where inaccurate data is deleted or modified to ensure completeness within the data warehouse.

The next layer to consider is the data architecture layer. This area is where the true design or schema of the enterprise data warehouse is completed. Data warehousing in not a combination of all the data sets within an enterprise, but instead it is a newly defined database built to enable an overview of all business entities within the enterprise.

This requires the data architecture to answer the questions that will be posed by the business in the area of business intelligence and data mining. By creating the data architecture in this manner, the raw data sets will be transformed into fact tables that will allow the users to perform ad-hoc reporting on the entire enterprise view rather than a specific database. This is also the area that will maintain metadata about the data from the raw system, which could include the source system name or primary keys.

The next area to consider is the business intelligence and reporting requirements. This layer can be thought of as the user-facing requirement for the data warehousing. Typically, this area contains canned reports, ad-hoc reporting capability, and enterprise dash boards or alerts. The business intelligence layers normally get the most consideration, as it is the only outward-facing component within the data warehouse.

The final layer for consideration is overall data storage requirements and maintenance. As a data warehouse continues to grow and expand, user base data storage must be strictly managed and maintained. Additionally, while creating the data warehouse architecture, the design should make realistic estimates as to what will be required form a data storage capacity as well as a band with data access capacity. These requirements will be critical as the data warehouse become widely used throughout the enterprise.

Data Warehouse Architecture

Data warehouse architecture is a design that encapsulates all the facets of data warehousing for an enterprise environment. Data warehousing is the creation of a central domain to store complex, decentralized enterprise data in a logical unit that enables data mining, business intelligence, and overall access to all relevant data within an organization. Data warehouse architecture is inclusive of all reporting requirements, data management, security requirements, band width requirements, and storage requirements.

When creating a data warehouse architecture, it is important to break the architecture into specific domains that are joined into a holistic final design. This design should be considered the blue print for the enterprise data architecture. In particular, several primary areas should be developed when considering data warehouse architecture. These areas are source system access, staging area process, data enrichment process, data architecture, business intelligence process, and storage requirements.

Data warehousing requires source data to be transferred from a transactional or database of record into the data warehouse. This process is simplified into the term Extract Transform and Load (ETL), which basically encapsulates the areas of source system access, data enrichment, and data architecture. For the sake of clarity, it is better to design these architectural areas in detail, which outlines how the ETL process will be achieved. While some data is required from the source systems, all data is not desirable as it would overburden the enterprise warehouse. The primary areas of concern when addressing the source system layer are data access methodologies, data required from the source system, and refresh requirements.

The next data warehousing architectural layer to consider is the staging area process. As most data from source systems will require validation and data cleansing, it is important to create a landing zone for source data to reside prior to loading into the business rules layer of the data warehouse. The staging area maintains raw data feeds from source systems that are typically time stamped to ensure the recentness of data.

The data enrichment or business rules process is where data is cleaned to meet the desired outcome of the data warehouse. A good example of this cleansing approach is using address cleansing tools; in the event the source system has incorrect data, the data enrichment process will run the address from the raw data set into a business rule system that would correct invalid addresses. This is also the time where inaccurate data is deleted or modified to ensure completeness within the data warehouse.

The next layer to consider is the data architecture layer. This area is where the true design or schema of the enterprise data warehouse is completed. Data warehousing in not a combination of all the data sets within an enterprise, but instead it is a newly defined database built to enable an overview of all business entities within the enterprise.

This requires the data architecture to answer the questions that will be posed by the business in the area of business intelligence and data mining. By creating the data architecture in this manner, the raw data sets will be transformed into fact tables that will allow the users to perform ad-hoc reporting on the entire enterprise view rather then a specific database. This is also the area that will maintain metadata about the data from the raw system, which could include the source system name or primary keys.

The next area to consider is the business intelligence and reporting requirements. This layer can be thought of as the user-facing requirement for the data warehousing. Typically, this area contains canned reports, ad-hoc reporting capability, and enterprise dash boards or alerts. The business intelligence layers normally get the most consideration, as it is the only outward-facing component within the data warehouse.

The final layer for consideration is overall data storage requirements and maintenance. As a data warehouse continues to grow and expand, user base data storage must be strictly managed and maintained. Additionally, while creating the data warehouse architecture, the design should make realistic estimates as to what will be required form a data storage capacity as well as a band with data access capacity. These requirements will be critical as the data warehouse become widely used throughout the enterprise.

Real Time Data Warehousing

Also known as active data warehousing, real time data warehousing is the process of storing and analyzing data in some type of storage system. Companies tend to make use of this approach in an ongoing effort to maximize the usefulness of various forms of business intelligence, especially in terms of positioning the company for growth through sales. By capturing the information at it becomes available and assimilating the data with historical information, it is possible to predict shifts in customer demand, as well as develop new marketing strategies that will draw in new customers.

The basic process of real time data warehousing requires that data added to a transactional database, such as an order placement or invoicing system, is immediately analyzed, classified, and related to information that is already warehoused from previous transactions. Ideally, the additional information will yield additional information that helps to point to trends within the purchase of goods or services offered by the company, the generation of profits or losses.

By assimilating and assessing transactions and other data as they occur, the company can move faster to take advantage of an upward trend that holds the potential to earn the business a significant return. Because the process of real time data warehousing is automatic, there is no need for anyone to activate this trickling down of data from various transactional databases into the central real time database. Thus, it is possible to access the updated bank of information at any time, and use that data to plan future projects or actions that will be in the best interests of the company.

This process of data mining in a real time fashion can also include automatic generation of reports that are customized to the needs of the end user. The data warehouse design often allows users to choose from a set of pre-programmed report formats, or to use tools built into the software package to create specialized reports that arrange data in any number of ways. This versatile data warehouse architecture makes it simple for corporations of different sizes and related to different fields to use the same basic software, but adapt the usage of that software to fit their individual needs.

Most real time data warehousing packages also allow for the generation of reports on-demand as well as on a set schedule. This can be extremely helpful, as it is possible to submit a query on the spur of the moment, and have an answer within a matter of seconds or minutes. For example, if a sales manager is presented with a question about the current day's sales of a given product line, he or she can simply frame the query, have the software pull the up-to-the minute data, and have a report that provides the information with ease. More conventional methods would require up to a half-hour or more to manage what the real time warehousing can manage in less than three minutes.

In an era when even a few minutes can mean the difference between success and failure, the use of real time data warehousing not only provides a simple means of storing all relevant data in a common repository. This approach also means having the information on hand at any time to make decisions with the potential to increase the bottom line for any company. For this reason, many businesses, both large and small, are integrating real time software into their overall business intelligence archiving and retrieval processes.

What are the Different Types of Data Warehousing Tools?

Data warehousing tools included in a standard software package can be divided into four primary categories: data extraction, table management, query management, and data integrity. A data warehouse is a repository for large sets of transactional data, which can vary widely, depending on the discipline and the focus of the organization. For example, many scientific research projects collect huge amounts of data for analysis and review. A data warehouse may be the best technology to manage and store this information. It is important to note that specific skill sets are required for all staff who work with data warehousing tools. This type of technology requires training in statistics, advanced math, processing logic, relational databases, and advanced computer skills. Many people in this field began their careers in statistics or computer science. The concepts used to create and manage the data flow are quite complex and require significant time and effort to master.

A data warehouse requires a method of adding data to it, and an extraction, transform, and load (ETL) tool is typically used for this purpose. The tool itself is a software program used to correctly identify the appropriate information from another computer system, based on the user's criteria. This data may need to be normalized or modified for consistency or to match the warehouse database structure. Loading the data is critical, as all the relationships and connections to other databases must be maintained to ensure the integrity of the database, so it can be used with other tools. Every data warehouse contains a vast number of database tables that are organized to work with each other in a logical, systematic way. The maintenance of these tables is essential to the continuing operation and accuracy of the data warehouse. Using the concept of relational databases, they must be maintained and validated on a regular basis because any faults or failures will result in inaccurate reporting. A query is simply a programmed question or report request, and there is an entire business process surrounding the creation of a data warehouse query. This process requires in-depth knowledge and understanding of the business needs, as well as the data structures within the data warehouse. Business intelligence specialists are trained professionals who have the combination of skills and training necessary to create and manage multiple, customized queries. A data integrity function is standard in most warehousing tools. These modules are often extremely complex to use, with multiple options and functions available, but they are absolutely essential to the creation and maintenance of a functioning, useful data warehouse. Data integrity tools check for consistency within the data, accurate connections between databases, and clean programming logic. Poor data integrity will result in a data warehouse that provides inaccurate reports, resulting is poor business decisions.

SECTION I: DATA WAREHOUSE TECHNOLOGY

1

CHAPTER

DATA WAREHOUSE DESIGN USING PROCESS-ORIENTED REQUIREMENT ANALYSIS

Palllavi Kalokhe and Kranti Gajmal

Keywords: Data Warehouse, Business Process, Process Orientation.

INTRODUCTION

A data warehouse is multidimensional modeled and is used for the storage of historicized, cleansed, validated, synthesized, operative, internal and external data. Stakeholders of a data warehouse system are interested in analyzing their business processes in a comprehensive and flexible way. What they actually need is a view of their business processes and its data. For this purpose data warehouses are modeled multidimensional, which corresponds to a typical view of its users. This analysis view of the business processes can be very different to the general view even though the underlying process is the same. Hence it is necessary to elicit requirements from the stakeholder of a data warehouse, which belong to their analysis views. The design of data warehouse system is highly dependent on these requirements. Often the users, the system analysts and developers don't speak the same language. Such communication problems can make it difficult to turn description of an analysis system into a technical specification of a data warehouse system that all parties can understand. Therefore, it will not deliver the expected effect to the company. In these cases often departments will develop data marts for their own purposes, which can be considered as stovepipes and makes an enterprise-wide analysis system impossible.

The challenge is to model a data warehouse system in a way that is both precise and user-friendly. Each symbol describing the analysis process should be intuitive for

Citation: Palllavi Kalokhe and Kranti Gajmal, Data Warehouse Design using Process-Oriented Requirement Analysis, ISSN: 2278-621X.

the user and have defined semantics, so that the developers can use the description as a general, but precise specification of the data warehouse system. Use cases have two advantages, which make them suitable for representing the requirements for a data warehouse system. Important characteristics that such a model should possess are:

- *A high level of abstraction.* The model should be at the level of the users' views of the desired system. It should not indiscriminately mix this high level information with information that is relevant to lower levels of the development process.
- *Human-readability.* The language in which the model is to be expressed will be used for validating the specification: that is, for presenting the specification to users for their views on its contents. Human understandability is thus the prime concern.
- *Precision.* A high-level specification language, for project scope agreement, delineating the system boundaries and naming major objects, rules and processes, is required.
- *Specification completeness.* It is important that the model captures all aspects of a specification.
- *Map ability to later phases.* A requirements definition phase will typically be followed by a detailed analysis and design phases. Therefore, the model should possess a structure suitable for mapping on the later phases.

This paper shows an object-oriented approach for a process-oriented requirement analysis, which grasps the stated model characteristics.

RELATED WORK AND BUSINESS PROCESS ORIENTATION

Building a data warehouse is different than developing transaction systems, whereby the requirement analysis process for the latter is supported by numerous methods. Up to now the data warehouse design process has not been supported by a formal requirement analysis method although there are some approaches for requirement gathering. Requirements can and must be gathered before the data warehouse design process otherwise only those parts are captured, which are in the basic corporate model. Data warehouse is designed to support the business process rather than specific query requirements. The process approach for data warehouse design enables organizations to focus on the performance of business processes and drift away from traditional task or department performance measurement. The change to process centering is not primarily a structural one, but process centering is a shift in perspective, in which tasks and processes exchange places. In practice this means that the traditional hierarchical organization remains and the process view is integrated into the industrial way of organizing. Therefore business processes cross organizational boundaries and often tends to be inefficient because of changing responsibilities, long delay times and so forth. The support of different views of the models is an opportunity to capture multidimensional and aggregated views of data warehouses. Basically use case models and object models can be applied to software processes and business processes, which use the same notation but represent different functionality. As argued above, we aim at analyzing business processes and focus therefore on the business process approach provided by these models and described in.

The use case model provides an overview of the area of interest, while the object model is an internal model and describes accurately each business process with its tasks and resources in order to make the model clearer. This paper presents the adaptation of the use case and object model in order to support the data warehouse requirement analysis. The aim is to provide a formal requirement engineering method that is easy to use, quickly to understand, covering all major data warehouse model characteristics and is therefore a means of communication between all involved parties in the requirement process.

DATA WAREHOUSE REQUIREMENTS

Requirements to the data warehouse system determine what data must be available, how it is organized, and how often it is updated. Furthermore the requirements enable the stakeholders to communicate the purpose. It is advantageous to start the requirement collection process with a macro business discovery (see Figure 1), which is necessary to identify the key business processes, key business metrics, measures and requirements. A highlevel model has to be developed depicting how business is conducted.

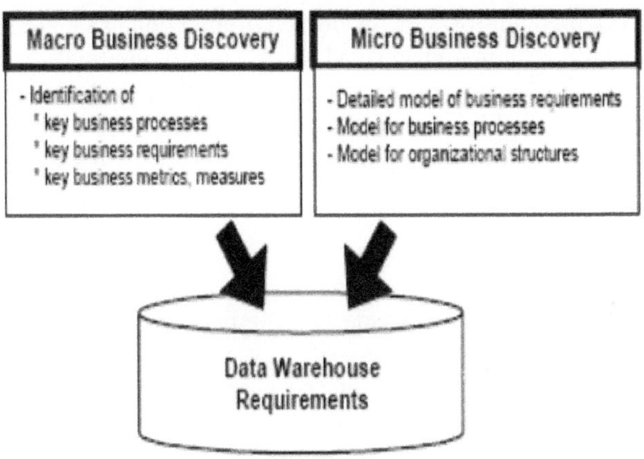

Figure 1: Requirement Discovery Process for Data Warehouse Requirements

The micro business discovery is an in-depth analysis of the requirements of the organization as defined by the macro business discovery. It describes the business requirements in more detail by considering these requirements in context of the models for the business processes and the organizational structures. Figure 2 shows the impacts of data warehouse requirements [4]. The figure demonstrates very well, that data warehouse requirements directly affect technical aspects of the data warehouse system.

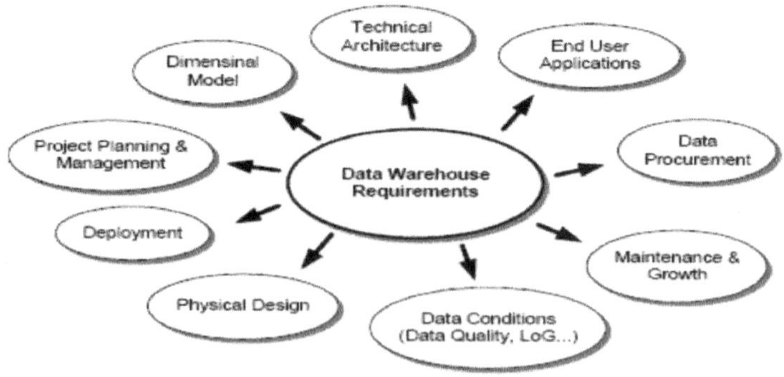

Figure 2: Impact of Warehouses Requirements

In the requirement collection process data warehouse requirements have to be driven by the business requirements. They arise from the macro and micro business discovery and result in a comprehensive technical specification. On the other hand data warehouse requirements are derived from the business requirements and their aim is to provide a comprehensive, precise specification for the data warehouse team. Current use case oriented approaches for the requirement analysis are used to describe technical aspects and ignore the business view. By integrating this central aspect in the requirement modeling process here present an approach of how to gather the business requirements from stakeholders corresponding to their business processes. In the requirement analysis process it is important to consider the organizational context of the stakeholders.

ORGANIZATIONAL CONTEXT

A data warehouse is intended to provide an enterprise-wide decision support for an organization. It should address the users of all hierarchy levels of the organization. This broad spectrum of different types of end users requires information at different granularity levels to meet their specific needs.

In the often-found structure of traditional organizations as figure 3(a) different requirements for data processing and data analysis can be identified, which correspond to the different layers of the organization. As we move upward through the layers of the hierarchy, for example, the level of granularity required decreases. Executives use highly summarized information, while line managers work at a detailed level. Administrative users need to create and maintain individual data items such as orders or customer records. Professional users and line managers require statistical analysis tools. Executives require systems that highlight anomalies or geographically show key indicators, and allow drill-down in problem areas. During the micro business discovery requirements of data warehouse users of all different levels in the hierarchy are identified.

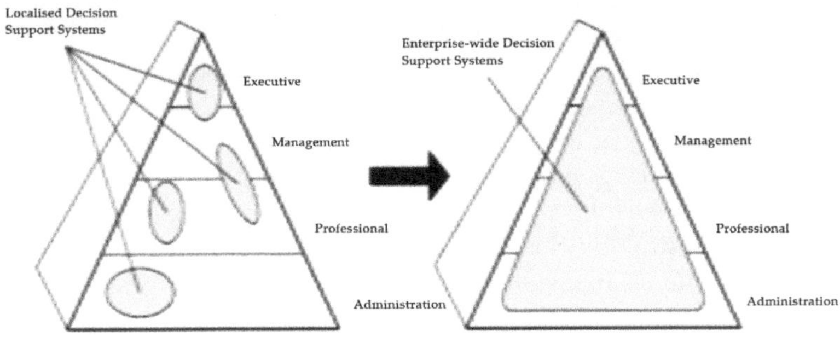

Figure 3: (a) structure of traditional organizations (b)an enterprise-wide decision support system

Figure 3 (b) shows an enterprise-wide decision support system with its organizational hierarchy, which can achieve these business goals. For gathering the meshed requirements of such a decision support system, it is necessary to use models which represent all business requirements on each hierarchy level and which allow requirement consolidation of all levels.

USE CASE MODEL

The Use Case model captures business processes in the company that satisfy the customer's interests and the interests of others outside the company (partners, suppliers, etc.). Our use case model describes business processes in the company that are analyzed and provide information to the data warehouse user and the company's staff.

Analysis System and Subsystems-The analysis system or subsystem is the modeling concept to symbolize the business or area of responsibility.

Analyst-The analyst represents a role that someone or something in the environment can play in relation to the analysis system. In our model analyst represent the environment that analyzes business processes belonging to the specified business system.

Use Case-The use case is constructing for a business process that is analyzed.

Uses Association-The uses association is a must association and describes use cases that are aggregated into other use cases. This concept must be applied when parts of the use case are analyzed by other analysts.

OBJECT MODEL

The object model provides a clear picture how the use case is structured internally in order to realize the analysis capabilities of the process (backward engineering) and to describe the analysis requirements of various actors (forward engineering). The internal structure consists of fact and dimension objects.

Dimension Objects

Davenport states in [3] that a process is a structured, measured set of activities designed to produce a specified output for a particular customer or market. He notes that a business process is a specific ordering of work activities across time and place, with a beginning, an end, and clearly identified inputs and outputs: a structure of action. Hammer argues in [7] that a business process is a group of tasks that together create a result of value to the customer. Hammer's definition consists of activity, result, customer and input objects, and Jacobson focuses on the customer, product, service, and deliverable and measure objects. Davenport provides the most comprehensive definition, which basically includes the objects of both other definitions. The objects in the process definitions highlight key business process characteristics, but represent also classical data warehouse dimensions (e.g. organization, customer, product, service, time, etc.) and data warehouse facts (measure). As these key business process objects can be found in any classical business process, we propose a standard set of dimension objects representing data warehouse dimensions (Figure 4):

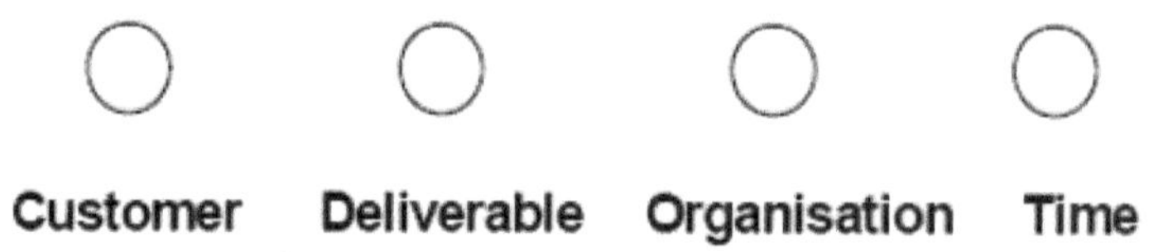

Figure 4: Data Warehouse Main Dimension Objects in Classic Business Processes

Customer Dimension Object. The single most important word in the definition of process is 'customer' and a process perspective on a business is the customer's perspective [8].

Deliverable Dimension Object. Davenport and Hammer do not specify the output [3] or result of value [7] of the process in their definition. The customer does not see or care about the company's organizational structure or its management philosophies; the customer sees only the company's products and services, all of which are produced by its processes. As the output or result of the value of a process might be the opposite of the defined process deliverables, and products or services are too specific for a requirement analysis model.

Organization Dimension Object

The analysis of the organizational structure detects occurrences that are caused by certain units and therefore organization dimension object is required.

Time Dimension Object

A business process is a specific ordering of work activities across time with a beginning and an end [3]. The end of the process represents a pointing time where the results of the process are delivered and cannot be changed anymore.

Fact Object

Performance is measured against cost, longevity, service and quality. These measures (e.g. turnover, profit, ratio rates etc.) represent facts in data warehouse notation and fact object in this paper.

CONCLUSION

This paper presents the adaptation of use case and object models for modeling business requirements for data warehouse systems to support the data warehouse design process. We showed how data warehouse requirements are derived from business requirements and their organization context. Use case model is an excellent means of both expressing requirements with regard to the data warehouse and providing a comprehensive picture of what the data warehouse is intended to perform. It illustrates the function of the business, the process analysts and the business process to be analyzed with its aggregations. The object model is an internal model that captures different analysis perspectives of the business process.

REFERENCES

1. Amatory, S. Murray, D., Data Warehousing in the real World – A practical Guide for Building Decision Support Systems, AddisonWesley Publishing 1997.
2. Coad, P., Yourdon, E., Object-Oriented Analysis. Englewood Cliffs, N.J.: Prentice Hall 1991.
3. Davenport, Th., Process Innovation: Reengineering Work through Information Technology, Harvard Business School Press 1993.
4. Davis, A., Hisa, P., Status Report: Requirements Engineering, IEEE Software November 1993.
5. Debevoise, N. T., The Data Warehouse Method, Prentice-Hall, 1999.
6. Finkelstein, A., Requirements Engineering Research: Coordination and Infrastructure, Requirements Engineering 1, 1996.
7. Hammer, M., Champy, J., Reengineering the Corporation – A Manifesto for Business Revolution, Harper Collins Publishers 1993.
8. Hammer, M., Beyond Reengineering, Harper Collins Publishers 1996.
9. IEEE, IEEE Guide to Software Requirements Specifications, IEEE Inc., 1984
10. Inmon, W. H., Building the Data Warehouse, Wiley & Sons 1996.

2
CHAPTER

IDENTIFICATION OF CATEGORICAL REGISTRATION DATA OF DOMAIN NAMES IN DATA WAREHOUSE CONSTRUCTION TASK

Rasim Alguliev, Rena Gasimova

Keywords: Domain, Domain Name System, Registrar, Registrant, Category Data, Data Warehouse, Data Clearing, Fuzzy Search Algorithms, Damerau-Levenstein Distance, Decision Tree

INTRODUCTION

Decision support systems (DSS) have been used for formation of administration decisions, i.e. discovery of the best alternative for a lengthy period of time. Majority of commercial, social and governmental organizations no longer make serious decisions without using elements of computer analysis [1]. At all stages of complex administrative decision making—from identification of the problem to control of realization of made decision—the more accurate, timely and complete is the appropriate information, the more effective will be the decision. Information support of the decision making process determines the effectiveness of decision at all stages [2].

Modern approach to automation of decision making support is based on use of data warehouse (DW) concept. Rampant development of information technologies, and data collection, storage and procession means in particular, allows to collect vast volumes of data which require analyzing. DW provides analysts, executives and top managers with capability to study large volumes of interdependent data using fast interactive information reflection on different levels of detailing from different points of view in accordance with notion of the user on subject field [3,4]. Bill Inmon, author of DW concept, defined them as "subject oriented, integrated, unchanged, supporting

Citation: R. Alguliev and R. Gasimova, "Identification of Categorical Registration Data of Domain Names in Data Warehouse Construction Task," Intelligent Control and Automation, Vol. 4 No. 2, 2013, pp. 227-234. doi:10.4236/ica.2013.42027.

data collection, organized to support management", designed to act as "unique and only source of truth", providing managers and analysts with trustworthy information necessary for operative analysis and decision making [5,6]. Richard Hackathorn, another founder of this concept, wrote that the objective of DW—is to provide "unique image of existing reality" for organizations [7]. Ralph Kimball, one of DW authors, described the warehouse as "a place, where people can access their data". He also formulated in [8,9] main requirements to data warehouses.

For correct comprehension of data concept, it is necessary to understand following principal moments: DW concept—is not a data analyzing concept; rather it is a concept of preparation for data analyzing; DW concept does not predetermine architecture of purposive analyticcal system. It describes the processes to be implemented in the system, but not the where precisely and how these processes must be implemented. The main objective of warehouses—is creation of a single logical presentation of data, contained in multitype data bases (DB) or in other words, a single corporate data model.

RELEVANCE

Apparently, at modern development level of information technologies, simple relocation of data from one DW to another does not cause difficulties. However if we simply relocate the data from all sources to a single DB, then we will obtain a "dump", an uncoordinated set of data. In order to create something more accessible for analysis by the final user, it is necessary to coordinate the data entering the DB from sources of data warehouse. In other words, to solve the main task of DW construction: to create the most coordinated, subject-oriented, integrated, time dependent data set.

Filling of warehouses, as a rule, is carried out by information from several data sources. Development or consequential support of qualitative information storage and processing systems is a complex problem. Human factor and partial absence of control at submittal lead to occurrence of distortions in data. Misprints and omissions are present almost in all details of saved objects, as well as in identification sets. During entrance stage of information into the data base, human factor is the main reason for occurrence of distortions. Damerau demonstrated that 95% of errors during typing by a person are transpositions [10].

Upon development of DW, very little attention is paid to cleaning of incoming information. Apparently, larger the volume of warehouse, the better it is considered. This is an erroneous practice and the best way to turn the data warehouse into a disposal dump. It is necessary to clean data. Information is heterogeneous and is collected from different sources.

Exactly presence of point sets of information collection makes the clearing process especially relevant. Generally speaking, errors are always committed, and it is impossible to completely dispose of them. Possibly, sometimes it is more reasonable to accept them, rather than spend money and time to get rid of them. But, in general cases, it is necessary to aim to reduce the amount of errors to an acceptable level so ever.

There are different kinds of errors. There are also errors characteristics to a certain subject field or task. Errors, which do not depend of task: contrariety of information;

data omissions, anomalous values; noise; data entry errors etc. There are different kinds of solutions for each of these problems. Data omissions are a very serious problem for majority of DW.

Due to lack of information, as a matter of actual practice, application of DW is realized poorly or with significant limitations. Quantity of errors during data input is excessive, for example misprints, deliberate data distortions, inconsistence of formats, excluding typical errors related to specifics of data input application operation.

OBJECTIVE

Domain is a domain namespace field and is characterized with independence of data allocation, inclusion of information system in domain contents, presence of special information systems (DNS servers) containing data on domain names allocated in domain and carries out the function of domain name space organization [11].

Registration data of domain include: domain name (domain), registry identifier (registrar), full name of the physical person (person), contact address of the physical person (address), domain administrator identifier (admino), organization identifier for administrative communication (admin-c), title of organization (organization), domain registration time (created), domain free date (freedate), telephone numbers with international codes (phone), e-mail address (e-mail), list of DNS servers supporting domain (nserver), domain type (type), information source (source), domain registration payment time (paid-till) [12].

Clearing of domain name registration data is carried out in the works and domain names registration data identification method is developed based on decision tree apparatus application. Decision trees are selected as the main algorithmic approach for construction of effective data integration system.

During construction of data warehouse, problems occur related to misprints and omission of data. As registration data of domain mainly consists of categorical data, it was decided to apply fuzzy search algorithms for cleaning of these data.

Following tasks are formulated for research purposes:

1) Processing of domain name registration data, data clearing using Damerau-Levenstain algorithm;

2) Identification of domain name registration data using decision tree construction.

SOLUTION

Algorithm Choice

Generalized string matching task which includes detection of substrings of text strings is also called fuzzy string matching task. This task is important for cases where errors are taken into account. Review of fuzzy comparison algorithms is provided in work [13-17].

Fuzzy search algorithms (also known as fuzzy string search) are the foundation of spell check and complete search systems such as Google or Yandex. There are many methods of analysis [18-25] and fuzzy (inexact) string matching [26-29]. The most popular of these fuzzy string matching methods are the methods of calculation of editing spacing [30-32]. Generally, metrics numerically calculating the value of transformation of one line to another is considered as spacing editing. There are different several operations, each of which can have a value of its own: character stuffing, deleting, replacement and transposition of proximate symbols. There are different fuzzy string matching algorithms, which are based on different editing distances. Hamming distance—is a number of positions, in which corresponding symbols of two words of the equal length are different [33]. In more general cases, Hamming distance is applied to lines of same length of any q alphabets and serves as the difference metrics of objects of equal dimensions. Hammings distance is usually used in bio-informatics and genomics.

If matching of two strings of different lengths is allowed, then as a rule, insertion and deletion are also required. If they are given the same weight as replacement, minimal general value of transformation will be equal to one of the metrics proposed by Levenstein [34]. As a result, a more general task for a voluntary alphabet was associated with his name. Gasfield made a significant contribution in study of this issue [35].

Levenstein distance and its generalization is actively applied for correction of errors in words (in search systems, data bases, during text input, during automatic detection of scanned text or speech), for comparison of text files, in bio-informatics for comparison of genes, chromosomes and proteins. From application point of view, determination of distance between words or text fields according to Levenstein has following disadvantages:

- Comparatively large distances are made upon rearrangement of words or parts of words;
- Distances among completely different short words become small, while distance between very similar long words become significant.

As a result of analysis of different DNS data bases, it is known that, contents of records of same fields of registration data of domain names can be expressed in forms different (not identical) in content. The reason for occurrence of difference of field value might be lack of information, misprints, use of abbreviations, duplication of records etc.

Upon entry of domain name registration data in DW, abbreviations, misprints, omissions, double recordings and other distortions are encountered. In order to increase the quality of input registration data such as "registrar", person", "address", "organization", "admin-o" etc., prevention of errors and inconsistencies of duplications in records is required. For example, in names of countries (cities) misprints can be as Kanata (Canada), Russian (Russia), Frankfrut Am Main (Frankfurt Am Main) etc.; organization identifier registration data (registrar) "MONIKER ONLINE SERVICES, INC." can be identified as "MONIKER, INC.", "MONIKER", "MONIKERS ONLINE SERVICES". In this case, words included in phrases must be processed separately. Despite difference of these strings, it is clear that, all of these titles stand for the same registrar. But let's also note that, upon comparing strings "MONIKER ONLINE

SERVICES, INC." and "MONIKER, INC." using Levenstein metrics, we receive a larger value for editing distance. In cases where it is necessary to process the words contained in phrases separately from each other and/or apply algorithms that can compare similar lines for equivalence (for example, full entrance of one line into another as subsequence) and detect them as "similar".

In reviewed paper, let's use Damerau-Levenstein distance—difference measure of two strings of symbols, defined as minimal quantity of insertion, deletion, replacement and transposition (rearrangement of two proximate symbols) operations necessary for transfer of one string to another. It is the modification of Levenstein distance, and differs from it by addition of transposition operation.

Editing distance determined in such way can be calculated using dynamic programming method [36]. Also, there is an algorithms for this, requiring O(MN) operations, where M and N—are lengths of compared lines, and it is required to calculate MN of elements of so called dynamic programming matrix in order to find the distance value.

Symbol Fields for Registration Data Recording

As a rule, symbol fields consist of a string which contains one or several words, divided in gaps and punctuation marks. Nonstandard phrases are used in fields. Data is entered manually by an operator, often in distorted condition. In this regard, punctuation marks such as ".", ",", ":", " ", "-" etc. that do not carry a functional significance, are replaced by "blank" sign.

Name of physical person (person), contact address of physical person (address), domain administrator identifier (admin-o), organization identifier for administrative communication (admin-c), organization title (organization) are the key fields upon identification of registration data.

Components of these fields can be present in random order, which is a difficult task for automatic processing of such information. In order to implement comparison of two lines containing such information, it is necessary to dismember each field to its contents, then compare only those which have identical meaning, for example in the address, compare the name of the city to the name of the city, name of the street to the name of the street. For content analysis, we enter so-called, samples. For example, sample address template is a combination of address components:

[apartment], [block], [building], [street], [city], [district], [index], [country].

For example, for domain—azerbaijan.info, sample address template is important:

, , 4676, Admiralty Way, Marina del Rey, California, 90292-660, US.

Difference measure of attributes' values, for example such as contact address of a person will be calculated using Damerau-Levenstein distance

Decision Tree

Decision trees is the most comfortable decision making method for record (object) identification, for their demonstrativeness while use, minimal calculation resources and simplicity of realization. Decision tree—is one the methods of automatic analysis of vast amounts of data. Decision trees—is a method of rule presentation in hierarchic, consecutive structure, where each object corresponds to single knot that gives decision. Under rule, we understand a logical construction, presented in "if…then" form. Main advantages of decision trees are generation of rules in fields where experts formalize their knowledge with difficulty; extraction of rules in natural language; intuitively understandable classification model; high forecast precision, comparable to other methods (statistics, neural networks); construction of non-parametric models [37].

Suppose that we are given any educating set of T, containing objects, each of which is characterized by m attributes, while one of them points at affiliation of the object o a certain class. Construction idea of decision tree from T set, first expresses by Hunt, is demonstrated in accordance with R. Queenlan [38].

Let's label classes (values of class marks) through $\{C_1, C_2, \cdots, C_k\}$, then there are 3 situations:

- Set of T contains one or more examples related to one class C_k. Then decision tress for T—is a list, determining the C_K class.
- Set of T does not contain any examples, i.e. it is an empty set. Then again, the list and the class associated with the list are selected from another set different from T, let's say from sets associated with the parent;
- The Set of T contains examples affiliated with different classes. In this case it is necessary to divide Set of T to some subsets. For this purpose, we choose one of the attributes that has two or more different values $O_1, O_2, \cdots, O_n$. T is divided into subsets of $T_1, T_2, \cdots T_n$, where each subset T_i; contains all examples that have a value of O_i for selected attribute. This procedure will be recursively continued until the final set will consist of examples related to the same class.

Above described procedure is the basis of many modern construction algorithms of decision trees. Obviously, upon using given methodology, construction of decision tree will be implemented from top downward. Currently, there is a significant number of algorithms, realizing decision trees CART, C4.5, Newld, ITrule, CHAID, CN2 etc. [39,40]. But following two are the most widespread and popular: CART (Classification and Regression Tree) and C4.5.

Decision tree will be generated following way: for exact identification of the objects, we will use fields univocally identifying the object. Domain registration data will be identified by following attributes: registrar, person, address, admin-o, admin-c, organization, created, updated, free-date, phone, e-mail, nserver, type, source. Intermediate nodes of the tree correspond to these attributes, and arches—to possible alternative comparison values of these attributes "+" (same), "±" (similar), and "–" (different). Tree leaves are indicated as one of three classes as "=" (compared objects are identical), "≠" (objects are different), "?" (unknown). The example of the tree for identification of registration data domain names is provided on **Figure 1**. Following are the most significant among attributes: registration identifier (registrar), full name of the physical person (person) contact address of the physical person (address), domain administrator identifier (admin-o), organization identifier for administrative communication (admin-c), title of organization (organization), list of DNS servers supporting domain (nserver).

Less significant, but as informative attributes are: domain registration time (created), domain update time (updated), domain free date (free-date), telephone numbers with international codes (phone), e-mail addresses (e-mail), domain type (type), domain registration payment time (paid-till), information source (source) etc.

Decision tree is formed based on the knowledge of experts of the subject field. Depth of the tree is selected based upon objects necessary for precise identification.

Software Implementation

Software implementation of identification algorithms of registration data of domain names is implemented on DRRacket language. Racket (former PLT Scheme) is the multi-paradigm programming language in Lisp/Scheme family, which also serves as a platform for creation of languages, design and realization. Programming language is known due to its extensive macro system, which allows creating built-in and subject-oriented languages, language constructions, such as classes or modules, as well as separate Racket dialects with different semantics. Distribution platforms of free and open software is spread under LGPL license [41-43].

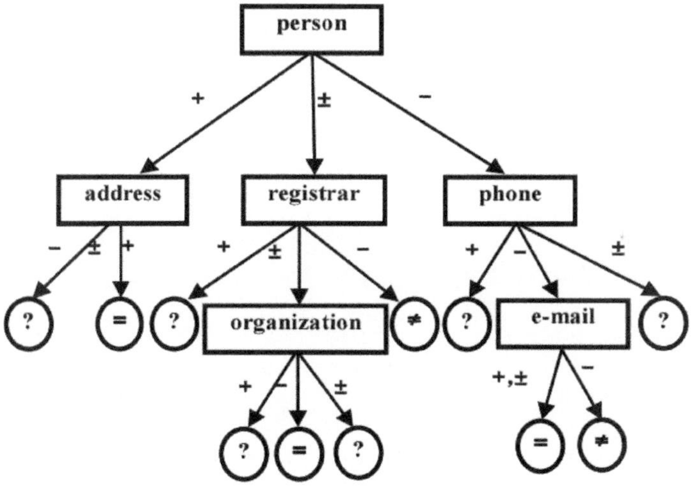

Figure. 1. Decision tree for identification of registration data of domain names.

We use Racket, in order to demonstrate that without crochets and other unused symbols, it is easy to understand complex program codes in programming language. Despite the fact that Racket language is simple and easy for perception, it is quite difficult to find errors committed in the program. a fraction of decision algorithm for identification of registration data in DRRacket language is provided in **Figure 2**. For comparison of results, the identical algorithm is implemented in Python language which is used for solution of wide range of tasks of applied programming [44-47]. Same algorithm is presented in Python program on **Figure 3**.

Conducted experiments with above described decision tree gave the identical positive results in DRRacket and Pythin programs.

CONCLUSIONS

Modern approaches to solution of this task are related with construction of DW allowing "liberating" of information from strict frames of operating systems and better comprehend the problems of real activity.

DW provides high speed of data reception, ability to receive and compare, as well as consistency, completeness and authenticity of data. After withdrawal from the source, data are loaded into the warehouse, in order to implement cleaning and simultaneously provide comprehensive support of data cleaning [48].

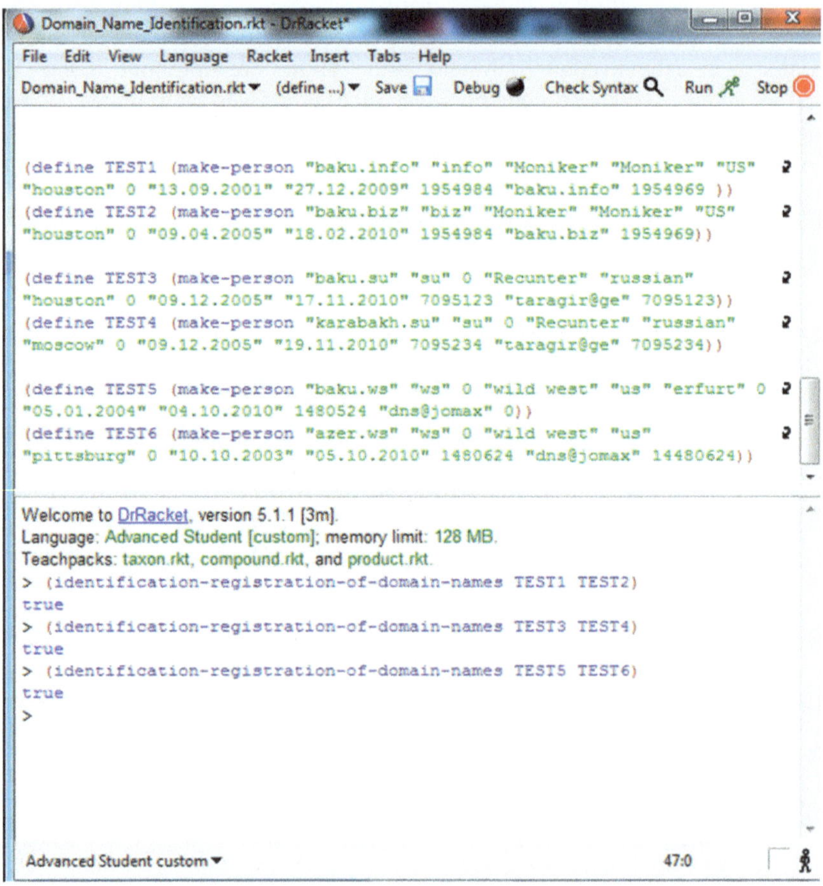

Figure 2. Decision algorithm for identification of registration data of domain names in DRRacket program.

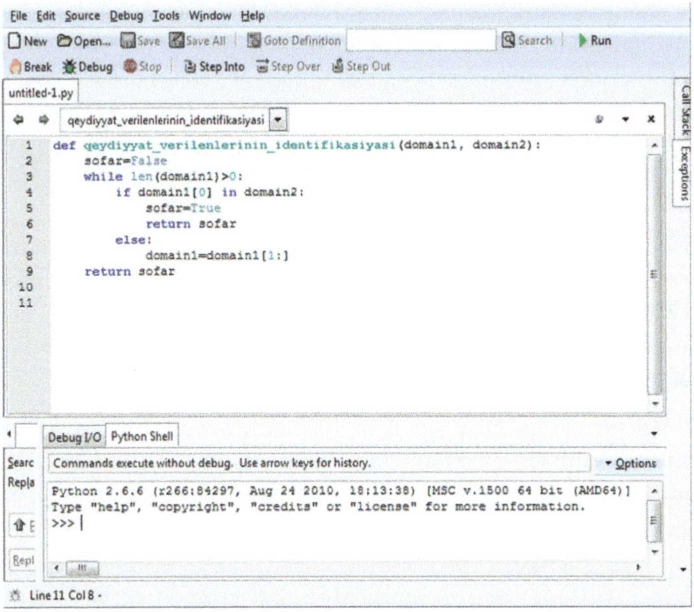

(a)

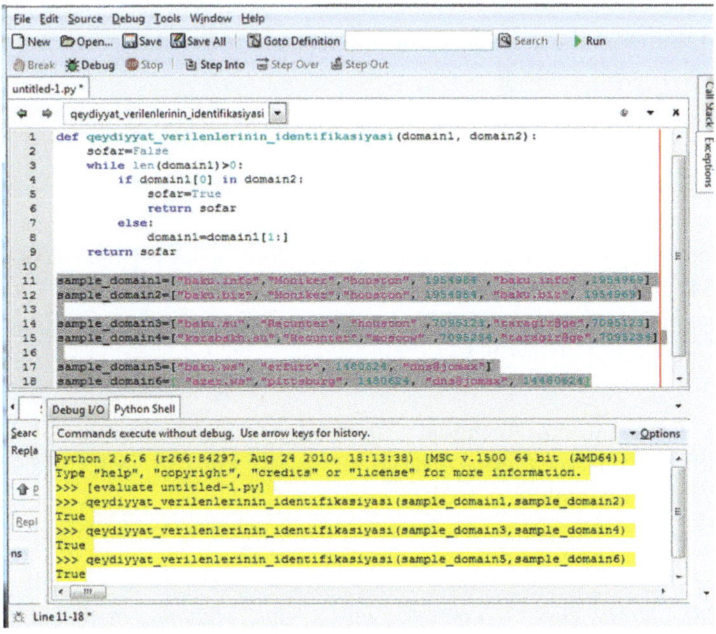

(b)

Figure 3. (a, b) Decision algorithm for identification of registration data of domain names in Python program.

Domain names registration data category identification was reviewed in this work. Abbreviations, misprints, omissions, conscious data corruption, record duplicates etc. which were allowed on information collection stage are considered as errors. Currently, variety of alternative proximity functions were proposed, but from our point of view, in order to conduct clearing and consistency checking, Damerau-Levenstein distance most accurately corresponds to intuitive similarity concept. Also, domain name registration data records identity method based on decision tree was proposed.

Developed identification method was implemented for creation of a DW on information from several DNS Servers based on the example of domain name registration data serving the interests of the Republic of Azerbaijan.

REFERENCES

1. E. A. Trachtengertz, "Evolution of Administrative Decision Making Support Systems of Computers," Information Technologies, No. 1, 2006, pp. 15-31.
2. I. P. Belyayev, "Art of Data Analysis," Information Technologies, No. 5, 2003, pp. 31-37.
3. V. V. Przhiakovski, "Complex Analysis of Large Volume Data: New Perspectives of Computerization," SUBD, No. 4, 1996, pp. 71-83.
4. A. A. Sakharov, "Construction Concept and Realization of Information Systems Oriented on Data Analysis," SUBD, No. 4, 1996, pp. 55-70.
5. W. H. Inmon, "Building the Data Warehouse," 2nd Edition, John Wiley & Sons, Inc., New York, 1993, p. 298.
6. W. H. Inmon, "Building the Data Warehouse," 3rd Edition, John Wiley & Sons, Inc., New York, 2002, p. 412.
7. W. H. Inmon and R. D. Hackathorn, "Using the Data Warehouse," John Wiley & Sons, New York, 1994, p. 285.
8. R. Kimball, "The Data Warehouse Toolkit," John Wiley & Sons, New York, 1996, p. 388.
9. R. Kimball and M. Ross, "The Data Warehouse Toolkit: The Complete Guide to Dimensional Modeling," 2nd Edition, John Wiley & Sons, New York, 2002, p. 464.
10. F. J. Damerau, "A Technique for Computer Detection and Correction of Spelling Errors," Communications of ACM, Vol. 7, No. 3, 1964, pp. 171-176. doi:10.1145/363958.363994
11. A. G. Sergo, "Domain Names," Bestseller, Moscow, 2006, p. 368.
12. A. A. Venedrukhin, "Domain Wars," Piter, Saint Petersburg, 2009, p. 224.
13. G. M. Landau and U. Vishkin, "Fast String Matching with k Differences," Journal of Computer and System Sciences, Vol. 37, No. 1, 1988, pp. 63-78. doi:10.1016/0022-0000(88)90045-1
14. G. M. Landau and U. Vishkin, "Fast Parallel and Serial Approximate String Matching," Journal of Algorithms, Vol. 10, No. 2, 1989, pp. 157-

169. doi:10.1016/0196-6774(89)90010-2

15. Z. Galil and R. Giancarlo, "Data Structures and Algorithms for Approximate String Matching," Journal of Complexity, Vol. 4, No. 1, 1988, pp. 33-72. doi:10.1016/0885-064X(88)90008-8
16. A. N. Borisov and A. V. Alekseyev, "Processing of Fuzzy Information in Decision Making Systems," Radio and Communication, Moscow, 1988, p. 304.
17. A. Y. Solodkov, "Object Identification Algorithms in Data Bases," System Integration, Vol. 12, No. 90, 2004, pp. 52-56.
18. A. E. Yermakov and V. V. Pleshko, "Parsing in Statistical Text Analysis Systems," Information Technologies, No. 7, 2002, pp. 15-17.
19. L. A. Zade, "The Concept of a Linguistic Variable and Its Application to the Adoption of Approximate Solutions," Mir, Moscow, 1976, p. 167.
20. K. Iberla, "Factoral Analysis," Statistics, Moscow, 1980, p. 398.
21. B. Carnigan and P. Pike, "Programming Practice," Nevsky Dialect, Saint Petersburg, 2001, p. 288.
22. T. Connolly, K. Begg and A. Strachan, "Data Bases. Design, Realization and Maintenance. Theory and Practice," Williams, Moscow, 2000, p. 1120.
23. T. H. Coremen, C. I. Laserson, R. L. Rivest and K. Stein, "Algorithms: Structure and Analysis," 2nd Edition, Williams, Moscow, 2005, p. 1296.
24. A. Coffman, "Introduction to Fuzzy Sets Theory," Radio and Communication, Moscow, 1982, p. 432.
25. O. I. Larichev and E. M. Moshkovich, "Qualitative Decision Making Methods," Fizmatlit, Moscow, 1996, p. 217.
26. A. Ehrenfeucht and D. Haussler, "A New Distance Metric on Strings Computable in Linear Time," Discrete Applied Mathematics, Vol. 20, No. 3, 1988, pp. 191-203.
27. U. Masek and M. S. Peterson, "A Faster Algorithm for Computing String-Edit Distances," Journal of Computer and System Sciences, Vol. 20, No. 1, 1980, pp. 785-807.doi:10.1016/0022-0000(80)90002-1
28. P. H. Sellers, "The Theory of Computation of Evolutionary Distances: Pattern Recognition," Journal of Algorithms, No. 1, 1980, pp. 359-373.
29. E. Ukkonen, "Approximate String Matching over SuffixTrees," Proceedings of the 4th Annual Symposium on Combinatorial Pattern Matching, Padova, 1993, pp. 229- 242.doi:10.1007/BFb0029808
30. D. M. Sunday, "A Very Fast Substring Search Algorithm," Communications of the ACM, Vol. 33, No. 8, 1990, pp. 132-142. doi:10.1145/79173.79184
31. A. Hume and D. Sunday, "Fast String Searching," Software—Practice and Experience, Vol. 21, No. 11, 1991, pp. 1221-1248. doi:10.1002/spe.4380211105
32. A. V. Aho, "Algorithms for Finding Patterns in Strings," In: J. van Leeuwen, Ed., Algorithms and Complexity, Handbook of Theoretical Computer Science, Elsevier Science Publishers, Amsterdam, 1990, pp. 255-300.

33. R. W. Hamming, "Coding and Information Theory," Englewood Cliffs, Prentice-Hall, Upper Saddle River, 1980, p. 239.

34. V. I. Levenstein, "Binary Codes Capable of Correction Deletions, Insertions and Reversals," Soviet Physics Doklady, Vol. 163, No. 4, 1965, pp. 845-848.

35. D. Gasfield, "Lines, Trees and Sequences in Algorithms," Informatics and Computational Biology, NEvsky Dialect, Petersburg, 2003, p. 654.

36. R. A. Wagner and M. J. Fischer, "The String-to-String Correction Problem," Journal of the ACM, Vol. 21, No. 1, 1974, pp. 168-173. doi:10.1145/321796.321811

37. O. G. Berestneva and E. A. Muratova, "Construction of Logical Models Using Decision Tree," Tomsk Polytechnic University News, Vol. 207, No. 2, 2004, pp. 55-61.

38. J. R. Quinlan, "Generating Production Rules from Decision Trees," Proceedings of the 10th International Joint Conference on Artificial Intelligence, Morgan Kaufmann, 1987, pp. 304-307.

39. J. R. Quinlan, "C4.5 Programs for Machine Learning," Morgan Kaufmann Pub., San Mateo, Vol. 240, 1993, p. 302.

40. J. R. Quinlan, "Improved Use of Continuous Attributes in C 4.5," Journal of Artificial Intelligence Research, Vol. 4, 1996. pp. 77-90.

41. R. B. Findler, C. Flanagan, M. Flatt, S. Krishnamurthi and M. Felleisen, "DrScheme: A Pedagogic Programming Environment for Scheme," Proceedings of the International Symposium on Programming Languages: Implementations, Logics, and Programs, September 1997, pp. 369-388.

42. R. B. Findler, J. Clements., C. Flanagan, M. Flatt, S. Krishnamurthi, P. Steckler and M. Felleisen, "DrScheme: A Programming Environment for Scheme," Journal of Functional Programming, Vol. 12, No. 2, 2002, pp. 159- 182.

43. S. Manuel and J. B. Hans, "Understanding Memory Allocation of Scheme Programs," ACM SIGPLAN International Conference on Functional Programming, Vol. 35, No. 9, 2000, pp. 245-256.

44. M. Lutz, "Programming in Python," 4th Edition, Symbol-Plus, Saint Petersburg, 2011, p. 992.

45. M. Dawson, "Programming in Python," Piter, Saint Petersburg, 2012, p. 432.

46. I. A. Khahaev, "Workshop on Algorithms and Programming in Python," Textbook, Alt Linux, Moscow, 2010, p. 126.

47. D. M. Beesley, "Python," 4th Edition, Detailed Directory, Symbol-Plus, Saint Petersburg, 2010, p. 864.

48. E. Spearley, "Corporate Data Warehouses. Planning, Development, Realization," Vol. 1, Williams Publishing House, Moscow, 2001, p. 395.

3

CHAPTER

COMPARATIVE STUDY OF DATA WAREHOUSE DESIGN APPROACHES

Rajni Jindal and Shweta Taneja

Keywords: Data warehouse design, Multidimensional modelling, Unified Modelling Language

INTRODUCTION

A Data Warehouse (DW) is defined as "a subject-oriented, integrated, time-variant, non-volatile collection of data in support of management's decision-making process" [1]. Data warehouses store huge amount of information from multiple data sources which is used for query and analysis. Therefore, the data is stored in the multidimensional (M D) structure [34]. A multidimensional model stores information into facts and dimensions. A fact contains the interesting concepts or measures (fact attributes) of a business process (sales, deliveries, etc.), whereas a dimension represents the perspective or view for analyzing a fact (product, customer, time, etc.) using hierarchically organized dimension attributes. Multidimensional modelling requires specialized design techniques that resemble the traditional database design methods [5] as shown in table 1.The database design consists of following five phases. The first phase is Analysis of operational systems whose aim is to collect the information concerning the pre existing operational system. It involves the designer, along with the people involved in managing the information system and produces in output the (conceptual or logical) schemes of either the whole or part of the information system. The next phase consists in gathering and filtering the user requirements. It involves the designer and users of the DW, and produces in output the specifications concerning the choice of facts and dimensions etc. Next is the Conceptual design [36] which aims at producing an implementation-

Citation: Rajni Jindal and Shweta Taneja, "Comparative Study of Data Warehouse Design Approaches," International Journal of Database Management Systems (IJDMS) Vol.4, No.1, February 2012, DOI: 10.5121/ijdms.2012.4104.

independent and expressive conceptual schema for the DW, according to the chosen conceptual model. Logical design takes as input the conceptual schema and creates a corresponding logical schema (which is more detailed) on the chosen platform by considering some set of constraints. And finally, a phase of physical design, that takes into account issues specifically related to the tools chosen for implementation –such as indexing and allocation.

Table 1. Database Design Methods

Step	Input	Output
Analysis of Operational System	Information regarding the operational systems	Database schemes
Requirements Elicitation	Database scheme	Specifications for data warehouse
Conceptual design	Database scheme and Specifications	Conceptual schema
Logical design	Conceptual schema	Logical schema
Physical design	Logical schema	Physical schema

Conceptual modelling is the necessary foundation for building a database that is well-documented and fully satisfies the user requirements. In this phase, the multidimensional schema of the data warehouse is defined. It is the beginning of the design process on which the success of entire data warehouse depends. Though several conceptual models have been proposed, none of them has been accepted as a standard so far, and all vendors propose their own proprietary design methods

Obviously, there is a need of existence of a standard conceptual model.

In this paper, we make a comparative study of various approaches and techniques for data warehouse design and propose an Object Oriented framework for the conceptual design of a data warehouse. We have used UML ([2], [3], [4]) in the design process as it has become a standard for object modelling during analysis and design steps of software system development. So, it reduces the effort of learning new notations or methodologies for every subsystem to be modelled.

BACKGROUND WORK OF DW DESIGN APPROACHES

In the literature, different data models [24, 25,26] both conceptual and logical have been proposed for data warehouse design .These approaches are based on their own visual modelling languages or make use of well-known graphical notation like ER model or UML, but to the best of our knowledge, there is no standard method or model that allows us to model all aspects of a DW. Moreover, during our survey we noticed that most of the research efforts in designing and modelling DWs have been focused on the development of MD data models and conceptual design, the interest on the physical design of DWs has been very poor.

The pioneer author in the field of data warehouse design is Juan Trujilio. He has made a major contribution. He proposed the use of UML for the design of data warehouse. He defined four UML profiles for modelling different aspects of data warehouse: the UML profile for Multidimensional Modelling, the Data Mapping profile, the ETL profile and Database Deployment profile. In [25],authors propose an approach that provides a theoretical foundation for the use of OO databases and Object relational databases in DW. This approach introduces a set of minimal constraints and extensions to UML for representing multidimensional modelling properties for DW. In [10,27], authors have proposed a multidimensional profile for the Data warehouse conceptual schema and Client conceptual schema. The author has also shown work in the field of physical schema. He has presented the database deployment profile in [13].

Another author who also has a significant role in the design of data warehouse is Stefano Rizzi. The author in [8] proposed a graphical conceptual model for data warehouses, called Dimensional Fact model, and gave a semi-automated methodology to build it from the pre-existing (conceptual or logical)schemes. Then in [11] based on the Dimensional Fact Model (DFM), he gave a general methodological framework for data warehouse design. Then he discussed some issues in Multidimensional modelling for the design of data ware house in [16].After that different authors gave different techniques and models for the design of data warehouse which we have discussed and compared in the next section.

COMPARITIVE ANALYSIS OF DW DESIGN TECHNIQUES

We have analyzed research work done in data warehouse design and its related issues. A brief tabular comparison has been provided below in table 1 on the basis of following criteria: Proposal, Framework/Architecture, Approach or technique proposed, schema used, whether the design can be extended to logical and physical design also, case study and tool used.

Table 1. Comparison of Work done by different Authors

Features → / Authors ↓	Proposal	Framework/Architecture	Approach/Technique	Schema used	Extended to Logical Level	Extended to Physical level	Case Study	Tool Support
1.S.Rizzi, Golfareli (1998) [11]		They propose a graphical conceptual model for DW called Dimensional Fact model	Gave a methodology to build it from the pre existing schemes.	Star	Yes	Yes	Sales DW	---
2. S.Rizzi, Golfareli (1999) [18]	They propose a general methodological framework for data warehouse design, based on Dimensional Fact Model (DFM).	----	After analyzing the existing information system and collecting the user requirements, a conceptual design is	Star	Yes	Yes	----	---

			carried out semi-automatic ally starting from the operationa l database scheme and then a workload is prepared.					
3.Juan Tujilio,Gome z (2000)	Object oriented approach to accomplish the conceptual modelling Of DW ,MD databases and OLAP application	----	They introduce d a set of constraint s and extensions to UML for showing MD modelling properties	Star	No	No	Sales DW	UML
4.Golfarelli, M., & Rizzi, S. (2001) [28]	They illustrated the main features of WAND, a prototype CASE tool for data warehouse design.	----	Implemen ted the tool WAND, which helps in structurin g a data mart and carrying out the Conceptu al design in a semi-automatic fashion.	----	Yes	-----	----	----
5. Juan Trujilio,E.Me dina and S.Lujan Mora [2002] [9]	They show how to manage the representation, manipulation and presentation of MD models on the web by means of extensible Style sheet Language Transformations (XSLT).	-----	They use Object-Oriented (OO) approach based on the Unified Modelling Language.	----	---	---	---	CASE tool
6.Abello, Saltor (2002) [6]	They present a MD conceptual object oriented model using extension of UML	-----	Used different structures of object oriented model like nodes,arcs ,detailed levels, stereotype s	----	---	----	---	---
7.Juan Trujilio , S.Lujan Mora and I.Song [2002] [10]	They present the development of multidimensiona l (MD) models for data warehouses using UML package diagrams	---	They present design guidelines and explain them with various examples.	---	----	-----	---	Ration al Rose 2000
8.Lujan Mora and Juan Trujilio (2003) [12]	They present a DW design method based on UML which is used to handle all DW design phases and steps from operational data sources to final implementation	Object oriented method based on UML	Used MD modelling ,MD databases and OLAP support	---	Yes	Yes	----	----
9. Lujan Mora and Juan Trujilio (2004)[13]	They proposed to model the physical design of a DW by using the component diagram and deployment diagram of UML	Framewo rk of a DW with 5 stages(i.e . source,int egration, DW,cust omisatio n and	Their approach reduces the overall developm ent time of a DW and covers all main	----	Yes	Yes	----	UML

		client) and 3 levels(conceptual, logical and physical). Each level is composed of diagrams -making a total of 15 diagrams	design phases of DW from conceptual modelling till final implementation					
10. Lujan Mora and Juan Trujilio,Vassiladis (2004) [14]	----	Framework for the design of DW back-stage including transformation rules at the attribute level and modelling of relationship between sources and targets in different levels of granularity	Their approach is based on usage of UML packages	---	Yes	Yes	----	Extend UML
11.Rizzi,Trujilio,Abello (2006) [16]	They aimed at discussing some open issues in modelling and design of data warehouses. Like issues regarding conceptual models, logical models, methods for design, interoperability etc.	----	-----	----	---	----	---	---
12.Medina,Trujilio et al.(2006) [31]	They gave a UML profile to represent MD and security aspects of conceptual modelling	-----	Use UML packages to group classes into higher level units	Star	----	----	Health system	UML
13.Deepti Mishra,Ali Yazici,Beril Pinar (2008) [17]	To compare various conceptual and logical DW design models and to find which is more suitable for implementing DW	---	-----	----	---	----	Sales and shipping system	---
14.Kamal Alaskar and Akhtar Shaikh (2009) [18]	Gave a UML profile for modelling DW usage on a conceptual level	Designed a conceptual UML model and translated it into XML logical model which is later converted into XML document as physical model	-----	Star	Yes	Yes	Hajj Pilgrim private tour	UML

15.Hui Ma,Yiping Yang and Fan Zhang (2009) [19]	They gave Anti-standardization technique in DW design	Converted ER model to multidimensional data model	Gave different anti standardization methods like increasing data redundancy, increasing derived columns etc.	Star	-----	----	Stock exchange	----
16.Fernandez Medina et al. (2010) [20]	Proposed a conceptual Multidimensional Data model(called as PIM)and transformed it into a secure XML DW as a logical model(called as PSM)	Model Driven Architecture(MDA) for developing secure DW.	Set of transformation rules to convert conceptual data model to logical model	---	yes	no	Airport DW	XML
17.Payal Pahwa and Shweta Taneja (2010) [23]	UML multidimensional model from various data sources based on UML schema	Conceptual level integration framework based on UML sources. First convert UML schema to UML class diagrams and then build multidimensional model from it	Object oriented approach for DW design. Mapping rules to convert UML class diagram to multidimensional model	Snowflake	----	---	Diabetic Interactive Electronic Treatment System(DIET)	UML
18.Francois Pinet et. al. (2010) [21]	Used UML to build a DW model	----	Gave an overview on UML based techniques and tools used in agricultural DW	-----	Yes	Yes	Pesticides in agriculture	UML
19.Anjana Gosain,Suman Mann (2010) [30]	-----	They extended the work of Alexander [7].They introduced seven operators over DW model.	Defined object oriented Md data model for description of data	----	No	No	----	UML
20.Jesus Pardillo and Jose Noberto Mazon (2011) [22]	They proposed that the use of ontologies will improve several aspects of the design of data Warehouses.	described several shortcomings of current data warehouse design approaches and discussed the benefit of using ontologies to overcome them	------	----	No	No	---	---

PROPOSED OBJECT ORIENTED FRAMEWORK FOR DATAWAREHOUSE CONCEPTUAL DESIGN

Components of the Framework

Our framework takes into account the requirements of the users. The framework is divided into two levels namely- Requirements level and Design level. At the Requirement level, the requirements are gathered from different users and a thorough analysis is made. The Integrator component integrates the collected requirements. Each level comprises of a number of components to control particular tasks along with detailed metadata repository to speed up the whole process.

In the next level, that is the design level; UML designer helps in extracting major objects and classes from data gathered from multiple data sources and constructs UML class diagrams. The UML class diagrams are converted to multi-dimensional model represented in the form of star or snowflake schema. The conversion is done by applying certain mapping rules that help in mapping the classes to facts and dimensions.

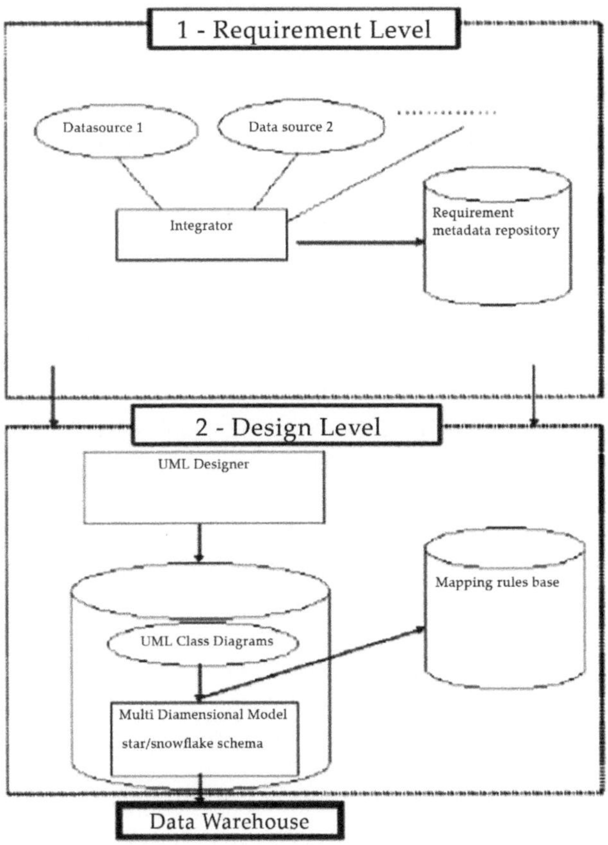

Figure 1. Proposed Framework.

CONCLUSION AND FUTURE SCOPE

In this paper, we make a comparative study of different approaches used for data warehouse design. In the literature survey, different authors [4, 5, 6, 7,8, 9,10,11,12,13] have proposed different techniques at different levels i.e. conceptual level ,logical level and physical level. Our comparative study is based on following criteria: Proposal, Framework/Architecture, Approach or technique proposed, Schema used, whether the design can be extended to logical and physical design also, Case study and Tool used.

We also propose an Object Oriented framework for data warehouse conceptual design. Our framework has many benefits. Firstly, the object oriented multidimensional approach [29] is the best as it satisfies all the criteria required for the data warehouse design and it is more adaptable as the user requirements are constantly changing. Secondly, we have used UML which is easy to learn and can model all real world objects. Thirdly, star and snowflake schemas are more efficient for data warehouse design as they are easy to learn and need fewer joins [18].

In the future, we are in the process of testing the proposed framework on a case study and implementing the same using JAVA at the front-end and Oracle 10g at the back-end.

REFERENCES

1. Inmon, W.H., Hackathorn, and R.D (1994) Using the data warehouse. Wiley-QED Publishing, Somerset, NJ, USA.
2. June 1999,UML Modelling Language Specification. Version 1.3, Available at http://www.rational.com/uml/resources/documention / (March 2009).
3. Booch G., Rumbaugh J., and Jacobson I.(1999) The Unified Modelling Language User Guide, Addison- Wesley Longman, p.482.
4. Vassiliadis P. and Sellis, T.,(1999) "A Survey of Logical Models for OLAP Databases". SIGMOD Record 28(4),pp 64–69.
5. S. Rizzi, A. Abelló, J. Lechtenbörger, J. Trujillo(2006) "Research in data warehouse modelling and design: dead or alive?" DOLAP, ACM, , pp. 3–10.
6. Abelló, J. Samos, and F. Saltor (2001) "A Framework for the Classification and Description of Multidimensional Data Models" In Proceedings of the 12th International Conference on Database and Expert Systems Applications (DEXA'01).
7. M. Blaschka, C. Sapia, G. Höfling, and B. Dinter,(1998) " Finding your way through ultidimensional data models" In Proceedings of the 9th International Conference on Database and Expert Systems Applications DEXA'98, volume 1460 of Lecture Notes in Computer science, pp 198–203, Vienna, Austria, August 1998. Springer-Verlag.
8. Stefano Rizzi, Matteo Golfarelli. (1998) "A Methodological Framework for Data Warehouse Design". DOLAP 98 Washington DC USA.Copyright ACM 1999 l-581 13-120-8/98/1 1...$5.00.
9. Juan Trujilio,E.Medina and S.Lujan Mora (2002) ,"A Web Oriented Approach

to manage Multidimensional Models through XML Schemas and XSLT '' EDBT 2002 Workshops, LNCS 2490, pp. 29–44, 2002. Springer-Verlag Berlin Heidelberg.

10. S.Lujan Mora and I.Song (2002),"Multidimensional Modeling with UML Package Diagrams " In Proc. of the 21st Int. Conf. on Conceptual Modeling.Lecture Notes in Computer Science pp 199-213,Finland,October 7-11,2002, . Springer-Verlag Stefano Rizzi, Matteo Golfarelli,D.Maio (1998) "The Dimensional Fact Model:A Conceptual Model for Data Warehouses." International Journal of Cooperative Information Systems(IJC IS),7(2-3):215-247.

11. Lujan Mora and Juan Trujilio (2003) "A Comprehensive Method for Data Warehouse Design."in Proceedings of 5th International Workshop on Design and Management of Data Warehose(DMDW'03), pp 1.1-1.14.

12. Juan Trujillo and Sergio LujánMora (2004) " Physical Modeling of Data Warehouses using UML" DOLAP'04, Washington, DC, USA.Copyright 2004 ACM 1581139772/04/0011 ...$5.00.

13. Sergio Luján-Mora1, Panos Vassiliadis and Juan Trujillo. (2004) " Data Mapping Diagrams for Data Warehouse Design with UML"in Proceedings of 23 rd International Conference on Conceptual Modeling (ER 04),volume 3288 of LNCS,China,Springer

14. Lujan Mora and Juan Trujilio (2006) ."Physical Modeling of Data warehouses by using UML Component and Deployment Diagrams:Design and implementation issues." Journal of Database Management 17(1)

15. Rizzi,Trujilio,Abello. (2006) " Research in Data Warehouse Modeling and Design:Dead or Alive?". DOLAP'06, Arlington, Virginia, USA.Copyright 2006 ACM 1-59593-530-4/06/0011 ...$5.00.

16. Deepti Mishra, Ali Yazici, Beri, Pinar Ba□aran. (2008) " A Casestudy of Data Models in Data Warehousing." 978-1-4244-2624-9/08/$25.00 ©2008 IEEE.

17. Kamal Alaskar1 and Akhtar Shaikh. (2009)" Object Oriented Data Modeling for Data Warehousing(An Extension of UML approach to study Hajj pilgrim's private tour as a Case Study). International Arab Journal of e-Technology, Vol. 1, No. 2.

18. Hui Ma,Yiping Yang and Fan Zhang (2009) "The Anti-standardized Design Research of Data Warehouse". IEEE.

19. Fernandez Medina et al. (2010)" Model Driven Development of Secure XML Data Warehouses: A Case Study" EDBT 2010, Lausanne, Switzerland. Copyright 2010 ACM 978-1-60558-945-9/10/0003 $10.00.

20. Francois Pinet et. al. (2010) "The use of UML to design agricultural data warehouses." AgEng 2010,International Conference on Agricultural Engineering. France

21. Jesús Pardillo and Jose-Norberto Mazón. (2011) " Using Ontologies for the Design of Data Warehouses." International Journal of Database Management Systems (IJDMS), Vol.3, No.2.

22. Payal Pahwa and Shweta Taneja. (2011) "Design of a Multidimensional model

using Object Oriented Features in UML." IARS International journal.

23. L. Cabibbo and R.Torlone(1998) "A Logical Approach to Multidimensional Databases" in Proceedings of 6th International Conference on Extending Database Technology EDBT 98 ,Volume 1337 of LNCS,pp 183-197, Spain,Springer.

24. J. Trujillo, M. Palomar, J. Gómez, I.-Y. Song(2001)," Designing data warehouses with OO conceptual models", IEEE Comput. 34 (12) (2001) 66– 75.

25. N.Tryfona,F.Busborg and J.G.Chriastiansen(1998) ,"StarER:A Conceptual Model for Data Warehouse Design",in Proceedings of the ACM 2 nd International Workshop on Data Warehousing and OLAP , DOLAP 99,pp 3-8 .

26. Luj´n-Mora S., Trujillo J., and Song, I.(2002), "Multidimensional modeling with UML package diagrams warehouses, " in Proceedings of 21 st International Conference on Conceptual Modeling, ER 02 ,Volume 2503 of LNCS,pp 199-213,Finland ,Springer.

27. Golfarelli, M., & Rizzi, S. (2001)." WanD: A CASE Tool for Data Warehouse Design". In Demo Proceedings 17th International Conference on Data Engineering (ICDE 2001), Heidelberg, Germany, 7-9.

28. Luj´n-Mora S., Trujillo J., and Song, I., "A UML profile for multidimensional modeling in data warehouses," Data Knowl. Eng. 59(3) 725–769.

29. Anjana Gosain,Suman Mann, (2010)"Object Oriented Multidimensional Model for a Data Warehouse with Operators", International Journal of Database Theory and Application Vol. 3, No. 4.

30. Rodolfo Villarroel, Emilio Soler, Eduardo Fernández-Medina, Juan Trujillo4,and Mario Piattini (2006)," Using UML Packages for Designing Secure Data Warehouses", ICCSA 2006, LNCS 3982, pp.1024 – 1034 .© Springer-Verlag Berlin Heidelberg.

31. Payal Pahwa, Shweta Taneja and Garima Thakur(2011)" Uclean: A Requirement based Object Oriented ETL Framework", International Journal of Computer Science & Engineering Survey (IJCSES) Vol.2, No.4, November 2011.

32. Sarkar, A., Choudhury, S., Chaki, N. & Bhattacharya, S, (2009) "Conceptual Level Design of Object Oriented Data Warehouse: Graph Semantic Based Model", INFOCOMP Journal of Computer Science, pp. 60-70.

33. Ponniah, P, (2001) Data Warehousing Fundamentals: A Comprehensive Guide for IT Professionals, pp. 402.

34. Elmasri, R. & Navathe, S.B, (2000) Fundamentals of Database Systems, Addison Weasely PubCo. ISBN 0201542633.

35. Nazri, Mior Nasir Mior,Noah, Shahrul Azman Mohd,Hamid, Zarinah (2008)," Automatic data warehouse conceptual design ",International Symposium on Information Technology,Malaysia.

36. Karen C. Davis Sandipto Banerjee (2007)," Teaching and Assessing a Data Warehouse Design Course", 24th British National Conference on Databases (BNCOD'07) 0-7695-2912-7/07 $20.00 © 2007 IEEE.

37. Mayank Sharma, Navin Rajpal and B.V.R.Reddy (2010)," Physical Data

Warehouse Design using Neural Network" . International Journal of Computer Applications 1(3):86–94, February 2010. Published By Foundation of Computer Science.

38. Abraham Silberschatz, Henry F. Korth, and Sudarshan (2002). Database System Concepts pp 445-489. 4th

39. Marotta, A., Ruggia, R.(2002)," Data warehouse design: a schema-transformation approach", Computer Science Society, 2002. SCCC 2002. Proceedings. 22nd International Conference of the Chilean.

4
CHAPTER

USING METADATA ANALYSIS AND BASE ANALYSIS TECHNIQUES IN DATA QUALITIES FRAMEWORK FOR DATA WAREHOUSES

Azwa Abdul Aziz, Md Yazid Mohd Saman and Mohd Pouzi Hamzah

Keywords: Data Warehouse (DW), Data Quality (DQ), metadata Analysis, DQ dimension

INTRODUCTION

The qualities of data contain in the Enterprise Information Systems have a significant impact and crucial to the decision maker. Many researchers have proved a lack of DQ may results failures in respective subject areas. As example, researchers have conducted the DQ impact in healthcare area, information system, IT management and many more. Sadiq *et al.* (2007) have stated that the hurricane protection in New Orleans failed because inadequate and incomplete using outdated elevation data. It has proved that the DQ problems may not just lead a lost of billion dollars in business transactions but can has a loss of hundred human life due to the decision made using a poor data.

As the scale in diversity of data grows in information system, the complexities of data grow multifold with it. The value and importance of knowledge, as seen by numerous organizations today, does without a doubt play a crucial role in the current ever-challenging and aggressive business environment (Ling, 2007).The last several years has introduce many of new technologies and tool to support the business process-grid systems, ETL applications, semantic web namely as a few. However, this technology can utilize and successes if a data resides in those of systems are qualities one. It is synonym with a sport car using a water to move its. The well-known principles of "Garbage In Garbage Out (GIGO)" indicates that regardless how much intelligence

Citation: Azwa Abdul Aziz, Md Yazid Mohd Saman and Mohd Pouzi Hamzah, "Using Metadata Analysis and Base Analysis Techniques in Data Qualities Framework for Data Warehouses," American Journal of Economics and Business Administration 3 (1): 112-119, 2011 ISSN 1945-5488.

and science is dedicated in new software solutions, DQ is still a major factor in the successful operation of IT systems.

Information systems within and between organizations are often highly distributed and heterogeneous. DW is the process of taking data from legacy and transaction database system and transforming it into organized information in a user friendly format to encourage data analysis and support fact-based business decision making (Kimball and Casserta, 2004). DW involves a lot of integration process of many databases into one large database. The DQ problems often been ignored in the process of data warehouse construction and utilization (Chen and Weng, 2009). Many DW projects are discontinued due to the insufficient DQ (English, 1999). It is not doubt that the successful of DW project depend to the qualities of data provided. This study proposes a DQ framework in DW architecture.

Definition of Data Quality and Its Measurement

Some researcher refer DQ as Information Quality (IQ) (Madnick *et al.*, 2009); (Diane *et al.*, 1997); (Wang, 1998) and (Lee *et al.*, 2002). There are tendency to use DQ to technical issues of DQ while IQ related to nontechnical issues. However in this study the term DQ refer to both technical and nontechnical issues of DQ.

The definition of DQ has subjective definitions across various fields. The simple definition of DQ is a data are "fit to use" (Wang, 1998). Some defines DQ as an accuracy of data or the freshness of data. Most of the DQ researcher and practitioner agree that DQ consist of several dimension to measure its. In early 1990's MIT propose Total Data Quality Management (TQDM) framework for measuring DQ. This becomes a pioneer work in DQ research which later most of the researcher using this framework to solve DQ problems (Madnick *et al.*, 2009). TQDM has classified the DQ dimension into 4 main categories which is Intrinsic, Accessibility, Contextual and Representational (Wang, 1998). Each category contains a several DQ dimension. As example accuracy and believability dimension is under intrinsic categories. However the basic sets of DQ dimension are accuracy, completeness, consistency and timeliness, which constitute the focus of the majority author (Batini *et al.*, 2009).

(Scannapieco *et al.*, 2009) have presented an architecture for managing data quality in cooperative information systems, by focusing on two specific modules, the Data Quality Broker and the Quality Notification Service. The Data Quality Broker allows for querying and improving data quality values. The Quality Notification Service is specifically targeted to the dissemination of changes on data quality values.

The dimensions propose in the framework of this study is emphasize on correctness (syntactic and semantic accuracy), consistency, completeness and timeliness (currency and volatility) of data. Those dimensions are important criteria to ensure the qualities of data in DW.

A DQ Framework for DW

Data Warehouse (DW) application systems are normally used to help top management of an organization to make a better decision for the company so as to survive in the competitive market. Business Intelligence applications have become a favorite tool that helps decision makers. The DQ problem often been ignored in the process of DW construction and utilization (Chen and Weng, 2009). Assessing ad improving DQ is a still complex task to do, especially in modern organizations where data are ubiquitous and diverse (Batini *et al.*, 2009). This framework is develops to improve the DQ in DW.

Figure 1 shows the propose framework. Basically the framework is following steps taken in TDQM method which are Define, Measure, Analyze and Improve. However the framework will use Metadata Analysis to gain the target qualities value and Base Analysis Techniques to view actual values in data sources. A gap analysis technique will provide the strategies to reduce the gap between the target and actual values. This study also proposes a DQ matrix strategy in DW design.

Define Sources System

Data sources refer to data that exist in legacies systems, Online Transaction Processing (OLTP) systems or an unstructured and semi structured data stores in files or external sources. OLTP record the daily transactions into operational databases. Data from sources will be extracted to the staging area. Staging area is a temporary area to perform cleansing, matching and transformation process. This is a standard procedure to be performs in any DW projects.

Analysis Phase

Analysis Phase is the critical process to ensure only qualities data available in DW. DQ researchers have proposed different idea how to perform data analysis. ETL tools available in market also provide several features to perform DQ assessment. Chen and Weng (2009) have proposed the analysis will be performs after the data are available in DW. A set of algorithm is created to verify integrity assessment and accuracy assessment. Yu *et al.* (2009) are suggested to clean the unwanted data base on user model framework. In this study the analysis phase is applies before a data are extract to DW. The analysis phase is divides into three type of analysis which are Metadata Analysis, Base Analysis and Gap Analysis. Metadata Analysis is the process of trying to understand what the data should be (target values) by analyzing both business metadata and technical metadata stores in metadata repositories. In contrast, the Base Analysis process is to gather what data look likes (actual values). Then a set of strategies to reduce the gap between these two values is gain from Gap Analysis.

Analysis Phase: Metadata analysis

The most simplistic definition of metadata is “data about data”. Metadata is all physical data and knowledge containing information about the business and technical processes and data used by corporation. Metadata Management Environment (MME) needs to be created in order to manage metadata efficiently. MME represents the architectural components, people and processes that are required to properly and systematically gather retain and disseminate metadata throughout the enterprise (Santoso and Kartika, 2006).

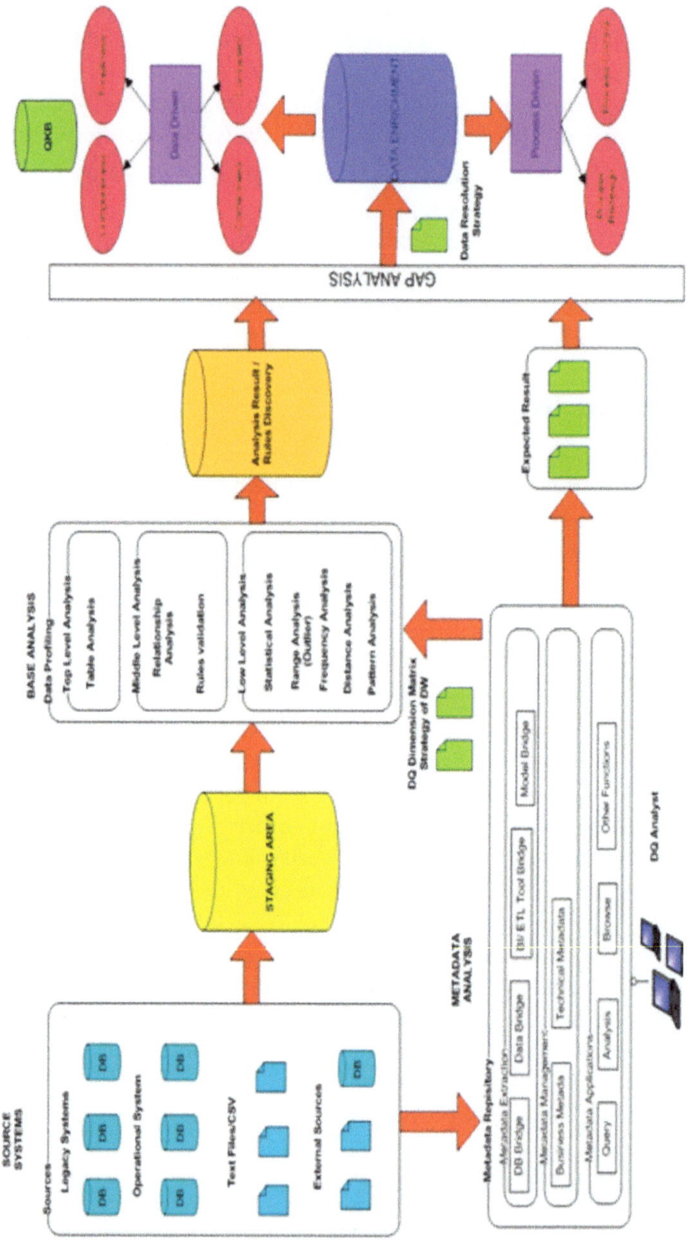

Figure 1: DQ Framework.

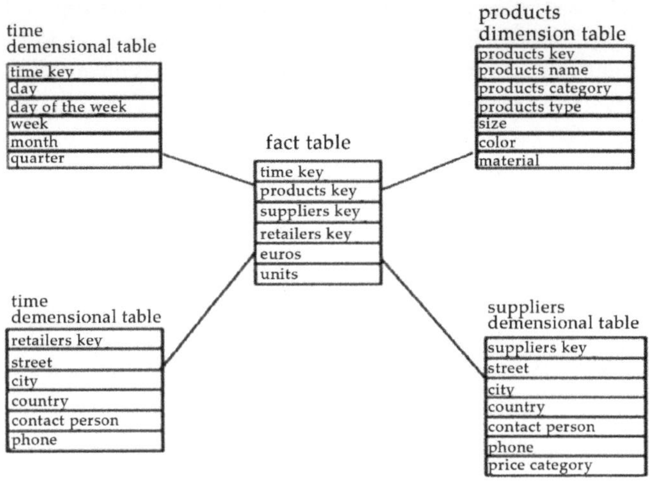

Figure 2: DW Star Schema Design.

Metadata repository propose in this study is summarize of what be done by (Chen and Weng, 2009). It contains three layers which is metadata extraction, metadata management and metadata applications. Metadata extraction acts as bridge to provide a driver connected to any Database Management System (DBMS) platform, text files, ETL tools or data modeler tool. Metadata Management stores the technical (user report, technical structure data mapping and transformation) and business metadata (business definition, subject area). Metadata application provides interface and functions for DQ Analyst to access metadata repository and perform metadata analysis.

Table 1: Fact tables

Attributes	Syntactic Acc	Semantic Acc	Complete	Consistent	Currency	Volatility
Time key						
Product key						
Supplier key						
Retailer key						
Euros	/				/	/
Unit	/				/	/
Supplier key	/		/			
Street	/	/		/		
City	/	/		/		
Country	/			/		
Contact per.						
Phone	/			/		/

DQ analyst tries to understand the flow and process of data both from technical and business perspective without looking on how the actual data been stored. The target values will be derived from Metadata Analysis. There are only four critical DQ dimensions propose in this framework. Accuracy dimension refer to the data values stored in the database correspond to real world values (Ballaou and Pazer, 1985). Syntactic accuracy defines the closeness of value *v* to the elements of corresponding definition domain, D (Batini *et al.*, 2009). Semantic accuracy is focus on same value which has different meaning. Completeness often related to missing values and null values. Consistency refers to the violation of semantic rules defined over a set of data items (Batini *et al.*, 2009).

Timeliness dimension divide into two categories which is currency and volatility. Currency factor captures the gap between the extractions of data from the sources and it delivery to users (Mokrane, 2004). Volatility is how frequent data been updated in sources system. DQ framework proposes a DQ dimension matrix strategies for DW design. As example, a Fig. 2 shows a star schema design for product information.

Metadata Analysis provides a DQ strategy on design above as shown in Table 1.

This will become a guideline during base analysis to verify the DQ dimension for selected attributes. Fact table contains Euros and Unit as fact unit. The most important information needed to verifies the quality of fact unit is whether the values are in the ranges (outlier analysis) or how frequency the values are changes (volatility). Attributes in dimension tables such street and contact person need to be a single meaning (semantic) and consistent. Loshin (2009) has proposed the prioritization matrix to provide clarity for deciding relative importance, getting agreement on priorities matrix and determining the best measure to handle the problems.

Analysis Phase: Base Analysis

Base Analysis also can be referring as data analysis. This is the process to determine the actual values store in the sources system using data profiling techniques. It will use a data store in staging area to perform data profiling. It will take a lot of time and cost if the analysis is done by scanning every single item in the tables. Therefore, a DQ Dimension Matrix Strategies is important document to ensure analysis is carrying efficiently. The researcher has develops a prototype known as Data Quality Analysis System (DQAS) to support Base Analysis using PHP programming and Oracle databases.

Table 2: Account

Attributes names	Prices
Data type	Double
Min value	-32990.0
Max value	898989.0
Mean	11423401973.0
Median	4848499.5

Generally, Base Analysis consists of three main analyses. It is a Top-Level Analysis (TLA), Middle-Level Analysis (MLA) and Low-Level Analysis (LLA). TLA investigating and verifying the upper view of data model such as table definition. MLA is checking the relationship between tables and the validation rules provide by sources system. LLA relates to the values of attributes profiling.

Table 3: Frequency analysis

Attributes names	Kuala Terengganu	70%
	K.T	10%
	Kuala Trg	9%
	K.Trg	8%
	Kla Trenganu	3%

Top-Level Analysis (TLA)

TLA will verify every tables or files which has been extract into staging area. This to ensure the tables contain in sources system are consistent in metadata technical definitions.

Middle- Level Analysis (MLA)

Two major sub analyses will be carry out in MLA are relationship analysis and rules validation analysis. Relationship analysis objective is to ensure the integrity rules of tables are not been violated. As example a foreign key exist in child table is exist in parent table. In contrast, rules validation ensures the logic of relationship between tables. Mokrane (2004) has given an example which stated the number of rows of a table depends on the number of rows of another table e.g., the number of accounts is equal or bigger than the number of customers.

Low-Level Analysis (LLA)

LLA related to the value analysis of an attributes. Some major process to be performs in LLA is statistical analysis, range analysis (outlier), frequency analysis, distances analysis and pattern analysis. Statistical Analysis provides mathematical information of data such as minimum/maximum values, mean, median, mode and standard deviation. This is to ensure the validity of the data and normally use against the metric in the tables. Table 2 shows an example of statistical analysis result using metric known as price.

Range Analysis determines whether the values contain in an attributes is within the range. Some refer as outlier analysis. As example a value of price items need to have maximum and minimum number. Age values are not appropriate if having a value which is more than 130 years. Frequency Analysis is the process to calculate percentage of value been enter into the system. This will helps to solve the semantic problems.

Table 4: Data Gap Analysis

Attributes	Target value	Actual value	Difference	Improve strategy
State	Kuala Lumpur	K.L K. Lumpur Kuala Lmpur	3difference value gather from frequency report or distance report	Change two incorrect value to correct value

Table 5: Rules Gap analysis

Target rules	Actual value	Difference	Improve strategy
Number of account table is should be less or equal than number customer table	Number of account is greater than number of customer	Account has content 100record more compare to the customer gather from MLA	Find PK exist in account tables not have FK in customer table. Apply integrity constraint in source system

However, it still needs human intervention to determine which values are correct as been proposed by. Instead, the correct value also can be store in Quality Knowledge Base (QKB) which acts as a synonym dictionary. The same concept of QKB has been mention by (Feng *et al.*, 2008) using Unified Traditional Chinese Medical Language System (UTCMLS) to tackle data inconsistency. Table 3 shows example of the result from statistical analysis using attributes city.

Distance Analysis is has been discussed by (Sadiq *et al.*, 2007) to overcome the problems of consistency and completeness. This framework proposes the correct values are store in QKB. Then a comparison will be applied to the value in store in sources system. The difference between this two value (e.g., ahmad, ahmd has distance values 1) will be verify. A set of algorithm is created to state that the number of distance value can be accepts as a same data. Distance Analysis is quick similar with a Hamming Code techniques in data communication to detect data error during transmission. The distance function can be successfully resolve the typo mismatch but there is and evident risk of matching two different terms which are similar in spelling, e.g,"Irin" and "Iris" should not be match as they may be intentionally different (Sadiq *et al.*, 2007). Here, the framework proposes a subject expert intervention to solve the problems arises.

Pattern Analysis is used to determine if the data values in a field are in the expected format. It will helps in developing the set of business rules for standardization. As an example, consider a pattern report for telephone numbers. There are many formats has been enter by users, but the valid formats should consist of three sets of numbers (three numbers for area code, three numbers for exchange and four numbers for station). The examples of formats enter by user are:

-9999999999- (999) 999-9999 - 999-999-9999 -999-999-AAAA- 999-999-Aaaa-99AA99999

(9-represents any digit, A- represents any upper case alpha (letter) character, a - represents any lower case alpha character).

Analysis Phase: Gap Analysis

Gap Analysis is verifying the comparison between target value gather from metadata analysis against actual value store in the sources system which is derived from base analysis. A set of improvement strategies is develop to closer the gap or ensure actual value same as target value. It can divide into data gap and rules gap analysis.

Data Gap Analysis is the process to identify the comparison between a data values contain in source systems with target quality values of the data. The values contained in source systems mostly are gathered from the result of LLA. Table 4 shows the result of Data Gap Analysis.

Rules Gap Analysis is a process to improve rules of data definitions. The rules of source systems need follow the definitions specified in the software requirements processes. Table 5 shows a sample of result from Rules Gap Analysis.

Improvement Phase: Data Enrichment

Data enrichment is the process to improve data and eliminate the fuzzy data exists in sources system. The improvements of the quality in the DW help to guarantee the reliability and help the enterprise to summarize and use the data for long period of time (Zhang *et al.*, 2009). Donald and Tayi (1999) have explores the factors that should be considered, such as current level of DQ, the level of DQ, the level of quality needed by the relevant decision process and the potential benefit of project designed to enhance DQ. The framework proposed classified the data enrichment process into two main categories which is data-driven and process-driven.

Improvement Phase: Data-Driven

Data-driven strategies improve a quality of data by directly modifying the value of data while process-driven strategies improve quality by redesigning the process that create or modify data. Data driven accentuate on how to improve four main dimensions that have been analyzed.

The first dimension is the accuracy with contains syntactic accuracy and semantic accuracy. Syntactic accuracy refer to the correctness of data such as redundant primary key refer to same objects, inconsistency attributes for similar records, relationship problem and human typo errors at sources system. Standardization techniques and transformation data to correct value is two steps can be taken to handles this problems. In additions, redesign the Entity Relationship Diagram (ERD) at sources system another measure can be taken to improve the quality of data. Of course the costs taken, the impacts of error and the priority of the improvement process needs to be study first.

A semantic problem refers to the same value which has different meaning. For handle this type of anomalies, subject expert need to add a new value that can be differentiate between those data. As example a two placed known as a "Taman Sentosa "exists in Kuala Terengganu area. This placed can be identifies if "Taman Sentosa "combines with postcode that make the value unique. Subject expert also can provide taxonomies as guidelines to recognize semantic values.

Inconsistency problems can be handle develops a complete dictionary that store the value expected such as Quality Knowledge Base (QKB). An algorithm can be develops to detect inconsistent value as mention before. Those values can transform into correct value by using Extract, Transform and Load (ETL) value available in market. A null value, missing values and uncompleted records can be solved once again by interferences from subject experts. They need to provide correct values or default value to transform the data.

Improving ETL jobs and schedule will helps to handle timeliness dimension problems. ETL developers can design a job the captures the information needed for currency dimension such as a time taken to extract data from sources systems to DW.

Volatility problem which deal with data that rapidly changes can be improved by increase the time to trigger ETL jobs. ETL tools provides by vendors has a capabilities to handle complex jobs with helps from powerful infra architecture and technologies. Now there are demand to provide report from DW which are not monthly basis or weekly basis, but a daily reports or even hour reports.

Improvement Phase: Process-Driven

Process-Driven proposes the improvement by changing the process to creating or modifying data at the sources system. It also can be refers as Business Process Reengineering (BPR). BPR is best method to handle DQ problem, however it will take a lot of cost and time to perform the activities. The worse case, redesign the sources system may lead to the failure of existing systems. Process- Driven techniques should be avoided in improving DQ in DW systems.

MATERIALS AND METHODS

The research is used TQDM method as a main reference in order to create a DQ framework life cycle in DW architecture. Then to support the framework, it is using a prototype known as DQAS which integrated with BI/ETL opens sources tools. A sample Oracle Schema known as Human Resource (HR) Schema is chose to study differences between applying the framework or not. Lastly, DQ framework is demonstrated in selected organizations in order to gain feedback from industrial.

RESULTS

The result has shows by applying DQ framework to HR schema, it is improved the quality of data. It avoiding data anomalies such as inconsistent data contain in the system applications. To get the feedback from selected companies, questionnaires have been given to respondents. The research questions have been divided into seven factors. They are "Understandable of Framework", "System Functionality", "DQAS Interface", "Commercial Values", "User Interest", "Technology Used in DQAS" and "OSS DW Interest". The result is shown in Fig. 3. The result show user interested in applying DQ processes in their organizations.

DISCUSSION

DW projects require high cost and involvement of many parties. Hence, introducing DQ Analysis make organizations need to provide additional budgets to buy DQ software tools. In addition, the ETL and BI tools are already required a high cost to own. However, the organizations need to understand that a DQ analysis is crucial process to ensure the quality of data in DW. Lack of quality data may lead to the failure in DW projects. By introducing DQ Life Cycle Framework for DW, it is proved that it helps to improve the quality of data reside in databases. However, the framework is still can be improve. The implementation of the framework in real life situation is important to analyze weaknesses of framework.

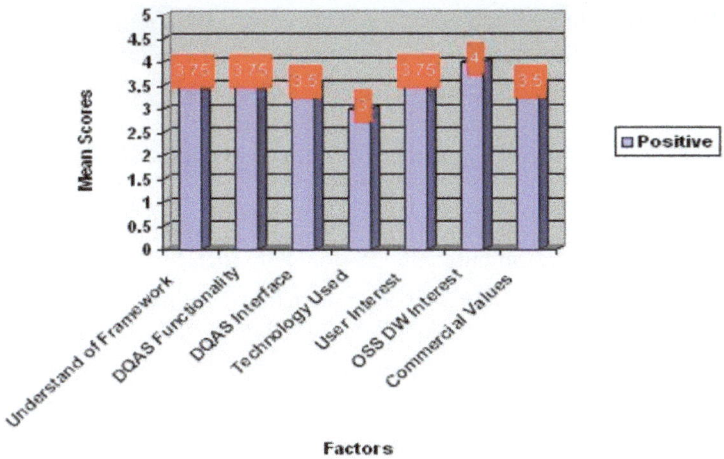

Figure 3: Result of the Analysis.

CONCLUSION

This study has discussed a framework for DQ measurement in DW architecture. To prove a concept in the framework, a prototype is develops using PHP known as DQAS. DQAS can use to perform Base Analysis techniques to any Oracle databases. Then, DQAS is integrates with Talend Open Studio (TOS) ETL and Eclipse Business Intelligence Reporting Tools (BIRT) to implement the DQ framework. Both TOS and BIRT are open sources tools. A schema provided by Oracle known as HR schema is selected as data sources. Then a multidimensional model is created in DW schema base on HR schema. A mapping document between sources to target table is prepared. Finally the differences applying the DQ framework and without using it is shown. It is hopes the implementation of the framework suggested in real situation can be conducted to obtain more accurate result.

REFERENCES

1. Ling, T.N., 2011. Knowledge management acceptance: factors amongst small and medium size enterprises. Am. J. Econ. Bus. Admin., 3: 73-80. DOI: 10.3844/ajebasp.2011.73.80
2. Ballaou, D. and H. Pazer, 1985. Modeling data and process quality in multi-input, multi-output information system. Manage. Sci., 31: 150-162. DOI: 10.1287/mnsc.31.2.150
3. Batini, C., C. Cappielo, C. Francalanci and A. Maurino, 2009. Methodologies for data quality assessment and improvement. ACM Comput. Surveys, 41: 1-52. DOI: 10.1145/1541880.1541883
4. Batini, C., F. Cabitza, C. Cappiello and C. Francalanci, 2006. A comprehensive

data quality for web and strurured data. Proceeding of the 1st International Conference on Management, Dec. 6-6, University Degli Studi di Milano Bococca, Bangalore, pp: 448-456. DOI: 10.1109/ICDIM.2007.369236

5. Chen, B. and B. Wang, 2009. Analysis and solution of data quality in data warehouse of Chinese materia medica. Proceeding of 2009 4th International Conference on Computer Science and Education, July 25-28, Nanning, China, pp: 823-827. DOI: 10.1109/ICCSE.2009.5228165

6. Diane, M.S., Y.W. Lee and R.W. Wang, 1997. 10 Potholes in the road to information quality. Computer, 30: 38-46. DOI: 10.1109/2.607057

7. Donald, P.B. and G.K. Tayi, 1999. Enhancing data quality in data warehouse environments. Communi. ACM, 42: 73-78. DOI: 10.1145/291469.291471

8. Loshin, D., 2009. Data Quality Remediation. Inform. Syst. Manage., http://www.information-management.com/white_papers/data_quality-10015359-1.htm

9. English, L., 1999. Improving data warehouse and business information quality. 1st Edn., John Wiley and Sons, New York, ISBN: 0471253839, pp: 518.

10. Feng, Y., Z. Wu, H. Chen, T. Yu and Y. Mao *et al.*, 2008. Data quality in traditional Chinese medicine. Proceeding of International Conference on Bio Medical Engineering and Informatics, May 27-30, Zhejiang University, Sanya, pp: 255-259. DOI: 10.1109/BMEI.2008.268

11. Kimball, R. and J. Caserta, 2004. The Data Warehouse ETL Toolkit. 1st Edn., Wiley and Sons, New York, ISBN: 0764567578, pp: 491.

12. Lee, Y.W., D.M. Strong, B.K. Kahn and R.K. Wang, 2002. AIMQ: A methodology for information quality assessment. Inform. Manage., 40: 133-146. DOI: 10.1016/S0378-7206(02)00043-5

13. Madnick, S.E. Y.W. Lee and H. Zhu, 2009. Overview and framework for data and information quality research. J. Data Inform. Qual., 1: 1-22. DOI: 10.1145/1515693.1516680

14. Mokrane, B., 2004. A framework for analysis of data freshness. Proceedings of the international workshop on Information quality in information system, (IWIQIS'04), ACM Press, New York. USA., pp: 59-67. DOI: 10.1145/1012453.1012464

15. Sadiq, S., X. Zhou and O. Maria, 2007. Data quality-the key success factor for data driven engineering. Proceeding of the International Conference on Network and Parallel Computing-Workshops, Sept. 18-21, IEEE Xplore Press, Liaoning, pp: 48-56. DOI: 10.1109/NPC.2007.176

16. Santoso, L.W. and G. Kartika, 2006. A proposal of Data quality for data warehouses environment. Jurusan Teknik Inform., 7: 143-148.

17. Scannapieco, M., A. Virgillito, C. Marchetti, M. Mecella and R. Baldoni, 2004. The DaQuinCIS architecture: A platform for exchanging and improving data quality in cooperative information systems. Inform. Syst., 29: 551-582. DOI: 10.1016/j.is.2003.12.004

18. Wang, R.Y., A product perspective on total data quality management. Comm. ACM, 41: 58-65. DOI: 10.1145/269012.269022

19. Yu, H., Z. Xiao-yi, Y. Zhen and J. Guao-quan, 2009 A universal data cleaning framework based on user model. Proceeding of the International Colloquium on Computing, Communication, Control and Management, Aug. 8-9, IEEE Xplore Press, Sanya, pp: 200-2002. DOI: 10.1109/CCCM.2009.5267946

20. Zhang, J., Q. Wen and H. Zhang, 2009. The research in improving the quality of DW data, the job-scheduling and checking based program in upgrading DW performance. Proceedings of the 5th International Conference on Wireless Communications, Networking and Mobile Computing. Sept. 24-26, IEEE Explore Press, Beijing, pp: 1-4. DOI: 10.1109/WICOM.2009.5303181

5
CHAPTER

THE CRITICAL FACTORS INFLUENCING THE ADOPTIONS OF DATA WAREHOUSE

Erappa G., Dr. K. Krishnamoorthy and Thippaswamy G.

Keywords – Data Warehousing, Network Management, Training and Communication, Materialized View

INTRODUCTION

Authors are encouraged to have their contribution checked for grammar. Abbreviations are allowed but should be spelt out in full when first used. Integers ten and below are to be spelt out. Italicize foreign language phrases (e.g. Latin, French). Over the years, firms have accumulated a large volume of data that potentially contain valuable information about their business. These data, which are stored in operational databases, are not easily accessible to decision makers due to most firms existing information technology (IT) infrastructure. Further, these operational databases are likely to be geographically or logically dispersed, thereby making it difficult and inconvenient to access.

Traditionally, the information systems Departments are the sole interface to firms' data stored in computer systems. Executives from various departments rely on the IS department to satisfy their needs for information that is necessary for decision making. The turnaround time is usually long and information is often not delivered on time to users, which in turn reduces the value of the information. Further, reports produced by the ARE departments usually pro-vide a one-dimensional (rather than multidimensional) view of the data. Executives will require different reports showing information in various dimensions (e.g., by product lines or by region.). Further, the ability to change dimensions and drill down enables more effective data analysis and

Citation: Erappa G., Dr. K. Krishnamoorthy and Thippaswamy G., "The Critical Factors Influencing the Adoptions of Data Warehouse," International Journal of Electronics Communication and Computer Engineering Volume 5, Issue 3, ISSN: 2249–071X.

decision making. However, since senior executives tend to ask for whatever they need, it is usually time consuming for the IS departments to deliver different reports customized to different executives. Consequently, only a subset of reports may be delivered on time. Even if the reports are delivered on time, it may not be exactly what the executive wants due to miscommunication or lack of clarity in specifying the information he/she needs. Further, on receiving the reports, the executive may discover that he/she needs further detailed information, which in turn may require more time for the IS department to provide. Even if further information is not needed, the executive may still need to seek clarification from the IS department regarding various aspects of the information provided. This is likely to result in further delay, thereby hindering timely and effective decision making.

With the appropriate user friendly query tools, staff members can experiment with different views of the data, thereby enabling him/her to understand the situation and make better decisions. Further, if necessary, staff members can drill down to obtain more detailed data about certain areas. This ability to change views and drill down greatly enhances the value of a data warehouse for decision making since detailed data can be readily accessed, whenever required. Past research has often focused on the technology required to establish and support data warehouses [14]. Previous work has also provided both technical [16] and non-technical prescriptions [18] for building and implementing data warehouses. The factors affecting data warehouse implementation [14], warehouse issues [13, 15], as well as the pitfalls of data warehouse development [19] have also been investigated. In addition, comparative cases of data warehousing [13] and businesses, which successfully deploy data warehouse, are often described.

The text is to be typeset in 10 pt roman, single spaced with baselineskip of 13 pt. Text area is 5 inches in width and the height is 8 inches (including running head). Final pagination and insertion of running titles will be done by the publisher. Upon acceptance, authors are required to submit their data source file including postscript files for figures.

PERFORMANCE EFFECT FACTOR

A Data ware house system is actually about strongly combine different business functions, so the close co-operation and communication across disparate business functions would be a natural prerequisite in a Data ware house project. Some authors have described the co-ordination and communication between departments as the oil that keeps everything working properly in these contexts. [7, 8] An effective communications program keeps people informed and generates interest in using the data warehouse. Organizational rules to rationalize inconsistencies had to be established. Clear and consistent communication of company-wide warehouse goals and policies fosters employee participation on three critical fronts: First, it reinforces the front-line employees' contribution of information to the warehouse. Second, it encourages information sharing to support ongoing business activities. Third, it inspires mid-level managers to use the data warehouse to inform key stakeholders regarding decisions, and new projects. The cooperation between the departments in an organization has a large effect on the smooth flow of the required information and expertise among the departments, which strongly influences the successful adoption of data warehouse technology. Interdepartmental cooperation and communication is a must for any project.

Education, Training and Documentation

Training and education of the employees are required in a successful data warehouse project. A data warehouse is not a simple project or an easy-to-learn system. It demands time to educate and transfer the knowledge to users by setting up training courses and distributing related-material. In most computing projects, management identifies the need for training, but does not always fund training. With every new database there is a need for another training course, complete with reference materials. Every enhancement or change to the warehouse must be documented and communicated to warehouse users.

Training expands the communication process by maintaining a level competence in both the business and IT community as to the tools and mechanisms of the data warehouses. The quality of employees and their development through training and education are major factors in determining long-term profitability of a small business. If you hire and keep good employees, it is good policy to invest in the development of their skills, so they can increase their productivity. Training often is considered for new employees only.

This is a mistake because ongoing training for current employees helps them adjust to rapidly changing job requirements. Training and updating the employees' knowledge of data ware house is a major challenge. Data ware house implementation requires a huge mass of knowledge to enable people to use, cope and solve problems within the framework of the system. Training employees to use ERP is not as simple as training them in any other packaged-software such as a Microsoft package. An ERP system is extremely complex and demands intensive training; it is difficult for the trainers to pass the knowledge to the users within a short period of time. Top management should understand this aspect and should be willing to spend adequate money on educating and training the end users. [9]

Call Center

Another role of the data warehouse support and protection group is the problem resolution when some problem is encountered in the data warehouse. In the case of data warehouses, the expensive and the risky nature of data warehouses have forced the potential adopters to pay extra attention in selecting appropriate vendors to increase the possibility of having successful data warehouse initiatives.

The Call Center is an important division for any organization as it serves as the primary interaction point between customers and the company. In many situations, it is the only interaction point and therefore, responsible for the customer's experience and satisfaction. Due to this heightened level of importance, it is critical that the contact handling process is conducted both efficiently and effectively. This process specifies how to collect, document, answer and/or escalate calls, requests, and queries related to issues with the data warehousing environment. Problem documentation can be completed either by the Call Center representative and/or in conjunction with a form completed by the end user or IT support person requesting a service or action. All inquiries, no matter how trivial should be logged, especially during the start of a new data warehouse or mart. These bits of information can form clues to taking proactive action to bigger problems before they emerge.

Network Management

If there is a heterogeneous group of platforms for the data warehouse implementation, network management is going to be one of the most demanding tasks [6]. Modern communication networks create large amounts of operational data, Including traffic and utilization statistics and alarm/fault data at various levels of detail. These massive collections of network-management data can grow the order of several Tera bytes per year, and typically hide "knowledge" that is crucial to some of the key tasks involved in effectively managing a communication network (e.g., capacity planning and traffic engineering).Besides providing easy access to people and data around the globe, modern communication networks also generate massive amounts of operational data throughout their life span. As an example, Internet Service Providers (ISPs) continuously collect traffic and utilization information over their network to enable key network- management applications. Not only are users coming constantly on-line, but users and equipment are invariably moving to new locations. The networking hardware is proliferating with LANs, WANs, hubs, routers, switches and multiplexers. Leaving behind all this is the next stage – users wanting to access internet based data sources along with the corporate data, requiring even greater bandwidth and network management resources. Managing this environment is one big challenge, capacity planning for the future is another. If the data warehouse team is not quite good in networking technology than there should be at least one person in the organization who understands technology.

Extract Transform and Load (ETL)

The ETL process is much more than code written to move data. The ETL architect also serves as the central point for understanding the various technical standards that need to be developed if they don't already exist. These might include limits on file size when transmitting data over the company intranet, requirements for passing data through firewalls that exist between internal and external environments, data design standards, standards for usage of logical and physical design tools and configuration management of source code, executables and documentation. The ETL architect must also ensure that the ETL design process is repeatable, documented and put under proper change control.

Extract, transform and load (ETL) is the core process of data integration and is typically associated with data warehousing. ETL tools extract data from a chosen source, transform it into new formats according to business rules, and then load it into target data structure. [VG10] ETL which stands for extract, transform, and load is a three-stage process in database usage and data warehousing. It enables integration and analysis of the data stored in different databases and heterogeneous formats. After it is collected from multiple sources (extraction), the data is reformatted and cleansed for operational needs (transformation). Finally, it is loaded into a target database, data warehouse or a data mart to be analyzed. If source data taken from various sources is not cleanse, extracted properly, transformed and integrated in the proper way, the extracted data will often be stored in a central staging area where it will cleanse and otherwise transformed before loading into the warehouse. An alternative approach to information integration is that of mediation: data is extracted from original data sources on demand when a query is posed, with transformation to produce a query result

Materialized View

A view can be materialized by storing the tuples of the view in the database. Index structures can be built on the materialized view. Consequently, database accesses to the materialized view can be much faster than recompiling the view. A materialized view is thus like a cache {a copy of the data that can be accessed quickly.} a materialized view provides fast access to data; the speed difference may be critical in applications where the query rate is high and the views are complex so that it is not possible to recomputed the view for every query.

Materialized views provide a framework within which to collect information into the warehouse from several databases without copying each database in the warehouse. Queries on the warehouse can then be answered using the materialized views without accessing the remote databases. Provisioning, or changes, still occurs on the remote databases, and are transmitted to the warehouse as a set of modifications. Incremental view maintenance techniques can be used to maintain the materialized views in response to these modifications.

Materialized views, and many recognize dependencies between base tables and the Materialized on of very efficient refresh expressions. This makes Database Server more manageable and user friendly

CONCLUSION

A data warehouse solution is not only a software package. It is a complex process to establish sophisticated and integrated information systems. The adoption of this technology requires massive capital expenditure, utilizes a certain deal of implementation time and has a very high likelihood of failure. Therefore, many adoption-related factors must be carefully assessed before the real adoption is actualized. I do study on BSNL its shows that the first and the most important part of a data warehouse maintenance program is the training of its users. The study shows that most business users are reluctant to adopt technology to carry out their work, therefore pursuing a business user to use data warehouse is inevitable. To pursue business users in using data warehouse the communication and training program is a must. The training program gives the users of data warehouse an insight into the qualities and capabilities of a data warehouse and teaches them the communication process keeps the business users and IT users in contact with each other to have exchange of views, suggestions and any guidance towards enhanced performance of a data warehouse. The services of help desk and problem management play an important role in taking valuable output from the data warehouse. Support is always required in any information system, same is the case with a data warehouse but here the support is needed 24 hours a day. Some of the processes like ETL are carried out during the night, which require presence of support staff to rectify any problem. The support team also points out if there is any loop hole or problem area within the data warehouse that should be addressed. Apart from help desk each data warehouse support team develops its own problem management process. The process defines necessary routines and instructions to counter any problem found in the warehouse. If the problems found in the data warehouse are not addressed at the right time, this leads to performance shortfalls, and usability and availability issues in near future. Thus help desk and problem management play a key role in improving data warehouse performance and getting the desired output from it. Network management also plays its part in improving data warehouse performance. From the case study we concluded that by having a fast and reliable network user queries get a much shorter response time especially in a distributed data warehouse.

REFERENCES

1. An investigation of the factors affecting data warehousing success by Roger L. Hayen et. al. in journal of Issues in Information Systems, Volume VIII, No. 2, 2007.
2. Developing a Data Warehouse Process that responds to the needs of the Enterprise,Peter R. Welbrock Smith-Hanley Consulting Group Philadelphia, PA
3. The data warehouse toolkit. 2nd edition. Ralph Kimball, Margy Ross. 2002 Wiley computer publishing..
4. Data Warehouse Management Handbook by Richard Kachur. 2000 Prentice Hall .
5. Building, using, and managing the data warehouse. Ramon Barquin, George Zagelow,Katherine hammer, Mark sweiger, George Burch, Dennis Berg, Christopher Heagele,Katherine Glassey-Edholm, David Menninger, Paul Barth, J.D. Welch, Narsim ganti, Herb Edelstein, Bernard Boar, Robert Small. Data warehousing institute series from Prentice Hall.Y.
6. Data warehouse, Practical advice from the experts. 1997. Prentice hall by Joyce Bischoff & Ted Alexander
7. Akkermans and Helden, Vicious and virtuous cycles in ERP implementation: A case study of interrelations between critical success factors, European journal of information systems, 2002, Vol.11 Iss. 1, p35..
8. Nah et al., Critical factors for successful implementation of enterprise systems, Business process management, Bradford: 2001, Vol.7 Iss.3, p285.
9. Bingi et al., Critical issues affecting an ERP implementation, Information systems management, 1999, Vol.16 Issue3.
10. Lessons from a successful data warehouse implementation. Dr. John D Porter and john. J Rome. Arizona State University.
11. Building a data warehouse for decision support. 1996 Prentice Hall. By Vidette Poe with contributions from Laura L. Reeves.

12. Fundamentals of database systems. 4th Edition. Persons international and Addison Wesley. Ramez Elmasri and Shamkant B. Navathe
13. N. Alur, Missing links in data warehousing, Database Programming and Design _1995. 21–23, September.
14. E. Appleton, The right server for your data warehouse, Datamation 41 _5. _1995. 56–58, March.
15. S. Atre, Rules for data cleansing, Computerworld _1998.69–72, March 8.
16. D.P. Ballou, G.K. Tayi, Enhancing data quality in data warehouse environments, Communications of the ACM 42 (1) (1999) 73–78.
17. J. Bischoff, Achieving warehouse success, Database Programming and Design (1994) 27–33, July.
18. S. Deck, Data warehouses: plan well, start small, Computer world _1998. 9, August 3.

SECTION II: BUSINESS-ORIENTED DATA WAREHOUSE APPLICATIONS

6

CHAPTER

DATA WAREHOUSING, DATA MINING, OLAP AND OLTP TECHNOLOGIES

G.Satyanarayana Reddy, Rallabandi Srinivasu, M. Poorna Chander Rao and Srikanth Reddy Rikkula

Keywords: Data Warehousing, OLAP, OLTP, Data Mining, Decision Making and Decision Support

INTRODUCTION

A data warehouse is a "subject-oriented, integrated, time varying, non-volatile collection of data that is used primarily in organizational decision making. (Inmon, W.H.,1992) Typically, the data warehouse is maintained separately from the organization's operational databases. There are many reasons for doing this. The data warehouse supports on-line analytical processing (OLAP), the functional and performance requirements of which are quite different from those of the on-line transaction processing (OLTP) applications traditionally supported by the operational databases.

Data warehousing is a collection of decision support technologies, aimed at enabling the knowledge worker (executive, manager, analyst) to make better and faster decisions. It serves as a physical implementation of a decision support data model and stores the information on which an enterprise needs to make strategic decisions.

The data can be stored in many different types of databases. One data base architecture that has recently emerged is the "data warehouse", a repository of multiple heterogeneous data sources, organized under a unified schema at a single site in order to facilitate management decision-making. Data warehouse technology includes data cleansing, data integration and online Analytical processing. OLAP stands for analysis techniques with functionalities such as summarization, consolidation and aggregation,

Citation: G. Satyanarayana Reddy, Rallabandi Srinivasu, M. Poorna Chander Rao and Srikanth Reddy Rikkula, "Data Warehousing, Data Mining, OLAP and OLTP Technologies," International Journal on Computer Science and Engineering Vol. 02, No. 09, 2010, 2865-2873. ISSN : 0975-3397.

as well as the ability to view information from different angles. Ten years ago, Data Warehousing was largely unknown. Today, many companies are receiving considerable business value from their warehousing efforts. First American Corporation (FAC), a regional bank located in the Southeast, lost $60 million in 1990 and was operating under letters of agreement with regulators. A new senior management team developed a customer intimacy strategy with a data warehouse at the heart of the strategy. Using warehouse data, FAC was able to determine the profitability of all of their clients and products; develop programs to attract, maintain, and enhance their customer base; create profitable new product and service offerings; and redesign their distribution channels to increase profitability and better meet customers' needs. Data warehousing helped FAC to become a profitable, innovative leader in the financial services industry.

Since the introduction of the data warehouse concept in the late 1980ies (e.g. Devlin/Murphy 1988), data warehouse systems are now an established component of information systems landscape in most companies. Due to high failure rates of data warehouse projects, several procedure models for building data warehouse systems were published considering their special requirements (e.g. Inmon 1996, Kimball 1996, Gardner 1998, Simon 1998). However, these methodologies were mainly focused on technical issues, like architectural concepts and data modeling. But according to studies about critical success factors of data warehouse projects organizational, political and cultural factors are at least as important as technical ones (Frolick/Lindsey 2003, Hwang et al. 2002, Finnegan/Sammon 1999). In addition, most development methodologies are lacking concepts to ensure long-term evolution and establishment of data warehouse systems (O'Donnell et al. 2002), which are both primarily organizational challenges (Meyer/Winter 2001). Up to now only few authors have adopted a mainly organizational-driven view on data warehouse systems. Kachur (2000) describes activities and organizational structures for data warehouse management.

DATA WAREHOUSING

Definition of Data Warehousing

According to W.H.Inmon, a leading architect in the construction of data warehouse systems, A data warehouse is a subject-oriented, integrated, time-variant and non-volatile collection of data in support of management's decision making process. So, data warehouse can be said to be a semantically consistent data store that serves as a physical implementation of a decision support data model and stores the information on which an enterprise needs to make strategic decisions. So, its architecture is said to be constructed by integrating data from multiple heterogeneous sources to support and /or adhoc queries, analytical reporting and decision-making. Data warehouses provide on-line analytical processing (OLAP) tools for the interactive analysis of multidimensional data of varied granularities, which facilitates effective data mining. The functional and performance requirements of OLAP are quite different from those of the on-line transaction processing applications traditionally supported by the operational databases.

Data can now be stored in many different types of databases. One type of database architecture that has recently emerged is data warehouse, which is a repository of multiple heterogeneous data sources, organized under a unified schema at a single site in order to facilitate management decision-making (Chaudhuri & Dayal 1997; Chawatte, Garcia-Molina, Hammer, Ireland, Papakonstantinou, Ullman & Wisdom 1994; Han & Kamber 2001). Data warehouse technology includes data cleaning, data integrating, and on-line analytical processing (OLAP) that is, analysis techniques with functionalities such as summarization, consolidation and aggregation, as well as the ability to view information from different angles.

A data warehouse is defined as a "subject-oriented, integrated, time variant, non-volatile collection of data that serves as a physical implementation of a decision support data model and stores the information on which an enterprise needs to make strategic decisions. In data warehouses historical, summarized and consolidated data is more important than detailed, individual records. Since data warehouses contain consolidated data, perhaps from several operational databases, over potentially long periods of time, they tend to be much larger than operational databases. Most queries on data warehouses are ad hoc and are complex queries that can access millions of records and perform a lot of scans, joins, and aggregates. Due to the complexity query throughput and response times are more important than transaction throughput.

Data warehousing is a collection of *decision support* technologies, aimed at enabling the *knowledge worker* (executive, manager, and analyst) to make better and faster decisions. Data warehousing technologies have been successfully deployed in many industries: manufacturing (for order shipment and customer support), retail (for user profiling and inventory management), financial services (for claims analysis, risk analysis, credit card analysis, and fraud detection), transportation (for fleet management), telecommunications (for call analysis and fraud detection), utilities (for power usage analysis), and healthcare (for outcomes analysis). This paper presents a roadmap of data warehousing technologies, focusing on the special requirements that data warehouses place on database management systems (DBMSs).

Data Warehousing Fundamentals

A data warehouse (or smaller -scale data mart) is a specially prepared repository of data designed to support decision making. The data comes from operational systems and external sources. To create the data warehouse, data are extracted from source systems, cleaned (e.g., to detect and correct errors), transformed (e.g., put into subject groups or summarized), and loaded into a data store (i.e., placed into a data warehouse).

The data in a data warehouse have the following characteristics:

- *Subject oriented* — The data are logically organized around major subjects of the organization, e.g., around customers, sales, or items produced.
- *Integrated* — All of the data about the subject are combined and can be analyzed together.
- *Time variant* — Historical data are maintained in detail form.
- *Nonvolatile* — The data are read only, not updated or changed by users.

A data warehouse draws data from operational systems, but is physically separate and serves a different purpose. Operational systems have their own databases and are used for transaction processing; a data warehouse has its own database and is used to support decision making. Once the warehouse is created, users (e.g., analysts, managers) access the data in the warehouse using tools that generate SQL (i.e., structured query language) queries or through applications such as a decision support system or an executive information system. "Data warehousing" is a broader term than "data warehouse" and is used to describe the creation, maintenance, use, and continuous refreshing of the data in the warehouse.

Adelman/Moss (2000) explains how to design and manage data warehouse systems focusing on project management aspects. In addition, they give an overview of organizational roles involved in a typical data warehouse project. Meyer (2000) and Meyer/Winter (2001) present organizational requirements for data warehousing and the concept of data ownership. A two-dimensional organizational structure for large financial service companies combining infrastructural competencies and content competencies is derived. Auth (2003) develops a process-oriented organizational concept for metadata management providing detailed activity chains and organizational roles. As shown above the organizational domain of data warehouse systems still lacks attention of data warehouse researchers compared to technical aspects. Therefore this paper aims at providing deeper insights in the current organizational situation of data warehouse departments in practice. The organizational domain of companies can be divided in a structural, human resource, political, and symbolic dimension and each dimension requires different design instruments (Bolman/Deal 2003, Mueller-Stewens 2003). The structural dimension focuses on goals, formal roles and relationships. Structures are created to achieve the company's goals considering technological and environmental factors. Rules, policies, processes, and hierarchies are the design elements of the structural dimension. Drawing from psychology, the human resource dimension takes care about the needs, feelings, prejudices, and limitations of all individuals. The political dimension sees organizations as arenas. Different interest groups cause conflicts while competing for power and resources and the organizational life is characterized by bargaining, negations and compromises. The symbolic dimension abandons the assumptions of rational behavior and views organizations as some kind of theatres. Rituals, ceremonies and stories are more important than rules or managerial authority (Bolman/Deal 2003). Many studies on critical success or failure factors of data warehouse projects have been published (e.g. Wixom/Watson 2001, Little/Gibson 1999, Frolick/Lindsey 2003). Most studies comprise technical as well as organizational factors. In the organizational domain issues like management support, sponsorship, user participation, and organizational politics are often mentioned. But these studies do not explicitly distinguish the different organizational dimensions and they only provide a general overview of relevant organizational factors. However, more detailed insights are needed to design and apply appropriate instruments and measures to implement these success factors.

The OLAP Council (http://www.olapcouncil.org) is a good source of information on standardization efforts across the industry, and a paper by Codd, et al. defines twelve rules for OLAP products. Finally, a good source of references on data warehousing and

OLAP is the Data Warehousing Information Center (http://pwp.starnetinc.com/larryg/articles.html).

Architecture and End-to-End Process

Figure 1 shows a typical data warehousing architecture.

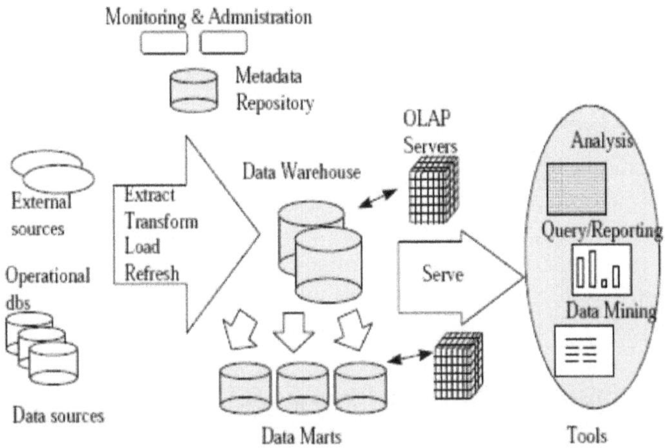

Figure 1: Data Warehousing Architecture.

It includes tools for extracting data from multiple operational databases and external sources; for cleaning, transforming and integrating this data; for loading data into the data warehouse; and for periodically refreshing the warehouse to reflect updates at the sources and to purge data from the warehouse, perhaps onto slower archival storage. In addition to the main warehouse, there may be several departmental data marts. Data in the warehouse and data marts is stored and managed by one or more warehouse servers, which present multidimensional views of data to a variety of front end tools: query tools, report writers, analysis tools, and data mining tools. Finally, there is a repository for storing and managing metadata, and tools for monitoring and administering the warehousing system.

Designing and rolling out a data warehouse is a complex process, consisting of the following activities (Kimball, R, 1996):

- Define the architecture, do capacity planning, and select the storage servers, database and OLAP servers, and tools.
- Integrate the servers, storage, and client tools.
- Design the warehouse schema and views.
- Define the physical warehouse organization, data placement, partitioning, and access methods.
- Connect the sources using gateways, ODBC drivers, or other wrappers.

- Design and implement scripts for data extraction, cleaning, transformation, load, and refresh.
- Populate the repository with the schema and view definitions, scripts, and other metadata.
- Design and implement end-user applications.
- Roll out the warehouse and applications.

OLTP AND OLAP

The job of earlier on-line operational systems was to perform transaction and query processing. So, they are also termed as on-line transaction processing systems (OLTP). Data warehouse systems serve users or knowledge workers in the role of data analysis and decision-making. Such systems can organize and present data in various formats in order to accommodate the diverse needs of the different users. These systems are called on-line analytical processing (OLAP) systems.

Major Distinguishing Features between OLTP and OLAP

i) Users and system orientation: OLTP is customer-oriented and is used for transaction and query processing by clerks, clients and information technology professionals. An OLAP system is market-oriented and is used for data analysis by knowledge workers, including managers, executives and analysts.

ii) Data contents: OLTP system manages current data in too detailed format. While an OLAP system manages large amounts of historical data, provides facilities for summarization and aggregation. Moreover, information is stored and managed at different levels of granularity, it makes the data easier to use in informed decision-making.

iii) Database design: An OLTP system generally adopts an entity –relationship data model and an application-oriented database design. An OLAP system adopts either a star or snowflake model and a subject oriented database design.

iv) View: OLTP system focuses mainly on the current data without referring to historical data or data in different organizations. In contrast, OLAP system spans multiple versions of a database schema, due to the evolutionary process of an organization. Because of their huge volume, OLAP data are shared on multiple storage media.

v) Access patterns: Access patterns of an OLTP system consist mainly of short, atomic transactions. Such a system requires concurrency, control and recovery mechanisms. But, accesses to OLAP systems are mostly read-only operations, although many could be complex queries.

Need of Data Warehousing and OLAP

Data warehousing developed, despite the presence of operational databases due to following reasons:

- An operational database is designed and tuned from known tasks and workloads, such as indexing using primary keys, searching for particular records and optimizing 'canned queries'. As data warehouse queries are often complex, they involve the computation of large groups of data at summarized levels and may require the use of special data organization, access and implementation methods based on multidimensional views. Processing OLAP queries in operational databases would substantially degrade the performance of operational tasks.

- An operational database supports the concurrent processing of multiple transactions. Concurrency control and recovery mechanisms, such as locking and logging are required to ensure the consistency and robustness of transactions. While and OLAP query often needs read-only access of data records for summarization and aggregation. Concurrency control and recovery mechanisms, if applied for such OLAP operations, may jeopardize the execution of concurrent transactions.

- Decision support requires historical data, whereas operational databases do not typically maintain historical data. So, the data in operational databases, though abundant, is always far from complete for decision-making.

- Decision support needs consolidation (such as aggregation and summarization) of data from heterogeneous sources; and operational databases contain only detailed raw data.

DATA FLOW

The steps for building a data warehouse or repository are well understood. The data flows from one or more source databases into an intermediate staging area, and finally into the data warehouse or repository (see Figure 2). At each stage there are data quality tools available to massage and transform the data, thus enhancing the usability of the data once it resides in the data warehouse.

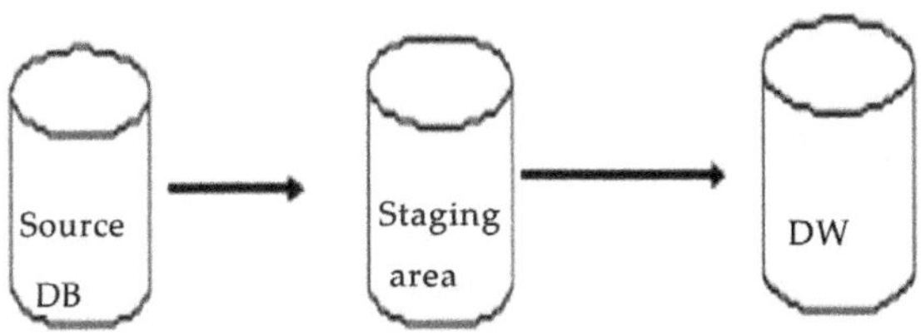

Figure 2: Data Flow.

DATA MINING

Data Mining is the extraction or “Mining” of knowledge from a large amount of data or data warehouse. To do this extraction data mining combines artificial intelligence, statistical analysis and database management systems to attempt to pull knowledge form stored data. Data mining is the process of applying intelligent methods to extract data patterns. This is done using the front-end tools. The spreadsheet is still the most compiling front-end application for Online Analytical Processing (OLAP). The challenges in supporting a query environment for OLAP can be crudely summarized as that of supporting spreadsheet operation effectively over large multi-gigabytes databases. To distinguish information extraction through data mining from that of a traditional database querying, the following main observation can be made. In a database application the queries issued are well defined to the level of what we want and the output is precise and is a subset of operational data. In data mining there is no standard query language and the queries are poorly defined. Thus the output is not precise (fuzzy) and do not represent a subset of the database. Beside the data used not the operational data that represents the to day transactions. For instance during the process of building a data warehouse the operational data are summarized over different characteristics, such as borrowings during 3 months period. Queries can be of the type of “identify all borrowers who have similar interest” or “items a member would frequently borrow along with movies”, which is not a precise as the list of books borrowed by a member. The nature of the database and the query result in extracting nonsubset of data. In supermarkets such relationships have already been identified using data mining. Thus related items such as “bread and milk’ or “beer and potato chips” would be kept together. Mobile companies decide on peak hours, rates and special packages based similar market research. Users can use data mining techniques on the data warehouse to extract different kinds of information which would eventually assist the decision making process of an organization (figure 3). For example, if certain books are rarely used by members of a particular library, while the same books are frequently used at other libraries then it is appropriate to transfer these books to respective libraries to ensure its effective use. Such knowledge could only be discovered through sharing experiences of librarians or by capturing the knowledge through database and integrating them as done when building data warehouses. Decision support tools assist users in discovering knowledge.

DECISION MAKING USING A DATA WAREHOUSE

A Decision Support System (DSS) is any tool used to improve the process of decision making in complex systems. A DSS can range from a system that answer simple queries and allows a subsequent decision to be made, to a system that employ artificial intelligence and provides detailed querying across a spectrum of related datasets. Amongst the most important application areas of DSS are those complicated systems that directly “answer” questions, in particular high level “what-if” scenario modeling.

Over the last decade there was a transition to decision support using data warehouses (Inmon 2002). The data warehouse environment is more controlled and therefore more reliable for decision support than the previous methods. The data warehouse environment supports the entire decision support requirements by providing high-quality information, made available by accurate and effective cleaning routines and using consistent and valid data transformation rules and documented presummarization of data values. It contains one single source of accurate, reliable information that can be used for analysis.

Data Warehouses (DW) integrate data from multiple heterogeneous information sources and transform them into a multidimensional representation for decision support applications. Apart from a complex architecture, involving data sources, the data staging area, operational data stores, the global data warehouse, the client data marts, etc., a data warehouse is also characterized by a complex lifecycle. In a permanent design phase, the designer has to produce and maintain a conceptual model and a usually voluminous logical schema, accompanied by a detailed physical design for efficiency reasons. The designer must also deal with data warehouse administrative processes, which are complex in structure, large in number and hard to code; deadlines must be met for the population of the data warehouse and contingency actions taken in the case of errors. Finally, the evolution phase involves a combination of design and administration tasks: as time passes, the business rules of an organization change, new data are requested by the end users, new sources of information become available, and the data warehouse architecture must evolve to efficiently support the decision-making process within the organization that owns the data warehouse. All the data warehouse components, processes and data should be tracked and administered via a metadata repository. In [M. Jarke, M.A.Jeusfeld, C. Quix, P. Vassiliadis,1998 & 1999], we presented a metadata modeling approach which enables the capturing of the static parts of the architecture of a data warehouse. The linkage of the architecture model to quality parameters (in the form of a quality model) and its implementation in the metadata repository.

The combination of all the data warehouse viewpoints is depicted in Fig. 3.

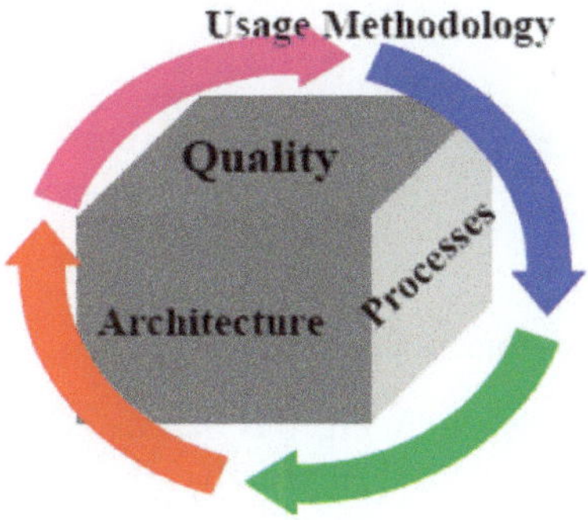

Figure 3. The different viewpoints for the metadata repository of a data warehouse.

Concept Base have been formally described in [M.A. Jeusfeld, C. Quix, M. Jarke, 1998]. [P. Vassiliadis, M. Bouzeghoub, C. Quix, 1999 & 2000] Presents a methodology for the exploitation of the information found in the metadata repository and the quality-oriented evolution of a data warehouse based on the architecture and quality model. In this paper, we complement these results with meta models and support tools for the dynamic part of the data warehouse environment: the operational data warehouse processes.

In [M. Jarke, M.A.Jeusfeld, C. Quix, P. Vassiliadis, 1998 & 1999] a basic meta model for data warehouse architecture and quality has been presented as in Fig. 3. The framework describes a data warehouse in three perspectives: a conceptual, a logical and a physical perspective. Each perspective is partitioned into the three traditional data warehouse levels: source, data warehouse and client level.

On the meta model layer, the framework gives a notation for data warehouse architectures by specifying meta-classes for the usual data warehouse objects like data store, relation, view, etc. On the metadata layer, the meta model is instantiated with the concrete architecture of a data warehouse, involving its schema definition, indexes, table spaces, etc. The lowest layer in Fig. 4 represents the actual processes and data.

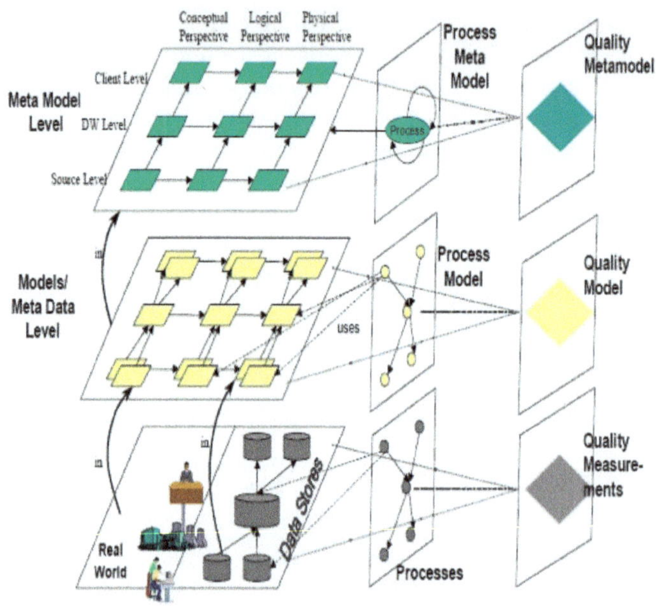

Figure 4: Frame work for Data Warehousing Architecture.

Another important issue shown in Fig. 5 is that we can observe a data flow in each of the three perspectives. In the logical perspective, the modeling is concerned with the functionality of an activity, describing what this particular activity is about in terms of consumption and production of information. In the physical perspective, the details of the execution of the process are the center of the modeling. The most intriguing part, though, is the conceptual perspective covering why a process exists. The answer can be either due to necessity reasons (in which case, the receiver of information depends on the process to deliver the data) and/or suitability reasons (in which case the information provider is capable of providing the requested information).

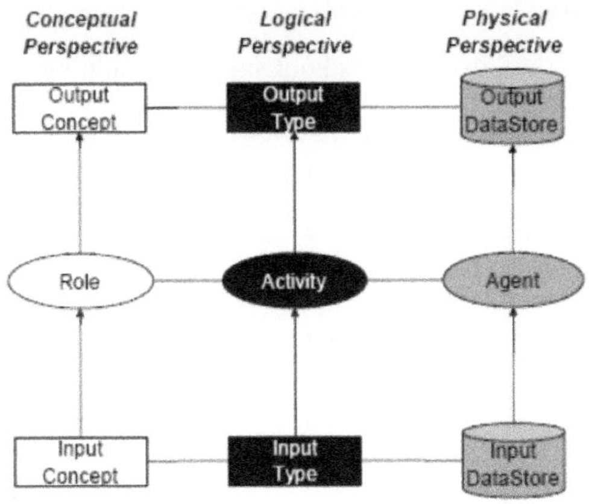

Figure 5: The reasoning behind the 3 perspectives of the process meta model.

STEPS FOR DESIGNING DATA WAREHOUSE

Designing a data warehouse is a complex process, which consists of following activities:

- Define the architecture, do capacity planning and select the storage servers, database and OLAP servers, and tools.
- Integrate the servers, storage and client tools.
- Design the warehouse schema and views.
- Define the physical warehouse organization, data placement, and partitioning and access methods.
- Connect the sources using gateways, ODBC drivers or other wrappers.
- Design and implement scripts for data extraction, cleaning, transformation, load and refresh.
- Populate the repository with the schema and view definitions, scripts, and other metadata.
- Design and implement end-user applications.
- Roll out the warehouse and applications.

DATA WAREHOUSE MODELS

There are 3 data warehouse models, according to architecture point of view-

Enterprise Warehouse

- Collects all of the information about subjects spanning the entire organization.
- Provides corporate-wide data integration, usually from one or more operational systems or external information providers, and is cross-functional in scope.
- Typically contains detailed data as well as summarized data, and can range in size from a few gigabytes to terabytes or beyond.
- May be implemented on traditional mainframes, UNIX super servers, or paralleled architecture platforms.

Data Mart

- Contains a subset of corporate-wide data that is of value to a specific group of users, however, scope is confined to specific selected subjects.
- Are usually implemented on low-cost departmental servers that are UNIX or windows/NT –based.
- Are categorized as independent or dependent, depending on the source of data operational systems or external information providers, or from data generated locally within a particular department. But, dependent data marts are sourced directly from enterprise data warehouse.
- The data contained in data mart tend to be summarized.

Virtual Warehouse

- Is a set of views over operational databases.
- Only some of the possible summary views may be materialized for efficient query processing.
- Is easy to build but requires excess capacity on operational database servers.

WHY OLAP IN DATA WAREHOUSE

Simply told, a data warehouse stores tactical information that answers "who?" and "what?" questions about past events. While OLAP systems have the ability to answer "who?" and "what?" questions, it is their ability to answer "what if?" and "why?" that sets them apart from Data warehouses.

- OLAP enables decision making about future actions. In contrast to Data warehouse, this is usually based on relational technology. OLAP uses a multidimensional view of aggregate data to provide quick access to strategic information for further analysis.

- OLAP and data warehouses are complementary. A data warehouse manages and stores data. OLAP transforms data warehouse "data" into "strategic information". It ranges from basic navigation and browsing (often known as 'slice and dice') to calculations, to more serious analysis such as time series and complex modeling.

CONCLUSION

Data warehouse can be said to be a semantically consistent data store that serves as a physical implementation of a decision support data model and stores the information on which an enterprise needs to make strategic decisions. So, its architecture is said to be constructed by integrating data from multiple heterogeneous sources to support and /or adhoc queries, analytical reporting and decision-making. Data warehouses provide on-line analytical processing (OLAP) tools for the interactive analysis of multidimensional data of varied granularities, which facilitates effective data mining. Data warehousing and on-line analytical processing (OLAP) are essential elements of decision support, which has increasingly become a focus of the database industry. OLTP is customer-oriented and is used for transaction and query processing by clerks, clients and information technology professionals. The job of earlier on-line operational systems was to perform transaction and query processing. Data warehouse systems serve users or knowledge workers in the role of data analysis and decision-making. Such systems can organize and present data in various formats in order to accommodate the diverse needs of the different users. OLAP applications are found in the area of financial modeling (budgeting, planning), sales forecasting, customer and product profitability, exception reporting, resource allocation, variance analysis, promotion planning, market share analysis. Moreover, OLAP enables managers to model problems that would be impossible using less flexible systems with lengthy and inconsistent response times. More control and timely access to strategic information facilitates effective decision -making. This provides leverage to library managers by providing the ability to model real life projections and a more efficient use of resources. OLAP enables the organization as a whole to respond more quickly to market demands. Market responsiveness, in turn, often yields improved revenue and profitability. And there is no need to emphasize that present libraries have to provide market-oriented services.

REFERENCES

1. Devlin, B. & Murphy, P. (1988) An Architecture for a Business and Information System, IBM Systems Journal, 27 (1), 60-80.
2. Inmon, W.H. (1996) Building the Data Warehouse, Second Edition, New York: John Wiley & Sons.
3. Kimball, R. (1996) The Data Warehouse Toolkit: Practical Techniques for Building Dimensional Data Warehouses, New York: John Wiley & Sons.
4. Gardner, S.R. (1998) Building the Data Warehouse, Communications of the ACM , 41 (9), 52-60.
5. Simon, A. (1998) 90 Days to the Data Mart, New York: John Wiley & Sons.

6. Frolick, M.N. & Lindsey, K. (2003) Critical Factors for Data Warehouse Failure, Journal of Data Warehousing, 8 (1).

7. Hwang, H.-G., Kua, C.-Y., Yenb, D. C., & Chenga, C.-C. (2002) Critical factors influencing the adoption of data warehouse technology: a study of the banking industry in Taiwan, Decision Support Systems, In Press, Corrected Proof.

8. Finnegan, P. & Sammon, D. (1999) Foundations of an Organisational Prerequisites Model for Data Warehousing, Proceedings of the 7th European Conference on Information Systems (ECIS 1999), Copenhagen, June.

9. O'Donnell, P., Arnott, D., & Gibson, M. (2002) Data warehousing development methodologies: A comparative analysis, Working Paper, Melbourne, Australia: Decision Support Systems Laboratory, Monash University.

10. Meyer, M. & Winter, R. (2001) Organization of Data Warehousing in Large Service Companies: A Matrix Approach Based on Data Ownership and Competence Centers, Journal of Data Warehousing, 6 (4).

11. Kachur, R. (2000) Data Warehouse Management Handbook, Paramus: Prentice Hall.

12. Adelman, S. & Moss, L. (2000) Data Warehouse Project Management, Boston: Addison-Wesley.

13. Auth, G. (2003) Prozessorientierte Organisation des Metadatenmanagements für Data- Warehouse-Systeme, Doctoral Thesis, University of St. Gallen, Bamberg: Difo-Druck (in German).

14. Bolman, L.G. & Deal, T.E. (2003) Reframing Organizations: Artistry, Choice, and Leadership, San Francisco: Jossey-Bass.

15. Mueller-Stewens, G. (2003) Die Organisation als Gegenstand von Veränderungsprozessen, in H. Oesterle & R. Winter (Eds.), Business Engineering: Auf dem Weg zum Unternehmen des Informationszeitalters (pp. 133-145), Berlin: Springer (in German).

16. Wixom, B.H. & Watson, H.J. (2001) An Empirical Investigation of the Factors Affecting Data Warehouse Success, MIS Quarterly, 25 (1), 17-41.

17. Little, R. & Gibson, M. (1999) Identification of Factors Affecting the Implementation of Data Warehousing, Proceedings of the 32nd Annual Hawaii International Conference on System Sciences (HICSS-32), Maui, Hawaii.

18. Inmon, W.H., Building the Data Warehouse. John Wiley, 1992.

19. http://www.olapcouncil.org

20. Codd, E.F., S.B. Codd, C.T. Salley, "Providing OLAP (On-Line Analytical Processing) to User Analyst: An IT Mandate." Available from Arbor Software's web site http://www.arborsoft.com/OLAP.html.

21. http://pwp.starnetinc.com/larryg/articles.html

22. Kimball, R. The Data Warehouse Toolkit. John Wiley, 1996.

23. Inmon, William H. *Building the Data Warehouse,* New York: John Wiley & Sons, 1992.

24. Chaudhuri, S & Dayal, U 1997, An Overview of Data Warehousing and OLAP Technology, SIGMOD Record 26:1, Mar, pp 65-74.

25. Chawatte, SS, Garcia-Molina H, Hammer J, Ireland K, Papakonstantinou Y, Ullman J & Wisdom J 1994, The TSIMMIS Project: Integration of Heterogeneous Information Sources, Proc. of IPSJ Conf., Tokyo, Japan, Oct., pp. 7-18.

26. Han, J & Kamber, M 2001, Data Mining Concepts and Techniques, Morgan Kaufmann.

27. Inmon, WH 2002, Building the Data Warehouse, 3rd Edition, Wiley.

28. M. Jarke, M.A.Jeusfeld, C. Quix, P. Vassiliadis: Architecture and quality in data warehouses: An extended repository approach. Information Systems, **24**(3): 229-253 (1999). A previous version appeared in Proc. 10th Conf. of Advanced Information Systems Engineering (CAiSE '98), Pisa, Italy (1998).

29. M.A. Jeusfeld, C. Quix, M. Jarke: Design and Analysis of Quality Information for Data Warehouses. In Proc. of the 17th Intl. Conf. on Conceptual Modeling (ER'98), pp. 349-362, Singapore (1998).

30. P. Vassiliadis, M. Bouzeghoub, C. Quix. Towards Quality-Oriented Data Warehouse Usage and Evolution. Information Systems, **25**(2): 89-115 (2000). A previous version appeared in Proc. 11th Conf. of Advanced Information Systems Engineering (CAiSE '99), pp. 164-179, Heidelberg, Germany (1999).

31. Chaudahari, Surajit and Dayal, Umeshwar. An overview of Data warehousing and OLAP technology. SIGMOD Record, 26(1), March 1997 Full text (pdf) available, as on 02/10/03: http://portal.acm.org/results.cfm?coll=portal&dl=ACM&CFID=1370 1999&CFTOKEN=8934106

32. Han, Jiawei and Kamber, Micheline. Data Mining: Concepts and techniques. Academic Press, 2001.

33. Witten, Ian H. and Frank, Eibe. Data mining: Practical machine learning tools and techniques with Java implementation. Academic Press, 2000.

34. OLAP council white paper, accessed on 15/10/03. http://www.olapcouncil.org/research/whtpaply.htm

35. OLAP application, accessed on 10/10/03. http://www.olapreport.com/Applications.htm

36. http://www.intelligententerprise.com/030320/605warehous1_1.shtml

37. http://www.cdacindia.com/html/dwh/dwhegov.asp

7

CHAPTER

A DATA WAREHOUSE DESIGN FOR THE DETECTION OF FRAUD IN THE SUPPLY CHAIN BY USING THE BENFORD'S LAW

Cornelia Kraus and Raul Valverde

Keywords: Supply Chain Fraud, Supply Chain Management Systems, Benford's law, Fraud Detection, Data Mining for Fraud, Accounting Information Systems

INTRODUCTION

The amounts of data produced each day increase steadily and demand companies to either surrender or rise to the challenges and opportunities that this trend brings along. Large data volumes and the inability to analyze or even process then, enables fraudulent tendencies to go unnoticed, even when new tracking devices or automatic scans are introduced and are determined to prevent those tendencies, but also add to the amount of data. Business areas like Supply chains become more complex as the world is getting smaller, trading and shipment is done throughout the globe and the number of involved parties, systems and transactions is rising. Design and Implementation methodologies for systems to process that data must be aligned to keep pace and systems must offer new concepts to not only process the volumes of data, but also in terms of velocity and variety. Generic approaches that enable analysts to apply algorithms fast without re-implementing them but to concentrate on the definition of the analytical dataset and the interpretation of the results are necessary for effective and successful data warehouse design and implementation. Solutions to address these challenges are more or less non-existent, data warehousing mostly focuses on reporting issues and a stable data basis, while forensic disciplines discuss algorithms and pretend the "perfect" data loaded, stored and ready for use. The goal of the project is to develop a data warehouse design

Citation: Cornelia Kraus and Raul Valverde, "A Data Warehouse Design for the Detection of Fraud in the Supply Chain by using the Benford's Law," American Journal of Applied Sciences 11 (9): 1507-1518, 2014, doi:10.3844/ajassp.2014.1507.1518.

to support analytics, reporting and data mining and forensic analytics by using the Benford's law within the area of supply chain. This is to detect fraud or to point out data anomalies that are worth further examination by subject matter experts.

Supply Chain Fraud and Data Mining

Risk consulting company Kroll indicates that "the same information technologies that help shippers manage global supply chains could make them more vulnerable to supply-chain fraud" (Hoffman, 2008). The detailed fraud report of 2008 points out that especially the increasing demand for natural resources often forced to act fast, exploring new sites, setting them up for production and find supplier and logistic companies to provide energy, staff and the like. As these sites are often in remote areas, the number of available suppliers are quite limited and this might lead responsible managers into situations where "flexibility" and the need to "make things happen" cause non-legal or at least questionable actions. Dependency on one supplier, conflict of interest or bribery may be some of those actions taken (Kroll Advisory, 2010).

Hesketh (2010) however points out that within the supply chain data is not uniformed, mostly not administrated properly and can be highly inaccurate or incomplete, which makes the whole process of the movement of goods in-transparent to both buyer and seller. Not describing the shipped goods creates a whole list of risks for all parties involved, like to the carrier if for example the weight is not properly defined, what seems to be common practice in the container ship industry (which is hereby the only sector of that industry) and "is due to many shippers deliberately under-declaring containers' weights in order to minimize import taxes calculated on cargo weight." This lack of information, data collection leads to a lack of knowledge, reduces the options for improvement and even enables criminals or shady operators to gain advantage of these deficits, causing damage of 20 billion USD annually.

The demand for data analytics in fraud prevention is high. Mayne (2010) points out and gives the example of enterprises that are using forensic methods to predict supply chain fluctuations, often driven by the need to improve their business, follow compliance rules or concerns regarding data breaches. Data analytics has a history of successful application in fraud detection; Massa and Valverde (2014) were able to implement a fraud detection system based of anomaly detection data analysis techniques to predict computer intrusion attacks in e-commerce web applications. Mishra *et al.* (2013) used data mining in the area of credit card transactional fraud for the Indian market. Forensics has become more and more the responsibility of IT departments, as they administer the data, maybe on multiple servers spread across the world, with virtual storage ("cloud solutions") involved, making forensic analysis not an easy task.

According to Hu (2009), the computer forensics process mainly consists of obtaining, identifying and analyzing evidence. The author points out that one problem with forensic evidence is that already the collection might alter the original state of the evidence (such as last-accessed timestamp for a file). This seems highly relevant when it comes to intrusion detection and other more network or system breech related issues, but for legacy supply chain management systems, tax-compliance and accounting in general, most transactions are still to be preserved on paper or at least in the form they were transmitted. Regarding the security of e-procurement solutions, security violations continue to rise, in number as well as frequency note Stephens and Valverde (2013). The more information technology is the basis to drive business value, the more important and critical transaction data becomes.

Data Mining is defined by Nirkhi *et al.* (2012) as "part of the interdisciplinary field of knowledge discovery in databases", which made its first steps in the 1980s and grew rapidly within the next decade and made its appearance within the area of digital forensics to gain insights from large volumes of data.

Hand *et al.* (2001), cited by Nirkhi *et al.* (2012) describe the formal methodology of data mining by the following steps:

- Determine type and structure of the datasets
- Decide how best to quantify the data
- Choose proper algorithmic processes for a scoring function
- Decide what data management principles are needed to implement the algorithms efficiently

Additionally Nirkhi *et al.* (2012) point out how important visualization is for the digital investigators, as it enables them to determine vital information "rap idly and efficiently".

Identifying data mining algorithms or methods to be used in the area of digital forensics in general and fraud detection in particular was either approached in general terms often by mere descriptions of the need of doing so or very detailed mathematical articles, demonstrating the statistical correctness of a method or algorithm. Both extremes were not included into the research for this project.

Benford's Law Theory

Benford's law may be categorized as a descriptive data mining method, as it discriminates data, but also as predictive, as it identifies characteristics of datasets that may help to predict future schemas.

There is a large amount of research on Benford's law, Durtschi *et al.* (2004) counted more than 150 articles over the period of 50 years, approaching it from many aspects, like mathematical integrity to use in the economics. As most of the mathematical theory is beyond the focus of this project, only articles discussing Benford in general or with relation to fraud detection were regarded.

These expected frequencies of digits in lists of numbers were described by Benford (1938) and verified but also controversially discussed in numerous papers until today. The use of the method is widespread, Geyer and Marti (2012) applied it to volcanological data and indicate their datasets follow Benford's law and that their "analysis shows that excessive data round-off, data errors, or anomalies may be detected when comparing the data with Benford's law expected frequencies". On the other end of the discipline scale, Nigrini and Mittermaier (1997) introduce in their study Benford's Law as a method for accounting auditing, where analytical procedures are required and successfully apply the law to a sample of data from an oil company. However, Özera and Babacanb (2013) found that the o ff-balance sheet account disclosures of a Turkish bank does not comply to Benford's law but admit that if "a da ta set does not comply with Benford Distribution is enough to be suspicious about that data set".

Nigrini (1999) listed multiple applications for Benford's law and digital analysis, some of which give a hint as to where the analysis might be helpful within the supply chain process:

- Estimations in the general ledger
- The relative size of inventory unit prices among locations
- Duplicate payments
- Processing inefficiencies due to high quantity/low dollar transactions
- Customer refunds

Benford found out that numbers with low first digits occurred more often, after he observed that in a book with logarithmic **Table 1** the pages with low first digits (1,2) were more worn out than the ones for high first digits (8,9). He then derived the expected frequencies of the digits:

$$P(d = d_1) = log_{10}(1 + 1/d_1)\ for\ d \hat{I} \{1, 2,...,9\}$$

where, d is a number {1,2..9} and P is the probability (Nigrini, 2012).

Table 1. Expected Frequencies for 1st to 4th digits (Source: Nigrini, 1996)

Digit	1st (%)	2nd (%)	3rd (%)	4th (%)	5th or greater (%)
0		11.97	10.18	10.02	10.00
1	30.10	11.39	10.14	10.01	10.00
2	17.61	10.88	10.10	10.01	10.00
3	12.49	10.43	10.06	10.01	10.00
4	9.69	10.03	10.02	10.00	10.00
5	7.92	9.67	9.98	10.00	10.00
6	6.69	9.34	9.94	9.99	10.00
7	5.80	9.04	9.90	9.99	10.00
8	5.12	8.76	9.86	9.99	10.00
9	4.58	8.50	9.83	9.98	10.00
	100.00	100.00	100.00	100.00	100.00

The first-two digit test is regarded as a more focused test than the first digit test by Nigrini (2012) and "is there to detect abnormal duplications of digits and possible biases in the data:

$$P(d = d_1 d_2) = log_{10}(1 + 1/[10 * d_1 + d_2])\ for\ d \hat{I} \{10,11,...,99\}$$

MATERIALS AND METHODS

The design approach for the data warehouse that was followed is described below:

- Discover the entities required for the data model for the data warehouse by examining the typical processes and events in supply chain management
- Interview two forensic consultants at Teradata Germany with experience in supply chain in order to identify a set of rules that will be use to identify attributes for the different entities of the data model for the data warehouse. This part of research will be focused on the warranty claims and inventory management processes. Although only two processes were selected for this part of the study, the same procedure can be followed for all the different processes of the supply chain
- Design a stored procedure that will dynamically create views for Benford Analysis
- Identify suitable datasets to test data warehouse and store procedure
- Generates a set of views for interpretation and visualization of the data

RESULTS

Based on the analysis of Hesketh (2010) that provides an excellent overview of the processes, events and involved parties within the supply chain management, the following subject areas were identified as the main source of entities for our data warehouse design:

- Party: All Individuals, companies, suppliers, buyers, consignors and the organization of the company itself
- Geography
- Locations like plants, distribution centers, ports, routes, GPS coordinates and street addresses
- Time
- Item: The parts produced, ordered, preassembled
- Item instance: Some items might be uniquely identified, like engines
- Procurement: Purchase order and associated Sales orders
- Inventory: Inventory state (snapshots), In and out Events, lot-sizes
- Shipment: The pre-order of containers, vessel space, the Advanced Shipment Notice, number of parts to be shipped with estimated time of arrival

- Issue Management (like Warranty and Returns) damaged part returns, the warranty process and terms

The major entities of every subject area were identified and an entity relationship data model for the data warehouse created (**Fig. 1**).

Two forensic consultants with Teradata Germany with experience in supply chain were interviewed in order to identify a set of rules that can be used to detect fraud in warranty claims and inventory management that is the main scope of this research. These rules will be use to identify attributes for the different entities of the data model for the data warehouse. The rules identified are summarized below:

Inventory: Unpacking a container that was delivered to a production plant implies transactions to the inventory of the plant. Boxes within the container might be damaged along with the contained goods. By comparing the content with the Purchase order and bill of lading deviations might become obvious. Claims to consignor, packaging facility or supplier might be created on this basis. Fraud can be concealed by the taking of a small amount of parts from a number of boxes, then blaming the supplier for shortages or declaring items as damaged and then blaming the consignor or packaging facility.

Returns and Warranty Claims: Claims may occur at certain stages of the supply chain or affect it end-to-end. For example, a car manufacturer uses spark plugs from a supplier to build its cars. The car is shipped to the dealer who sells it to a customer. Three months later the customer claims to the dealer that his car does not ignite. Inspection shows that the spark plugs are malfunctioning so the dealer will exchange the plugs but open a warranty claim to the manufacturer of the car. The car manufacturer then will raise another warranty claim to the manufacturer of the plug. Not all failed parts are sent back to the original supplier for inspection (regarding to the costs and amounts) but payments are granted either on a subset that was inspected or on good-will.

Receiving goods: Goods might be stolen or damaged on a frequent basis, maybe depending on the numbers of parts delivered or price of the parts.

Store Procedure Design

A stored procedure was designed to dynamically create four types views, based on the input-parameters handed over with the procedure call. The design is depicted in **Fig. 2**. The store procedure's in parameters are described in the **Table 2** below.

The store procedure has four views. The VV_BENFORD_STAT view contains statistical information about the dataset chosen. VV_BENFORD_DET view provides detailed information of the Bendford analysis and helps to determine the first and first two digits of a set of numbers. The VV_BENFORD_FIRST_RES counts how often the first digit appeared in the dataset while the VV_BENFORD_TWO_RES counts how often the first two digits appeared in the dataset. The results of the views provides a Z score that measures how statistically different the actual result is from the expected result and therefore attempts to help answer the question of how confident one can be about the observed relationship.

Data Collection

Two datasets were collected from projects developed by Teradata Germany. Both datasets are car manufacturer supply chain/quality data. As the data was not allowed to leave the company premises, all testing was done on-site and on anonymised production data. Therefore the developed objects were deployed to a sandbox on the production system and executed.

The first dataset (**Fig. 3**) reflects two years of warranty claims from dealers towards the car manufacturer regarding defective parts and consequential costs.

The second data set (**Fig. 4**) is much smaller dataset reflects one year of inventory data, filtered only for transactions that have a transaction type = 'LOST', which might include thefts, damaged or lost items.

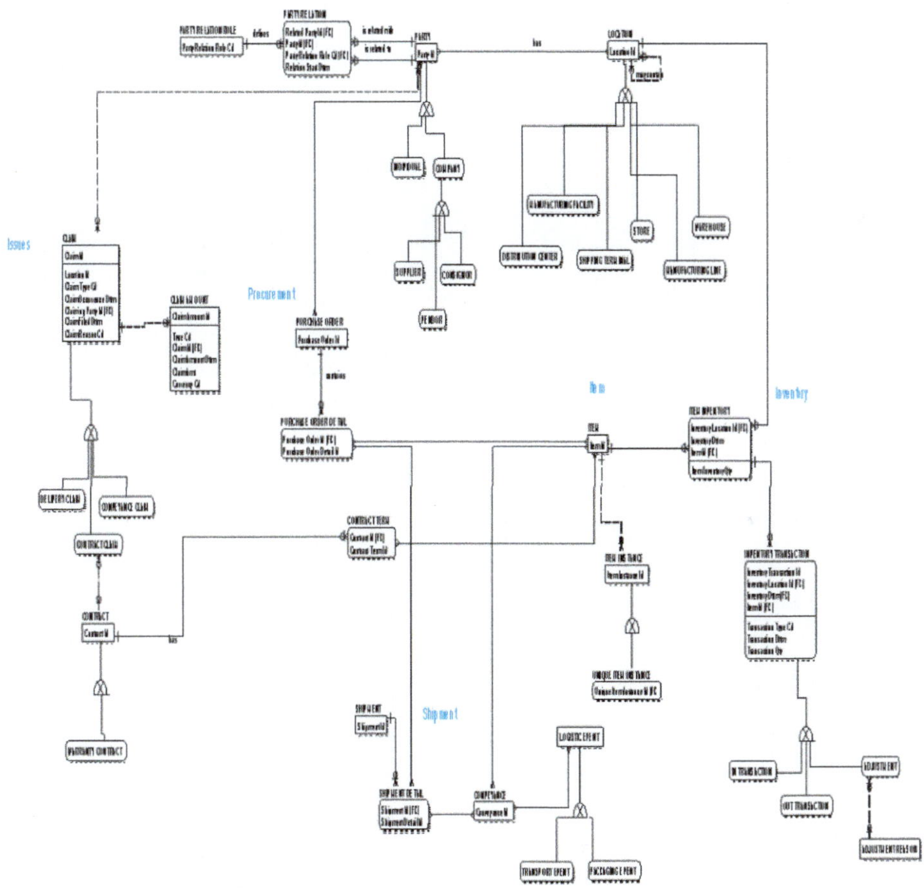

Figure 1. Data Warehouse Entity Relationship Diagram.

Table 2. Store procedure's in parameters

In-Parameters:	Description
source_db_nm:	The name of the database that contains the table to be analysed
table_nm:	The name of the table
key_col:	The name of the key column of that table.
value_col:	The column with the data to be analysed.
result_db_nm:	The database where the views will be created

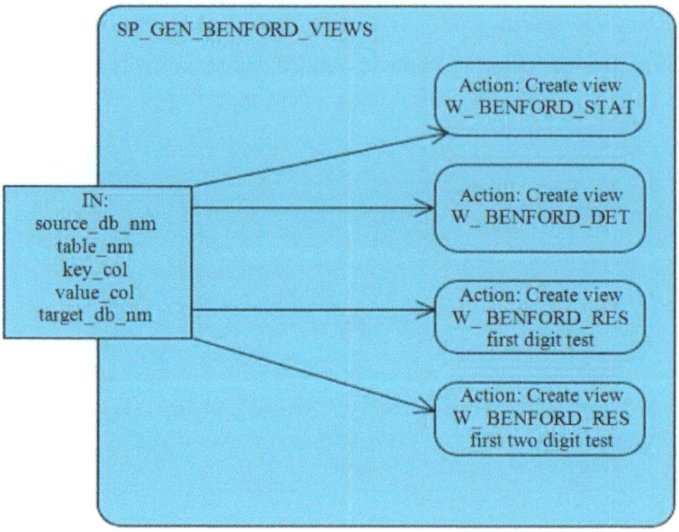

Figure 2. Activity diagram for stored procedure SP_GEN_BENFORD_VIEWS.

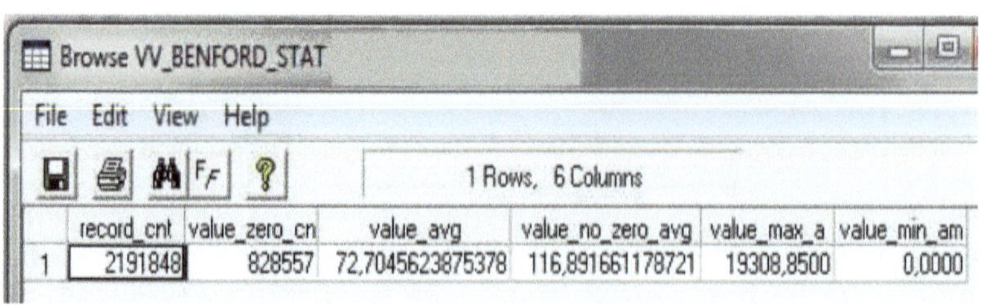

	record_cnt	value_zero_cn	value_avg	value_no_zero_avg	value_max_a	value_min_am
1	2191848	828557	72,7045623875378	116,891661178721	19308,8500	0,0000

Figure 3. Statistical information of dataset 1.

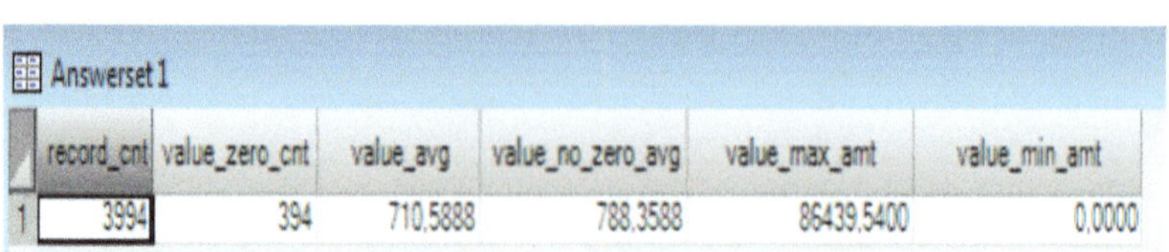

	record_cnt	value_zero_cnt	value_avg	value_no_zero_avg	value_max_amt	value_min_amt
1	3994	394	710,5888	788,3588	86439,5400	0,0000

Figure 4. Statistical information of dataset 2.

Query (14.0 VM)

```
REPLACE PROCEDURE benford.SP_GEN_BENFORD_VIEWS
(
    IN source_db_nm CHAR(30),
    IN table_nm     CHAR(30),
    IN key_col      CHAR(30),
    IN value_col    CHAR(30),
    IN result_db_nm CHAR(30)
)

BEGIN

CALL DBC.SYSEXECSQL('REPLACE VIEW '  || trim(both from : result_db_nm) ||'.VV_BENFORD_STAT
                    AS
                    SELECT
                          COUNT(*)          AS record_cnt,
                          SUM(CASE WHEN ' || : value_col || ' = 0 THEN 1 ELSE 0 END) AS value_zero_cnt,
                          AVG(' || : value_col || ') AS value_avg,
                          AVG(CASE WHEN '|| : value_col || ' = 0 THEN NULL ELSE ' || : value_col || 'END)
                                                                                   AS value_no_zero_avg,
                          MAX('|| : value_col ||') AS value_max_amt,
                          MIN('|| : value_col ||') AS value_min_amt
                    FROM ' || TRIM(BOTH FROM :source_db_nm) ||'.'|| TRIM(BOTH FROM :table_nm) ||' ;'
                   );
```

Figure 5. Call of dynamic SQL within a stored procedure.

Query (14.0 VM)

```
CALL benford.SP_GEN_BENFORD_VIEWS ('benford', 'T_SAMPLE_SET', 'sample_id', 'sample_amt', 'benford');
```

Figure 6. Stored procedure call.

Answerset 1

```
REPLACE VIEW benford.VV_BENFORD_STAT
    AS
    SELECT
                COUNT(*) AS record_cnt,
                SUM(CASE WHEN sample_amt = 0 THEN 1 ELSE 0 END) AS value_zero_cnt,
                AVG(sample_amt) AS value_avg,
                AVG(CASE WHEN sample_amt = 0 THEN NULL ELSE sample_amt END) AS value_no_zero_avg,
                MAX(sample_amt) AS value_max_amt,
                MIN(sample_amt) AS value_min_amt
    FROM benford.T_SAMPLE_SET ;
```

Figure 7. Result of dynamic SQL after procedure call.

Name	Type
SP_GEN_BENFORD_VIEWS	Procedure
T_BENFORD	Table
T_SAMPLE_SET	Table
VV_BENFORD_DET	View
VV_BENFORD_FIRST_RES	View
VV_BENFORD_FIRST_TWO_RES	View
VV_BENFORD_STAT	View

Figure 8. All used and generated database objects.

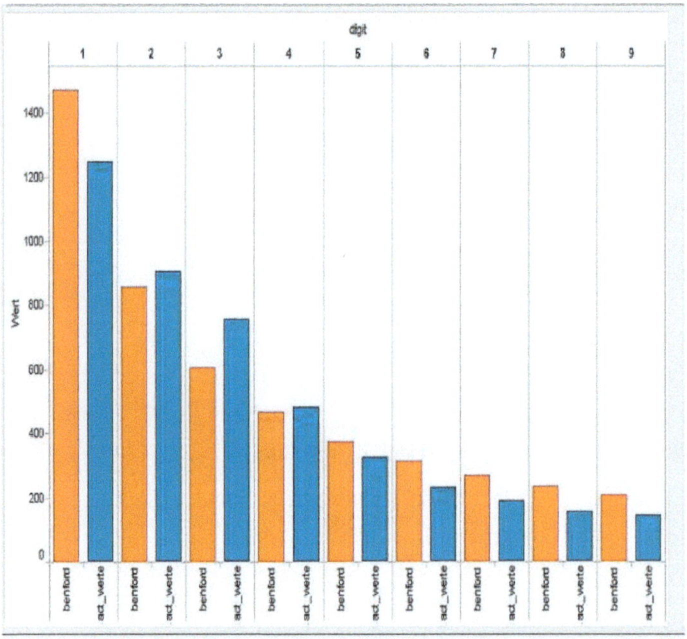

Figure 9. Dataset 1 frequencies (blue) compared to Benford's expected frequencies (orange).

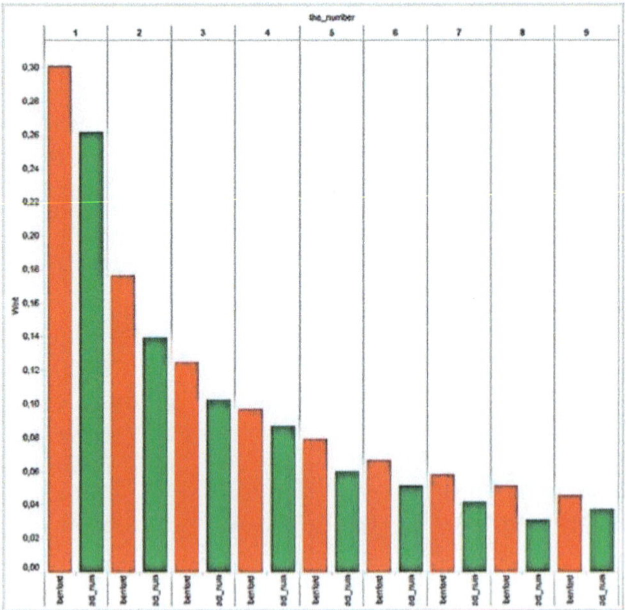

Figure 10. Dataset 2 frequencies (green) compared to Benford's expected frequencies (red).

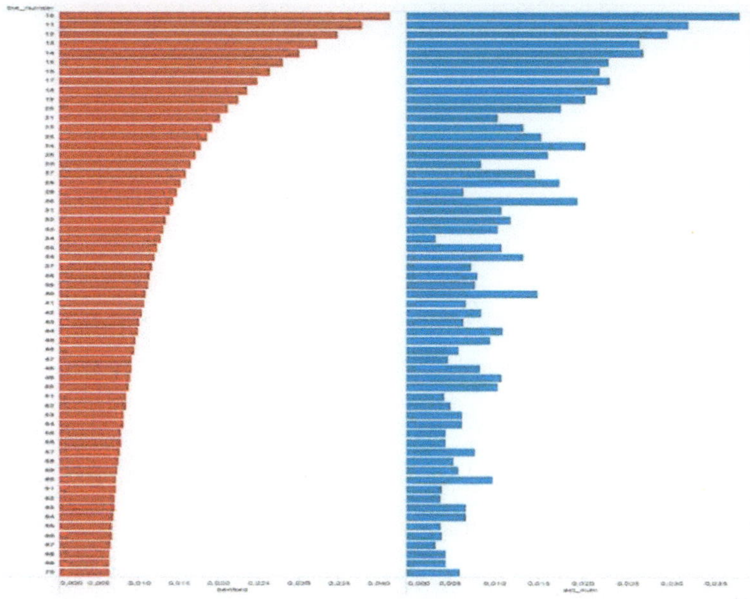

Figure 11. Dataset 2- first two digit test (Benford in red, actual values in blue).

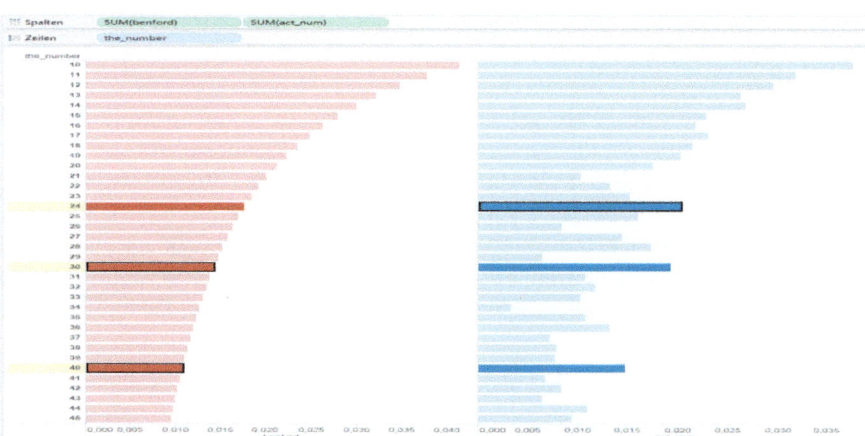

Figure 12. Dataset 2- some obvious deviations (range 10 to 45 for first two digits).

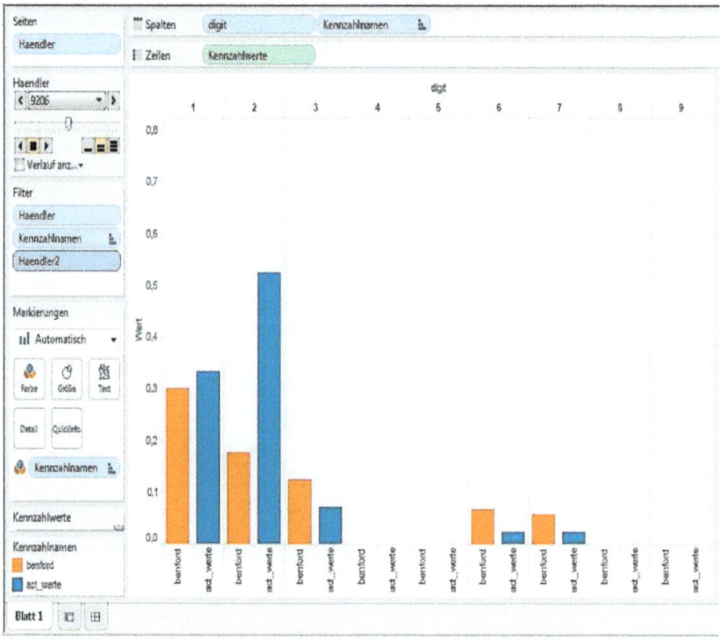

Figure 13. Tableau Screen showing one deviation from Benford.

Benford Implementation

The Benford probabilities were calculated and stored in a lookup table with SQL-Statements one at a time for the numbers from 1 to 9 and then from 10 to 99 so that the first digit test as well as the first-two digit test can be performed. In case also the second, third or fourth digit test needs to be performed, the used pattern can be extended easily. As described in section 3.1, the stored procedure is intended to create 4 views, which is where the Dynamic SQL is used. For the first view (Statistical information about the chosen dataset) the call for generating the view within the stored procedure is depicted in **Fig. 5.**

The stored procedure is called handing over the IN-Parameters as depicted in **Fig. 6.**

The IN-Parameters are replaced upon execution within the SYSEXECSQL call, creating a valid SQL statement which is executed directly and results in the creation of the view as depicted in **Fig. 7.**

Once the stored procedure is successfully executed with a first set of data (in T_ SAMPLE_SET), all used and created database objects are shown below in **Fig. 8.**

Third or fourth digit tests might be implemented following the same pattern.

Visualization

Tableau (www.tableausoftware.com) was used for visualization. The views provided by the stored procedure were the basis for reporting and via the VV_BENFORD_DET view any connection to related information could be achieved. Following these guidelines, three visualization-sets where created and used to display the three datasets available.

Figure 11 Dataset 2-first two digit test (Benford in red, actual values in blue).

The Visualization in Fig. 9 depicts dataset 1. Benfords Values for first digits are in orange, the result set values in blue. As the pattern of the actual values align with the Benford-values, this dataset obeys to Beford's Law, however some values step out marginally, like for the digits 1, 2 and 3. The Visualization in Fig. 10 depicts dataset 2. Benford Values for first digits are in red, the result set values in green. As the pattern of the actual values align with the Benford-values, this dataset obeys close to Benford's Law, even more than Dataset 1. For a more detailed look into large datasets, two options were chosen for dataset 2 to find peculiarities. This can be regarded as the next step after identifying peculiarities in Fig. 12.

Example for groupings applied next:

- A grouping based on vendors
- Only vendors having a deviation from Benford's law > 0.15 for at least one digit

While reviewing the result, vendors with low numbers of claims had high deviations from Benford. Therefore a filter was applied that only vendors with more than 20 claims in the period where considered.

Figure 13 shows the result of applying those to filters for one particular vendor (#9206).

DISCUSSION

For Benford's first digit test, both datasets show no outstanding peculiarities and follow the pattern of Benford's law. According to Nigrini (1996), if the complete dataset follows Benford, then also subsets (not grouped by digits, of course) should also comply.

In Fig. 11, the first two digit test is depicted with Tableau. Here, a slightly different chart type was chosen, as the number of digits was too high to assign them to the x-axis and still get a chart to fit on the screen without scrolling.

Overall, the dataset obeys also to Benford's law (first two digit test), as the pattern matches for most of the first two digits to Benford's numbers. The visualization is much more granular and more details need to be reviewed to find peculiarities.

The analyst would use this chart to identify deviations and "drill" down for some to review the source of the deviation. In Fig. 12 three of the values that deviate from Benford's value are highlighted.

Overall, the dataset obeys also to Benford's law (first two digit test), as the pattern matches for most of the first two digits to Benford's numbers. The visualization is much more granular and more details need to be reviewed to find peculiarities. The analyst would use this chart to identify deviations and "drill" down for some to review the source of the deviation. In Fig. 12 three of the values that deviate from Benford's value are highlighted.

The advantage of a drill-down option or further groupings & filters is obvious when looking at the many deviations that might be worth to investigate further, as not only the highlighted values but even more might be worth to investigate.

The chart in Fig. 13, shows that especially the first digit 2 was highly frequented in his claim amounts, much more than others and having a high deviation from Benford for this digit. This observation makes an analysis on the lowest level necessary, the actual records underneath. A drill down to the detail data for dataset 1 lists all the amounts claimed in Fig. 13 by vendor #9206.

Answerset 1

	party_id	clm_amt_a	amt_links
4	9.206	16.5500	16.55
5	9.206	16.5500	16.55
6	9.206	17.0800	17.08
7	9.206	17.0800	17.08
8	9.206	22.0600	22.06
9	9.206	22.0600	22.06
10	9.206	22.0600	22.06
11	9.206	22.0600	22.06
12	9.206	22.0600	22.06
13	9.206	22.0600	22.06
14	9.206	22.7700	22.77
15	9.206	22.7700	22.77
16	9.206	22.7700	22.77
17	9.206	22.7700	22.77
18	9.206	22.7700	22.77
19	9.206	22.7700	22.77
20	9.206	22.7700	22.77
21	9.206	22.7700	22.77
22	9.206	27.5800	27.58
23	9.206	27.5800	27.58
24	9.206	28.4700	28.47
25	9.206	28.4700	28.47
26	9.206	28.4700	28.47
27	9.206	28.4700	28.47
28	9.206	34.1600	34.16
29	9.206	39.8500	39.85

Figure 14. Dataset 1-drill down to granular data

Repeating numbers of relatively small amounts can be observed in the details, see red box in Fig. 14. After some further research into this it was identified that these claims were part of a product recall campaign, where a huge amount of faulty parts had to be replaced, ordered by the manufacturer but taken out by the vendors. No actual case of fraud was identified, but a case quite out of the ordinary was detected without knowing about it beforehand.

CONCLUSION

By applying the method to two datasets for the business area, the following aspects surfaced and can be projected to all data within the supply chain:

- The chosen approach (apply the method on full sets of data, in-database style) is applicable; performs well in terms of query response time and can be applied repeatedly on either newer datasets or other datasets without change

- Even if data is available, it might not be eligible for applying Benford's law if the dataset is too small or is of such poor quality that interpretation would only generate effort but no proper results
- Both datasets followed Benford's law for the first digit, with some deviations also for the first two digits. As the datasets are different in size, origin and type of data this is a very interesting observation and gives room for the assumption that also other data from the area of supply chain might be worth to test against Benford.

The results of the research were consistent with Tödter (2009), who states that "Benford's law is a potentially useful instrument to discover fraud and manipulation" as the implementation and application to the datasets documented showed the general obedience to Benford's law (first and first-two digits) overall and enables the researcher to detect anomalies, maybe only in the form of peculiarities for further analysis.

Tödter (2009) states that "in every single case there may be other plausible reasons for deviations from Benford's law, such as insufficient variability of the underlying data, rounding effects or other irregularities. This was consistent with the results of this study as it was observed that more the data was filtered and the smaller and less diverse the datasets was, the bigger the diversion to Benford's law was.

Supply chain data as well as any other data environment requires a detailed business know how for interpretation and to prevent misinterpretations. Additionally, mathematical and statistical skills are vital for choosing the most promising dataset and the appropriate method to test it with.

One limitation of this study is that focused mainly in inventory management and warranty claims, future research in this area should explore other supply chain processes such as procurement and warehouse management in order to test the generalizability of the data warehouse design. Future research should also focus on the development of a generic approach using parameterized stored procedures with Dynamic SQL that could provide the possibility to operationalize data mining methods and implement other different fraud detection algorithms such as neural networks, frequent pattern analysis or classification methods in order to ease the workload of the analyst and check data on a frequent basis rather than one-time only.

ACKNOWLEDGMENT

Special thanks to Dr. Michael Benz from Teradata for his support and expertise in the area forensic analysis and data mining.

REFERENCES

1. Benford, F., 1938. The law of anomalous numbers. Proc. Am. Philosophical Society, 4: 551-572.
2. Durtschi, C., W. Hillison and C. Pacini, 2004. The effective use of Benford's law to assist in detecting fraud in accounting data. J. Forensic Account., 5: 17-34.

3. Geyer, A. and J. Marti, 2012, Applying Benford's law to volcanology. Geology, 40: 327-330. DOI: 10.1130/G32787.1

4. Hand, D., H. Mannila and P. Smyth, 2001. Principles of Data Mining. 1st Edn., MIT Press, Cambridge, ISBN-10: 026208290X, pp: 546.

5. Hesketh, D., 2010. Weaknesses in the supply chain: Who packed the box. World Customs J., 4: 3-20.

6. Hoffman, W., 2008. Fighting supply-chain fraud. Traffic World.

7. Hu, D., 2009. Exploratory study on computer forensics technology. Proceedings of the 2nd International Conference on Computer and Electrical Engineering, Dec. 28-30, IEEE Xplore Press, Dubai, pp: 608-611. DOI: 10.1109/ICCEE.2009.258

8. Kroll Advisory, 2012. Global fraud report. Kroll Consulting, USA, Fall.

9. Massa, D. and R. Valverde, 2014. A fraud detection system based on anomaly intrusion detection systems for e-commerce applications. Comput. Inform. Sci., 7: 117-140. DOI: 10.5539/cis.v7n2p117

10. Mayne, M., 2010. Elementary, my dear Watson? For IT Security Professionals, SC Magazine.

11. Mishra, J.S., S. Panda and A.K. Mishra, 2013. A novel approach for credit card fraud detection targeting the Indian market. Int. J. Comput. Sci., 10: 172-179.

12. Nigrini, 1996. A taxpayer compliance application of Benford's Law. J. Am. Taxat. Assoc., 18: 72-91

13. Nigrini, M. J.,Mittermaier, L. J. 1997. The use of Benford's law as an aid in analytical procedures. Auditing, 16: 52-67.

14. Nigrini, M.J. 1999. 'I've Got Your Number'. J. Accountancy, 187: 79-83.

15. Nigrini, M., 2012. Benford's Law: Applications for Forensic Accounting, Auditing and Fraud Detection. 1st Edn., John Wiley and Sons, Hoboken, New Jersey, ISBN-10: 1118152859, pp: 330.

16. Nirkhi, S.M., R.V. Dharaskar and V.M. Thakre, 2012. Data mining: A prospective approach for digital forensics. Int. J. Data Min. Knowl. Manage. Process, 2: 41-48.

17. Özera, G. and B. Babacanb, 2013. Benford›s Law and Digital Analysis: Application on Turkish Banking Sector. Bus. Econom. Res. J., 4: 29-41.

18. Stephens, J. and R. Valverde, 2013. Security of e-procurement transactions in supply chain reengineering. Comput. Inform. Sci., 6: 1-20. DOI: 10.5539/cis.v6n3p1

19. Tödter, K.H., 2009. Benford's law as an indicator of fraud in economics. German Econom. Rev., 10: 339-351. DOI: 10.1111/j.1468-0475.2009.00475.x

8
CHAPTER

DATA LOAD MANIFESTATION IN PROCESS CHAINS IN SAP BUSINESS WAREHOUSE

M. Victoria Hebseeba, Dr. T. Bhasakara Reddy, Prof. B. Lakshma Reddy and Dr. T. Venkateswarulu

Keywords: Process Type, Variant, Business Warehouse, ETL

DATA EXTRACTION, TRANSFORMATION AND LOADING

A process chain is a mechanism that controls extraction, transformation, and loading (ETL) activities execution at a scheduled time in a defined Sequence. Since in many support project environments in IT industry multiple process chains are run you come across some issues with the system executing them at appropriate times. A process chain is a BW objects which has scheduled sequence of processes linked together and are executed in a specified order.

Process chain waits in the back ground for an event. Some of these processes trigger a separate event that can start other processes in turn. In an operating system there are a multitude of processes in addition to the loading process that occur regularly [1] [2]. Process chain is a mechanism that controls extraction, transformation, and loading (ETL) activities execution at a scheduled time in a defined manner. Process chains are used to automate the complex structures with the help of the controlled processing, visualize the schedule by using network applications and centrally control and monitor the processes [3] [4].

Openness is applied to the theory behind process chains, in that both user-defined programs and processes can be implemented. In addition, you can include process chains in other process chains, so-called Meta chains. In doing so you have the option of integrating process chains from the BW system, in which the Meta chain is found,

Citation: M. Victoria Hebseeba, Dr. T. Bhasakara Reddy, Prof. B. Lakshma Reddy and Dr. T. Venkateswarulu, "Data Load Manifestation in Process Chains in SAP Business Warehouse," Advanced Computing: An International Journal (ACIJ), Vol.3, No.2, March 2012, DOI : 10.5121/acij.2012.3209.

or from other BW systems [5] [6]. In this context, local or remote process chains are concerned. Processes are scheduled before your run and can be monitored with the standard batch monitor. You start subsequent processes by using background events. Short dumps and terminations are recognized and handled respectively [7] [9].

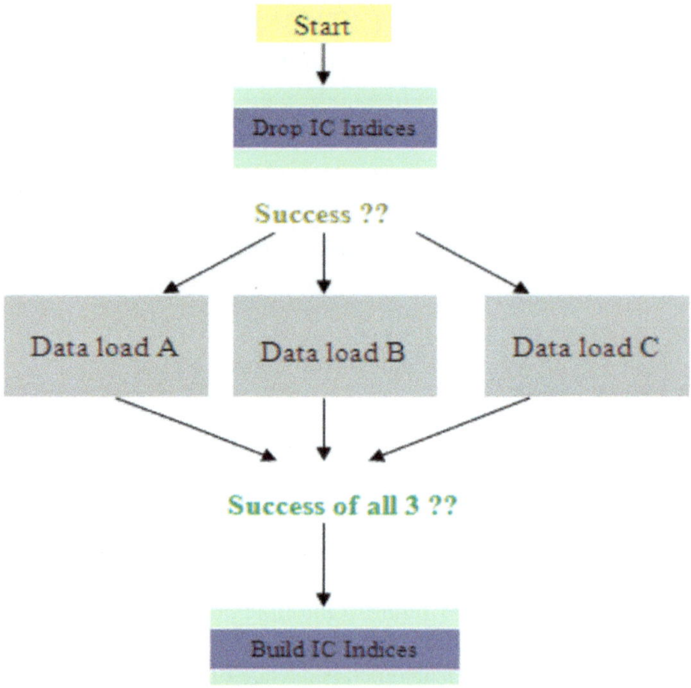

Figure 1: Building a process flow: Data loading from Info packages in parallel to 1 Info cube.

DATA LOAD MANIFESTATION

One of the BW's strongest selling points is its business objects developed by SAP based on predefined business roles and their tasks. For instance a sales general manager needs reports to get business information and conduct analysis. SAP provides set of BW objects developed called as business content objects to support operation level application programming tasks. It contains roles, work books, queries, info cubes, key figures, characteristics, update rules, info sources, and extractors for SAP R/3.

A multi provider C_YTCT_M is created by the union of basic cubes. The multi provider created does not contain any data by itself; rather the data reside in the basic cubes 0TCT_C21, 0TCT_C22, and 0TCT_C23.

To a user multi provider resembles a basic cube. The below figure displays the multi provider created by selecting the business content cubes to derive the DTP, info package and process details included in various process chains in the system.

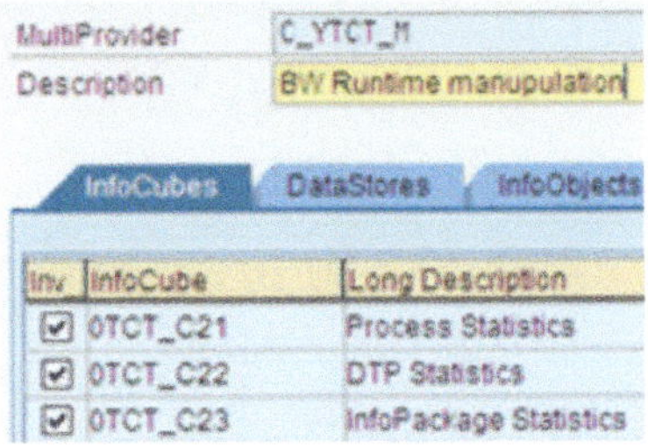

Figure 2: Multi provider BW Run time manipulation.

The data from transactional data from data sources is extracted to the destination info cubes after the data pass through the info sources from various info cubes which pick the data from Info sources.

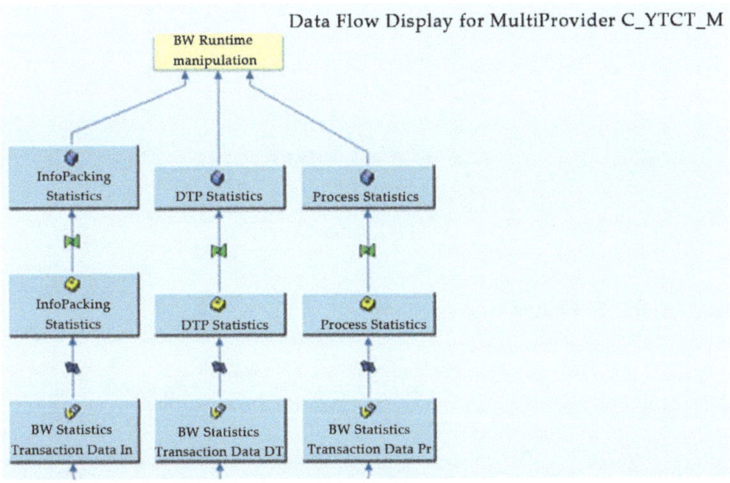

Figure 3: Data flow for Multi provider C_YTCT_M.

Fields Display

On the multi provider a new report is created in the system to capture the no. of iteration of PCs, records from IP and DTP etc. details. Chosen duration, frequency, number of records, data transfer process records, calendar day in key figures to be displayed in columns in the output of the report. Arranged rows to display the system details and then process chain id, process chain type, process variant. Selected UTC time stamp is free characteristics. Time stamp being a free characteristic allows further drill down. This helps in reducing the input/ out put volume for the initial query result, thereby improving the query performance.

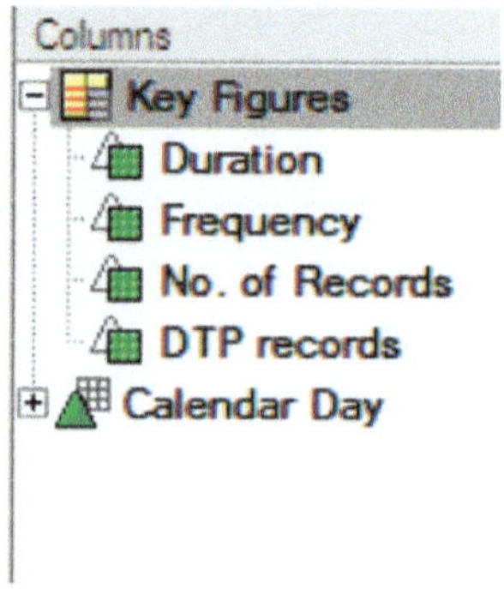

Figure 4: Columns.

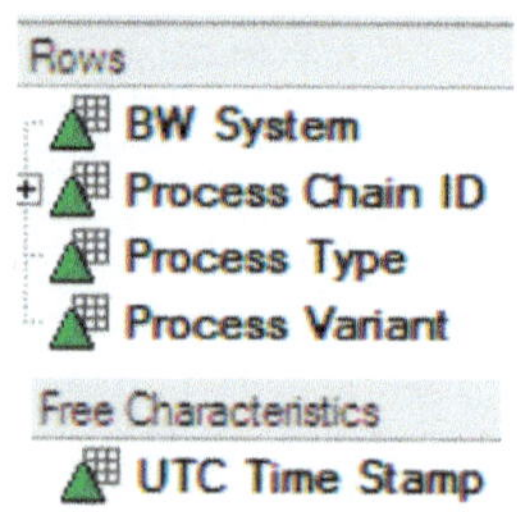

Figure 4: Rows and Free Characteristics.

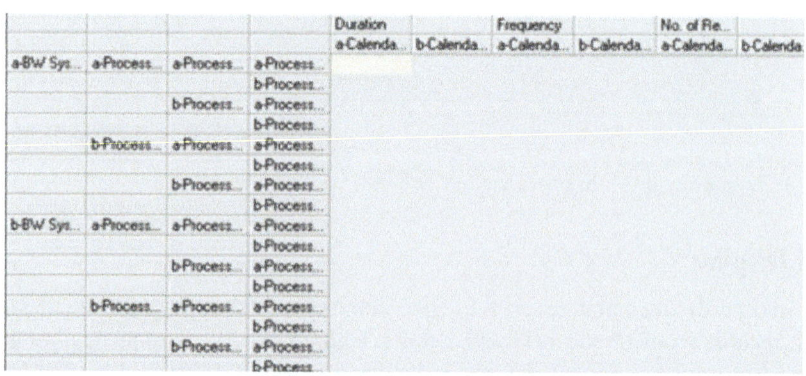

Figure 5: Result format

Test Results

- Performed several lab tests. Executed the process chains. Compared the result displayed with that of the info packages inside the process chain.

- The status displayed was exactly matching in both the scenarios.
- Enter the date range. For example: 1/11/2011 to 30/11/2011 and give process chain technical name if required in the variables screen.

CONCLUSIONS

Process Chains are the new generation of job scheduling and monitoring tools for tasks such as data loads, reporting agent jobs, or index rebuilds.

The proposed approach is best suited for to be executed daily or whenever required to get the complete data load details. This approach very helpful to the ETL team in Business Ware house support project environments to view and analyze the data load status and system performance for multiple process chains in the system collated in one sheet. This approach has demonstrated good results in our preliminary experiments.

REFERENCES

1. Olaf Klostermann and Milco Osterholm, (2006) " SAP Net weaver BW Administration and Monitoring", *1st ed., Galileo Press,* Germany.
2. [2] Andrew J. Ross, (2009)" SAP Net weaver BI Accelerator", *1st ed., Galileo Press, Boston (MA),* USA.
3. Christian Merwald, Sabine Morlock, (2009) " Data Ware Housing with SAP BW7, BI in SAP Net Weaver 2004s" *1st ed., Rocky Nook Inc.*,
4. Biao Fu and Henry Fu. (2002) "SAP BW a step by step guide".
5. Arshad Khan,(2005) " SAP and BW Data Warehousing. How to plan and implement".
6. Frank K. Wolf and Stefan Yamada, "Data Modeling in SAP Net weaver BW", *1st ed., Galileo Press,* Boston,(MA)
7. Kevin McDonald, Andreas Wilmsmeier, David C. Dixon and W.H Inmon,(2002) "Mastering the SAP Business Information Ware house" *Wiley Publishing Inc,* USA .
8. Elizabeth Vitt and Michael Luckevich and StaciaMisner, "Making better Business Intelligence Decisions faster", *Microsoft Press,* USA
9. Daniel Knapp, "Practical Data modeling with SAP Net Weaver BW", *Galileo Press,* Boston (MA), USA
10. http://airccse.org/journal/ijngn/papers/3111ijngn04.pdf
11. http://www.ijmo.org/papers/13-P30001.pdf
12. http://airccse.org/journal/acij/papers/1111acij08.pdf

9
CHAPTER

BIG DATA USAGE IN THE MARKETING INFORMATION SYSTEM

Alexandre Borba Salvador, Ana Akemi Ikeda

Keywords: Big Data, Marketing Research, Marketing Information System

INTRODUCTION

A solid information system is essential to obtain relevant data for the decision-making process in marketing. The more correct and relevant the information is, the greater the probability of success is. The 1990s was known as the decade of the network society and the transactional data analysis [1] . However, in addition to this critical data, there is a great volume of less structured information that can be analyzed in order to find useful information [2] . The growth of generation, storage capacity, processing power and data analysis provided a technological phenomenon called big data. This phenomenon would cause great impacts on studies and lead to the development of solutions in different areas. In marketing, big data research can represent the possibility of a deep understanding of the consumer behavior, through their profile monitoring (geo-demographic, attitudinal, behavioral), the statement of their areas of interest and preferences, and monitoring of their purchase behavior [3] [4] . The triangulation of the available data in real time with information previously stored and analyzed would enable the generation of insights that would not be possible through other techniques [5] .

However, in order to have big data information correctly used by companies, some measures are necessary, such as investment on people qualification and equipment. More than that, the increase of information access may generate ethic-related problems, such as invasion of privacy and redlining. It may affect research as well, as in cases

Citation: Salvador, A. and Ikeda, A. (2014) Big Data Usage in the Marketing Information System. Journal of Data Analysis and Information Processing, 2, 77-85. doi: 10.4236/jdaip.2014.23010.

where information could be used without consent of the surveyed. Predictive analytics are models that seek to predict the consumer behavior through data generated by their purchase and/or consumption activities and with the advent of big data, predictive analytics grow in importance to understand this behavior from the data generated in on-line interactions among these people. The use of predictive systems can also be controversial as exemplified by the case of American chain Target, which identified the purchase behavior of women at the early stage of pregnancy and sent a congratulation letter to a teenage girl who had not yet informed her parents about the pregnancy. The case generated considerable negative repercussions and the chain suspended the action [4] .

The objective of this essay is to discuss the use of big data in the context of marketing information systems, present new possibilities resulting from its use, and reflect on its limitations. For that, the point of view of researchers and experts will be explored based on academic publications, which will be analyzed and confronted so we may, therefore, infer conclusions on the subject.

THE USE OF INFORMATION ON THE DECISION-MAKING PROCESS IN MARKETING

The marketing information system (MIS) was defined by Cox and Good (1967, p. 145) [6] as a series of procedures and methods for the regular, planned collection, analysis and presentation of information for use in making marketing decisions. For Berenson (1969, p. 16) [7] , the MIS would be an interactive structure of people, equipment, methods and controls, designed to create a flow of information able to provide an acceptable base for the decision-making process in marketing. The need for its implementation would derive from points that have not changed yet: 1) the increase in business complexity would demand more information and better performance; 2) the life cycle of products would be shortened, requiring more assertiveness from marketing managers to collect profits in shorter times; 3) companies would become so large that the lack of effort to create a structured information system would make its management impractical; 4) business would demand rapid decisions and therefore, in order to support decision making, an information system would be essential for marketing areas; 5) although an MIS is not dependent on computers, the advances in hardware and software technologies would have spread its use in companies, and not using its best resources would represent a competitive penalty [7] .

The data supplying an MIS can be structured or non-structured regarding its search mechanisms and internal (company) or external (micro and macro environment) regarding its origin. The classic and most popular way of organizing it is through sub-systems [8] -[10] . The input and processing sub-systems of an MIS are the internal registration sub-system (structured and internal information), marketing intelligence sub-system (information from secondary sources, non-structured and from external origins), and the marketing research sub-system (information from primary sources, structured, from internal or external origins, generated from a research question).

BIG DATA

The term big data applies to information that could not be processed using traditional tools or processes. According to an IBM [11] report, the three characteristics that would define big data are volume, speed and variety, as together they would have created the need for new skills and knowledge in order to improve the ability to handle the information (Figure 1).

The Internet and the use of social media have transferred the power of creating content to users, greatly increasing the generation of information on the Internet. However, this represents a small part of the generated information. Automated sensors, such as RFID (radio-frequency identification), multiplied the volume of collected data, and the volume of stored data in the world is expected to jump from 800,000 petabytes (PB) in 2000 to 35 zettabytes (ZB) in 2020. According to IBM, Twitter would generate by itself over 7 terabytes (TB) of data a day, while some companies would generate terabytes of data in an hour, due to its sensors and controls. With the growth of sensors and technologies that encourage social collaboration through portable devices, such as smartphones, the data became more complex, due to its volume and different origins and formats, such as files originating from automatic control, pictures, books, reviews in communities, purchase data, electronic messages and browsing data. The traditional idea of data speed would consider its retrieval, however, due to the great number of sensors capturing information in real time, the concern with the capture and information analysis speed emerges, leading, therefore, to the concept of flow. The capture in batches is replaced by the streaming capture. Big data, therefore, regards to a massive volume of zettabytes information rather than terabytes, captured from different sources, in several formats, and in real time [11] .

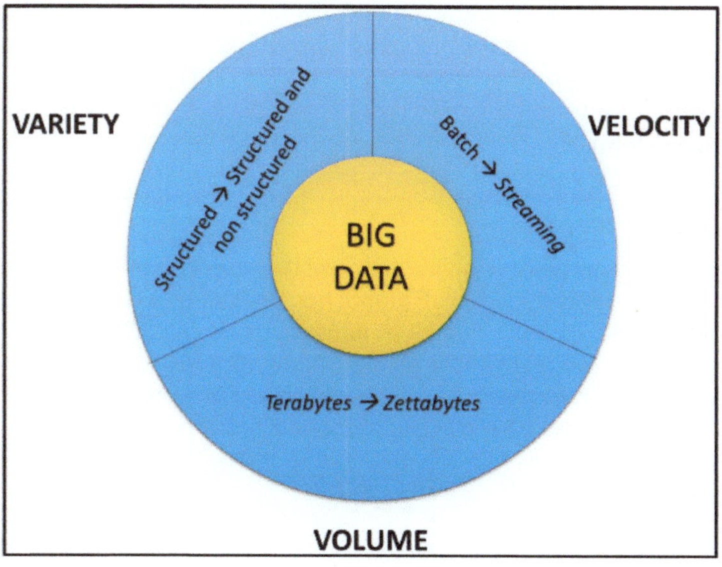

Figure 1. Three big data dimension. Source: Adapted from Zikopoulos and Eaton, 2012.

A work plan with big data should take three main elements into consideration: 1) collection and integration of a great volume of new data for fresh insights; 2) selection of advanced analytical models in order to automate operations and predict results of business decisions; and 3) creation of tools to translate model outputs into tangible actions and train key employees to use these tools. Internally, the benefits of this work plan would be a greater efficiency of the corporation since it would be driven by more relevant, accurate, timely information, more transparency of the operation running, better prediction and greater speed in simulations and tests [12] .

Another change presented by big data is in the ownership of information. The great information storages were owned only by governmental organizations and major traditional corporations. Nowadays, new corporations connected to technology (such as Facebook, Google, LinkedIn) hold a great part of the information on people, and the volume is rapidly increasing. Altogether, this information creates a digital trail for each person and its study can lead to the identification of their profile, preferences and even prediction of their behavior [5] .

Within business administration, new uses for the information are identified every day, with promises of benefits for operations (productivity gains), finance (control and scenario predictions), human resources (recruitment and selection, salary, identification of retention factors) and research and development (virtual prototyping and simulations). In marketing, the information on big data can help to both improve information quality for strategic planning in marketing and predict the definition of action programs.

USE OF BIG DATA IN THE MARKETING INFORMATION SYSTEM

Marketing can benefit from the use of big data information and many companies and institutes are already being structured to offer digital research and monitoring services. The use of this information will be presented following the classical model of marketing information system proposed by Kotler and Keller (2012) [10] .

Input-Sub-Systems

Internal Reports

Internal reports became more complete and complex, involving information and metrics generated by the company's digital proprieties (including websites and fanpages), which would also increase the amount of information on consumers, reaching beyond the data on customer profile. With the increase of information from different origins and in different formats, a richer internal database becomes the research source for business, markets, clients and consumers insights, in addition to internal analysis.

Marketing Intelligence

If in one hand the volume of information originated from marketing intelligence increases, on the other hand, it is concentrated on an area with more structured search and monitoring tools, with easier storage and integration. Reading newspapers, magazines and sector reports gains a new dimension with the access to global information in real time, changing the challenge of accessing information to selection of valuable information, increasing, therefore, the value of digital clipping services. The monitoring of competitors gains a new dimension since brand changes, whether local or global, can be easily followed up. The services of brand monitoring increase, with products such as GNPD by Mintel [13] and the Buzzz Monitor by e. Life [14] or SCUP and Bluefin.

Marketing Research

Since the Internet growth and virtual communities increase, studying online behavior became, at the same time, an opportunity and a necessity. Netnography makes use of ethnography sources when proposing to study group behavior through observation of their behavior in their natural environment. In this regard, ethnography (and netnography) has the characteristic of minimizing the behavior changes setbacks by not moving the object of study from its habitat, as many other study groups do. However, academic publications have not reached an agreement on technique application and analysis depth [15] -[17] . Kozinets (2002, 2006) [16] [17] proposes a deep study, in which the researcher needs to acquire great knowledge over the object group and monitor it for long periods, while Gerbera (2008) [15] is not clear about such need of deep knowledge of the technique, enabling the understanding of that which could be similar to a content analysis based on digital data. For the former, just as ethnography, the ethical issues become more important as the researcher should ask for permission to monitor the group and make their presence known; and, for the latter, netnography would not require such observer presentation from public data collected. The great volume of data captured by social networks could be analyzed using netnography.

One of the research techniques that have been gaining ground in the digital environment is the content analysis due to, on one hand, the great amount of data available for analysis on several subjects, and, on the other hand, the spread of free automated analysis tools, such as Many Eyes by IBM [18] , which offers cloud resources on terms, term correlation, scores and charts, among others. The massive volume of information of big data provides a great increase in the sample, and, in some cases, enables the population research, with "n = all" [4] .

Storage, Retrieval and Analysis

With the massive increase of the information volume and complexity, the storage, retrieval and analysis activities are even more important with big data. Companies that are not prepared to deal with the challenge find support in outsourcing the process [11] . According to Soat (2013) [19] , the attribution of scores for information digitally available (e-scores) would be one of the ways of working with information from different origins, including personal data (data collected from fidelity programs or e-mail messages), browsing data collected through cookies, and outsourced data, collected from financing institutes, censuses, credit cards. The information analysis would enable the company to develop the client's profile and present predictive analyses that would guide marketing decisions, such as identification of clients with greater lifetime value.

Information for the Decision-Making Process in Marketing

The marketing information system provides information for strategic (structure, segmentation and positioning) and operational (marketing mix) decision making. The use of big data in marketing will analyzed below under those perspectives.

Segmentation and Positioning

For Cravens and Piercy (2008) [20] , a segmentation strategy includes market analysis, identification of the market to be segmented, evaluation on how to segment it, definition of strategies of micro segmentation. A market analysis can identify segments that are unacknowledged or underserved by the competitors. To be successful, a segmentation strategy needs to seek identifiable and measurable, substantial, accessible, responsive and viable groups.

Positioning can be understood as the key characteristic, benefit or image that a brand represents for the collective mind of the general public [21] . It is the action of projecting the company's offer or image so that it occupies a distinctive place in the mind of the target public [10] . Cravens and Piercy (2008, p. 100) [20] connect the segmentation activity to the positioning through identification of valuable opportunities within the segment. Segmenting means identifying the segment that is strategically important to the company, whereas positioning means occupying the desired place within the segment. Digital research and monitoring tools enable studies on the consumer behavior to be used in behavioral segmentation. The assignment of scores and the use of advanced analyses help to identify and correlate variables, define predictive algorithmics to be used in market dimensioning and lifetime value calculations [19] [22] . The netnographical studies are also important sources to understand the consumer behavior and their beliefs and attitudes, providing relevant information to generate insights and define brand and product positioning.

Product

From the positioning, the available information should be used to define the product attributes, considering the value created for the consumer. Information on consumer preferences and manifestations in communities and forums are inputs for the development and adjustment of products, as well as for the definition of complementary services. The consumer could also participate in the product development process by offering ideas and evaluations in real time.

The development of innovation could also benefit from big data, both by surveying insights with the consumers and by using the information to develop the product, or even to improve the innovation process through the use of information, benefiting from the history of successful products, analyses of the process stages or queries to an idea archive [23] . As an improvement to the innovation process, the studies through big data would enable the replication of Cooper's studies in order to define a more efficient innovation process, by exploring the boundary between the marketing research and the research in marketing [24] .

Distribution

Internal reports became more complete and complex, involving information and metrics generated by the company's digital proprieties (including websites and fanpages), which would also increase the amount of information on consumers, reaching beyond the data on customer profile. With the increase of information from different origins and in different formats, a richer internal database becomes the research source for business, markets, clients and consumers insights, in addition to internal analysis.

In addition to the browsing location in the digital environment and the monitoring of visitor indicators, exit rate, bounce rate and time per page, the geolocation tools enable the monitoring of the consumers' physical location and how they commute. More than that, the market and consumer information from big data enables to assess, in a more holistic manner, the variables that affect the decisions on distribution and location [25] .

Communication

Big data analysis enables the emergence of new forms of communication research through the observation on how the audience interacts with the social networks. From their behavior analysis, new insights on their preferences and idols [3] may emerge to define the concepts and adjust details on the campaign execution. Moreover, the online interaction while displaying offline actions of brands enables the creation and follow up of indicators to monitor the communication [3] [26] , whether quantitative or qualitative.

The increase of information storage, processing and availability enables the application of the CRM concept to B2C clients, involving the activities of gathering, processing and analyzing information on clients, providing insights on how and why clients shop, optimizing the company processes, facilitating the client-company interaction, and offering access to the client's information to any company.

Price

Even offline businesses will be strongly affected by the use of online prices information. A research by Google Shopper Marketing Council [27] , published in April, 2013, shows that 84% of American consumers consult their smartphones while shopping in physical stores and 54% use them to compare prices. According to Vitorino (2013) [4] , the price information available in real time, together with the understanding of the consumers' opinion and factors of influence (stated opinions, comments on experiences, browsing history, family composition, period since last purchase, purchase behavior), combined with the use of predictive algorithmics would change the dynamics, and could, in the limit, provide inputs for a customized decision making on price every time.

LIMITATIONS

Due to the lack of a culture that cultivates the proper use of information and to a history of high costs for storage space, a lot of historical information was lost or simply not collected at all. A McKinsey study with retail companies observed that the chains were not using all the potential of the predictive systems due to the lack of: 1) historical information; 2) information integration; and 3) minimum standardization between the internal and external information of the chain [28] -[30] . The greater the historical information, the greater the accuracy of the algorithm, provided that the environment in which the system is implemented remains stable. Biesdorf, Court and Willmott (2013) [12] highlight the challenge of integrating information from different functional systems, legacy systems and information generated out of the company, including information from the macro environment and social networks.

Not having qualified people to guide studies and handle systems and interfaces is also a limiting factor for research [23] , at least in a short term. According to Gobble (2013) [23] McKinsey report identifies the need for 190,000 qualified people to work in data analysis-related posts today. The qualification of the front line should follow the development of user-friendly interfaces [12] . In addition to the people directly connected to the analytics, Don Schults (2012) [31] still highlights the need for people with "real life" experience, able to interpret the information generated by the algorithms. "If the basic understanding of the customer isn't there, built into the analytical models, it's really doesn't matter how many iterations the data went through or how quickly. The output is worthless (SCHULTZ, 2012, p. 9)."

The management of clients in a different manner through CRM already faces a series of criticism and limitations. Regarding the application of CRM for service marketing, its limitations would lie in the fact that a reference based only on the history may not reflect the client's real potential; the unequal treatment of clients could generate conflicts and dissatisfaction of clients not listed as priorities; and ethical issues involving privacy (improper information sharing) and differential treatment (such as redlining). These issues can be also applied in a bigger dimension in discussions about the use of information from big data in marketing research and its application on clients and consumers.

The predictive models are based on the fact that the environment where the analyzing system is implemented remains stable, which, by itself, is a limitation to the use of information. In addition to it and to the need of investing in a structure or expending on outsourcing, the main limitations in the use of big data are connected to three main factors: data shortage and inconsistence, qualified people, and proper use of the information. The full automation of the decision due to predictive models [5] also represents a risk, since that no matter how good a model is, it is still a binary way of understanding a limited theoretical situation. At least for now, the analytical models would be responsible for performing the analyses and recommendations, but the decisions would still be the responsibility of humans.

Nuan and Domenico (2013) [5] have also emphasized that people's behavior and their relationships in social networks may not accurately reflect their behavior offline, and the first important thing to do would be to increase the understanding level of the relation between online and offline social behavior. However, if on one hand people control the content of the intentionally released information in social networks, on the other hand, a great amount of information is collected invisibly, compounding their digital trail. The use of information without the awareness and permission of the studied person involves the ethics in research [15] -[17] . Figure 2 shows a suggestion of continuum between the information that the clients would make available wittingly and the information make available unwittingly to the predictive systems. The consideration of the ethics issues raised by Kozinets (2006) [17] , Nunan and Domenico (2013) [15] , and reinforces the importance of increasing the clients' level of awareness regarding the use of their information or ensuring the non-customization of the analysis of information obtained unwittingly by the companies.

FINAL CONSIDERATIONS

This study discussed the use of big data in the context of marketing information system, and, what was clear is that we are still in the beginning of a journey of understanding its possibilities and use, and we can observe the great attention generated by the subject and the increasing ethical concern. As proposed by Nunan and Domenico (2013) [5] , the self-governance via ESOMAR (European Society for Opinion and Market Research) [32] is an alternative to fight the abuses and excesses and enable the good use of the information. Nunan and Di Domenico (2013) [5] propose to include in the current ESOMAR [32] rules the right to be forgotten (possibility to request deletion of history), the right to have the data expired (complementing the right to be forgotten, the transaction data could also expire), and the ownership of a social graph (an individual should be aware of the information collected about them).

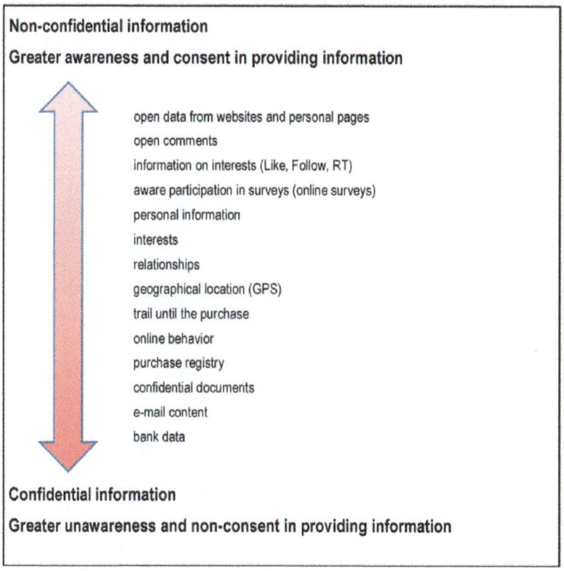

Figure 2. Continuum between the awareness and non-awareness regarding the use of information. Source: authors.

In marketing communication, the self-governance in Brazil has showed positive results, such as the examples in the liquor industry and kid's food industry, which, upon the pressure of public opinion, have adopted restrictive measures to repress abuses and maintain the communication of categories [33] . Industries such as the cigarette are opposite examples of how the excess has led to great restrictions to the categories. As in the prisoners' dilemma [34] , the self-governance forces a solution in which all participants have to give up on their best short-term individual options for the good of the group in a long term (Figure 3). On the other hand, if the consumer's consent in releasing the use of their information would solve the ethical issues, the companies would never have so much power to create value for their clients and consumers. Recovering the marketing application proposed in "Broadening the concept of marketing" [35] , the exchange of consent release could be performed by offering a major non-pecuniary value. This value offer could be the good use of the information to generate services or new proposals that increase the value perceived by the client [10] . Currently, many mobile applications offer services to consumers, apparently free of charge, in exchange for their audience for advertisements and access to their information in social networks. By understanding which service, consistent with its business proposal, the consumer sees the value in, and making this exchange clear, the service and consent of the information use could be a solution to access information in an ethical manner.

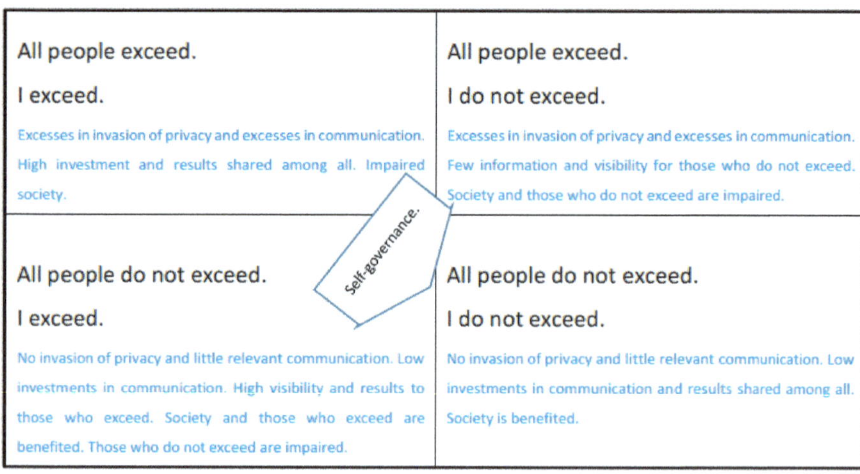

Figure 3. Free exercise of the prisoners' dilemma application. Source: Authors, based on Pindick and Rubinfeld (1994).

From the point of view of marketing research, the development of recovery systems and the analyses of great volumes of non-structured information could lead to the understanding of consumer behaviors. Issues regarding the findings and understanding of the consumers in marketing research are addressed qualitatively. However, due to the volume of cases, could the studies, through big data, provide at the same time the understanding on the consumer and the measurement of the groups with this behavior? A suggestion for the following research would be to study the combination of the qualitative and quantitative research objectives with the use of big data and analytical systems in understanding consumer behavior and measurement of group importance.

REFERENCES

1. Chow-White, P.A. and Green, S.E. (2013) Data Mining Difference in the Age of Big Data: Communication and the Social Shaping of Genome Technologies from 1998 to 2007. International Journal of Communication, 7, 556-583.
2. ORACLE: Big Data for Enterprise. http://www.oracle.com/br/technologies/big-data/index.html
3. Paul, J. (2012) Big Data Takes Centre Ice. Marketing, 30 November 2012.
4. Vitorino, J. (2013) Social Big Data. São Paulo, 1-5. www.elife.com.br
5. Nunan, D. and Domenico, M.Di. (2013) Market Research and the Ethics of Big Data Market Research and the Ethics of Big Data. International Journal of Market Research, 55, 2-13.
6. Cox, D. and Good, R. (1967) How to Build a Marketing Information System. Harvard Business Review, May-June, 145-154. ftp://donnees.admnt.usherbrooke.ca/Mar851/Lectures/IV
7. Berenson, C. (1969) Marketing Information Systems. Journal of Marketing, 33, 16. http://dx.doi.org/10.2307/1248668
8. Chiusoli, C.L. and Ikeda, A. (2010) Sistema de Informação de Marketing (SIM): Ferramenta de apoio com aplicações à gestão empresarial. Atlas, São Paulo.
9. Kotler, P. (1998) Administração de marketing. 5th Edition, Atlas, São Paulo.
10. Kotler, P. and Keller, K. (2012) Administração de marketing. 14th Edition, Pearson Education, São Paulo.
11. Zikopoulos, P. and Eaton, C. (2012) Understanding Big Data: Analytics for Enterprise Class Hadoop and Streaming Data. McGraw Hill, New York, 166. Retrieved from Malik, A.S., Boyko, O., Atkar, N. and Young, W.F. (2001) A Comparative Study of MR Imaging Profile of Titanium Pedicle Screws. Acta Radiologica, 42, 291-293. http://dx.doi.org/10.1080/028418501127346846
12. Biesdorf, S., Court, D. and Willmott, P. (2013) Big Data: What's Your Plan? McKinsey Quarterly, 40-41.
13. MINTEL. www.mintel.com
14. E. Life. www.elife.com.br
15. Gebera, O.W.T. (2008) La netnografía: Un método de investigación en Internet. Quaderns Digitals: Revista de Nuevas Tecnologías y Sociedad, 11. http://dialnet.unirioja.es/servlet/articulo?codigo=3100552
16. Kozinets, R. (2002) The Field behind the Screen: Using Netnography for Marketing Research in Online Communities. Journal of Marketing Research, 39, 61-72. http://www.jstor.org/stable/10.2307/1558584 http://dx.doi.org/10.1509/jmkr.39.1.61.18935
17. Kozinets, R.W. (2006) Click to Connect: Netnography and Tribal Advertising. Journal of Advertising Research, 46, 279-288. http://dx.doi.org/10.2501/S0021849906060338
18. Many Eyes. http://www.manyeyes.com/software/analytics/manyeyes/

19. Soat, M. (2013) E-SCORES: The New Face of Predictive Analytics. Marketing Insights, September, 1-4.

20. Cravens, D.W. and Piercy, N.F. (2008) Marketing estratégico. 8th Edition, McGraw Hill, São Paulo.

21. Crescitelli, E. and Shimp, T. (2012) Comunicação de Marketing: Integrando propaganda, promoção e outrs formas de divulgação. Cengage Learning, São Paulo.

22. Payne, A. and Frow, P. (2005) A Strategic Framework for Customer Relationship Management. Journal of Marketing, 69, 167-176. http://dx.doi.org/10.1509/jmkg.2005.69.4.167

23. Gobble, M.M. (2013) Big Data: The Next Big Thing in Innovation. Research-Technology Management, 56, 64-67. http://dx.doi.org/10.5437/08956308X5601005

24. Cooper, R.G. (1990) Stage-Gate Systems: A New Tool for Managing New Products, (June).

25. Parente, J. (2000) Varejo no Brasil: Gestão e Estratégia. Atlas, São Paulo.

26. Talbot, D. (2011) Decoding Social Media Patterns in Tweets A Social-Media Decoder. Technology Review, December 2011.

27. Google Shopper Marketing Agency Council (2013) Mobile In-Store Research: How Is Store Shoppers Are Using Mobile Devices, 37. http://www.marcresearch.com/pdf/Mobile_InStore_Research_Study.pdf

28. Bughin, J., Byers, A. and Chui, M. (2011) How Social Technologies Are Extending the Organization. McKinsey Quarterly, 1-10. http://bhivegroup.com.au/wp-content/uploads/socialtechnology.pdf

29. Bughin, J., Livingston, J. and Marwaha, S. (2011) Seizing the Potential of "Big Data." McKinsey …, (October). http://whispersandshouts.typepad.com/files/using-big-data-to-drive-strategy-and-innovation.pdf

30. Manyika, J., Chui, M., Brown, B. and Bughin, J. (2011) Big Data: The Next Frontier for Innovation, Competition, and Productivity. 146. www.mckinsey.com/mgi

31. Schultz, D. (2012) Can Big Data Do It All ? Marketing News, November, 9.

32. ESOMAR. http://www.esomar.org/utilities/news-multimedia/video.php?idvideo=57

33. CONAR. Conselho Nacional de Auto-regulamentação Publicitária. http://www.conar.org.br/

34. Pindyck, R.S. and Rubinfeld, D.L. (1994) Microeconomia. Makron Books, São Paulo.

35. Kotler, P. and Levy, S.J. (1969) Broadening the Concept of Marketing. Journal of Marketing, 33, 10-15. http://www.ncbi.nlm.nih.gov/pubmed/12309673 http://dx.doi.org/10.2307/1248740

SECTION III: BIO-MEDICAL DATA WAREHOUSE USE CASES

10
CHAPTER

BUILDING A HEALTH CARE DATA WAREHOUSE

Dr.Osama E.Sheta and Ahmed Nour Eldeen

Keywords: Health care data warehouse, Extract-Transformation-Load (ETL), Health care Decision Support System (DSS) and Cancer

INTRODUCTION

The healthcare industry is one of the world's largest, fastest-developing and most information-rich industries [1].The growing need for integrated healthcare has led this industry to open towards adoption of extensive healthcare decision support systems. Information technology in health care is still a topical subject, has stimulated developments in physician order entry, decision support systems and shared patient records. Despite all the efforts, many health care organizations still have stand-alone information systems that do not communicate with each other. More importantly, clinical information systems (CIS) such as electronic patient records, are often designed to support hands-on care for individual patients, but are not well suited for analyses on an aggregated level, for example on groups of patients with the same disease[2].

In this paper we work in the cancer diseases, the cost of treatment for these diseases, Death rate in specific type of cancer and the impact of a particular drug on the disease.

Cancer known medically as a malignant neoplasm, is a broad group of various diseases, all involving unregulated cell growth. In cancer, cells divide and grow uncontrollably, forming malignant tumors, and invade nearby parts of the body. The cancer may also spread to more distant parts of the body through the lymphatic system or bloodstream. Not all tumors are cancerous. Benign tumors do not grow uncontrollably,

Citation: Dr.Osama E.Sheta and Ahmed Nour Eldeen,"Building a Health Care Data Warehouse," International Journal of Database Management Systems (IJDMS) Vol.4, No.5, October 2012. DOI: 10.5121/ijdms.2012.4503.

do not invade neighboring tissues, and do not spread throughout the body. Determining what causes cancer is complex. Many things are known to increase the risk of cancer, including tobacco use, certain infections, radiation, lack of physical activity, poor diet and obesity, and environmental pollutants. These can directly damage genes or combine with existing genetic faults within cells to cause the disease. Approximately five to ten percent of cancers are entirely hereditary.

People with suspected cancer are investigated with medical tests. These commonly include blood tests, X-rays, CT scans and endoscopy [3].

DATA WAREHOUSE ARCHITECTURE

The concept of "data warehousing" arose in mid 1980s with the intention to support huge information analysis and management reporting [4]. Data warehouse was defined According to Bill Inmon a "subject-oriented, integrated, time variant and non-volatile collection of data in support of management's decision making process" [5].

According to Ralph Kimball "a data warehouse is a system that extracts, cleans, conforms, and delivers source data into a dimensional data store and then supports and implements querying and analysis for the purpose of decision making".[6]

Today, data warehouses are not only deployed extensively in banking and finance, consumer goods and retail distribution and demand-based manufacturing, it has also became a hot topic in noncommercial sector, mainly in medical fields, government, military services, education and research community etc.

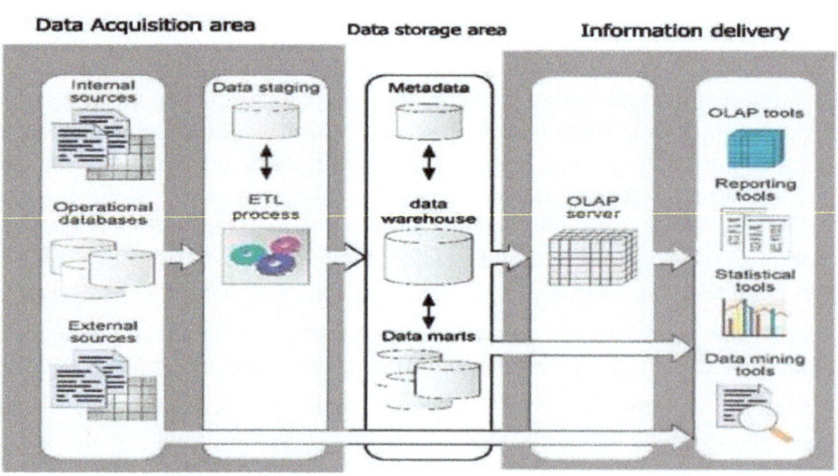

Figure 1. Data Warehouse Architecture

Data warehouse architecture is a description of the components of the warehouse, with details showing how the components will fit together [7]. Figure 1 shows a typical architecture of a data warehouse system which includes three major areas that consist of tools for extracting data from multiple operational databases and external sources for cleaning, transforming and integrating this data; and loading data into the data warehouse [8]. Data are stored and managed in the warehouse and data marts which present multidimensional views of data to a variety of front end tools: query tools, report writers, analysis tools, and data mining tools [8].

There are three major areas in the data warehouse architecture as following:

- Data acquisition.
- Data storage.
- Information delivery.

Then we will explain in details each area as following: [9]

- **Data Acquisition**: This stage covers the process of extracting data from the multi sources, moving all the extracted data to the staging area, and preparing the data for loading into repository. The two major architectural components of this area are source data and data staging which is the place where all the extracted data is put together and prepared for loading into the data warehouse.

  The function and services for this area are:

  1. *Data Extraction*: Select data sources from multi sources and determine the types of data.

  2. *Data Transformation:* transform extracted data to data for data warehouse repository. Clean data, de-duplicate, and merge. De-normalize extracted data structures as required by the dimensional model of the data warehouse

- **Data storage**: This stage covers the process of loading the transformed data from the staging area into the data warehouse repository.

  The function and services for this area are the following:

  1. Load a data into data warehouse tables.
  2. Optimize the loading process.

- **Information delivery**: The information delivery component makes it easy for the users to access the information directly from the data warehouse.

  The function and services for this area are the following:

  1. Allow users to browse data warehouse content.
  2. Enable queries of aggregate tables for faster results and analysis.
  3. Provide multiple levels of data granularity.
  4. Easy to perform complex analysis using online analytical processing (OLAP).

BUILDING CANCER DATA WAREHOUSE

Many healthcare processes involve a series of patient visits or a series of outcomes. The modeling of outcomes associated with these types of healthcare processes is different from and not as well understood as the modeling of standard industry environments. The process of cancer patient in healthcare can be thought of as a value circle the center of this circle are data related to patient treatment [10, 11]. The treatment is measured or generated by all the processes and organizations around the circle show in Figure 2. This is quite different from typical processes in other industries, which usually follow a linear chain model in which a product moves through a series of steps from raw material to finished goods or from customer order to delivery [10].

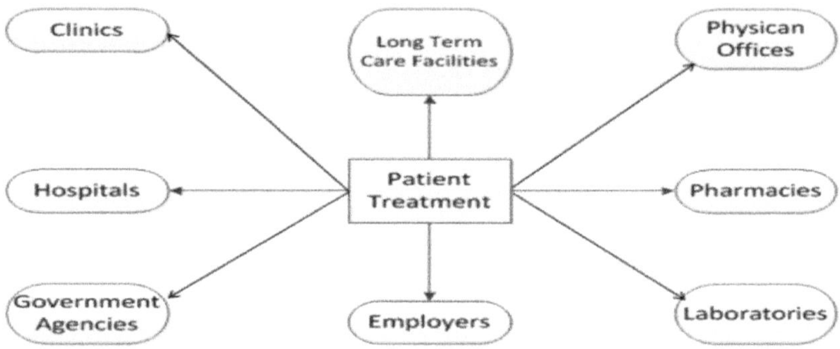

Figure 2. Health care value circle

In this paper we proposes a 2 stages approach for the building cancer data warehouse

- Business Analysis.
- Architecture Design.

We will explain in details each stage as following:

Business Analysis

Is the discipline of identifying business needs and determining solutions to business problems. Solutions often include a systems development component, but may also consist of process improvement, organizational change or strategic planning and policy development [12].

The business analysis stage, consist of business process analysis and business requirement analysis

Business Process Analysis

Cancer data warehouse use case diagram as shown in Figure 3 depicts a high level overview of system functionality [13].

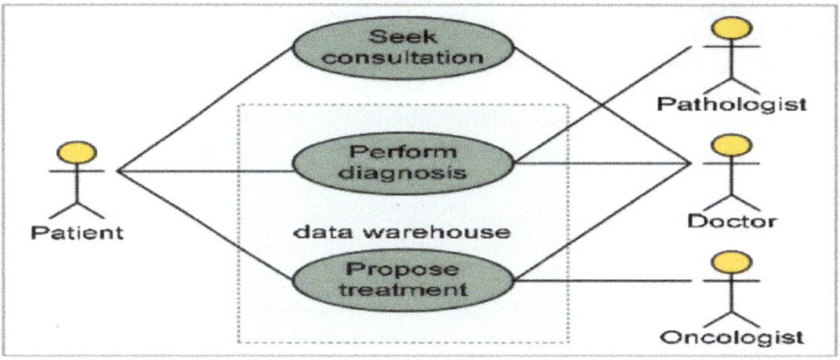

Figure 3. Cancer data warehouse use case diagram.

There are four actors in the process; Patient, Doctor, Pathologist, and Oncologist. The interactions between the actors and cases are demonstrated in the following paragraphs.

Case 1: Seek consultation

Patient go to doctor for consultation when certain symptoms are noticed.

Case 2: Perform diagnosis

The doctor together with pathologist will perform a series of tests on the patient to determine the type, stage and prognosis of the cancer.

Case 2.1: Determine the type of Cancer

First, the doctor will perform an excisional biopsy, by taking tissue sample from the affected organs for further examination. If other organs e.g. skin, brain, stomach are affected, a biopsy from these organs is also required. Next, pathologist will inspect the physical appearance of the biopsy sample under a microscope, or identify the special molecules on the Cancer cells using markets that result to determining the type of Cancer.

Case 2.2: Determine the stage of Cancer

The doctor will proceed with a number of tests to see how advanced the cancer is and how far it has spread.

Case 2.3: Determine the prognosis of Cancer

Next, the doctor will look into other factors to determine the prognosis of the disease.

Case 3: Propose treatment

When the above investigations are completed, the doctor and oncologist will counsel the patient regarding the best treatment options available, based on the type and the stage of the disease and some prognostic factors. There are three main types of treatment normally used to cure Cancers:

- Chemotherapy – Using drugs as infusions into the patient's veins.
- Radiotherapy – Using high energy rays over the affected areas.
- Biological therapy or antibiotic therapy – Using drugs like Rituximab to target special molecules on the cancer cells.

Besides proposing the treatment options to patient, the doctor also need to explain to the patient about the risks of taking the particular treatment and chance of recovery. Upon endorsement by the patient, the doctor will schedule the treatments for the patient.

Business Requirement Analysis

We will propose some of the standard requirements for a healthcare data warehouse to support Cancer diagnosis and treatment recommendation:

- The medical diagnosing function requires understanding of patient medical history, symptoms, drug-drug interactions, knowledge of diseases in general as well as the general population.
- Minimal level of demographic details about the patient need to be captured in the patient master record include: Full Name, Gender, Date of Birth, Marital Status, Address, Occupation and etc.
- All patient master records can be recognized by National ID number. The system must be able to detect duplication of patient master records. The system shall automatically merge the patient records, if duplication of master records for the same patient is found.
- The system must able to display data at both summary and detail levels, and allow users to drill down to analyze a specific result.
- The system must facilitate a multi-dimensional data model presentation. Patient and medical details can be queried by multiple factors, such as location, gender, age range, blood group, race etc.
- The system should have to be updateable and adapted to constant changes that accompany the scientific development.

Architecture Design

Figure 4 illustrates the overall architecture of the propose healthcare data warehouse specific to Cancer. Data is imported from several sources and transformed within a staging area before it is integrated and stored in the production data warehouse for further analysis.

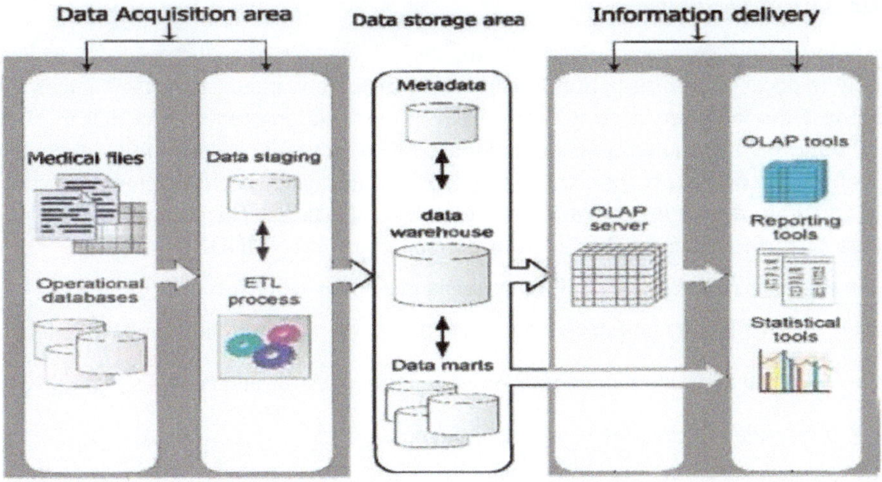

Figure 4. Cancer data warehouse Architecture.

Data Acquisition

This covers the entire process of extracting data from the Access database, medical files such as (patient medical records, blood tests, urine test results, x-ray results and etc.) then moving all the extracted data to the staging area and preparing the extracted data for loading into data warehouse repository.

In this stage there are a set of functions and services such as:

- *Data Extraction:* Select data from access DB and Medical files and determine the types of filters to be applied to Cancer data warehouse.
- *Data Transformation:* Map extracted data to data for data warehouse repository. Clean data, de-duplicate, and merge data from access DB and medical files.

Data Storage

This covers the process of loading the transformed data from the staging area into the data warehouse repository. All functions for transforming and integrating between the access data base and medical files are completed in the data staging area.

In this stage there are a set of functions and services such as:

- Load a health care data into data warehouse tables.
- Optimize the loading process.
- Perform incremental loads at regular prescribed intervals.
- Support loading integrated data into multiple tables.

Information Delivery

The information delivery component makes it easy for the doctors and decision making to access the information directly from the data warehouse. In the Cancer data warehouse model, after locating the sources of data, we proceeded to design the Data Warehouse; the star model was adopted, based on a fact table and multiple dimensions tables [14]. Then create hierarchy from dimension tables and specify the measure in fact table which used with this hierarchy to create useful reports. The doctors and decision makers perform analysis using the information cubes in the MDDBs.

In this stage there are a set of functions and services such as:

- Allow doctors and decision makers to browse data warehouse content.
- Enable queries of aggregate tables for faster results and analysis.
- Provide multiple levels of data granularity.
- Monitor doctors and decision making access to improve service and for future enhancements.

Finally the designed cancer data warehouse was done using the following:

- Relational database management system: Microsoft Sql Server 2008 and Microsoft Access
- ETL : Sql server integration service 2008 (SSIS).
- OLAP: Sql server analysis service 2008 (SSAS).
- Reporting: Sql server Reporting service 2008(SSRS) .
- C # language.

CONCLUSION

The healthcare industry is one of the world's largest, fastest-developing and most information-rich industries for take advantage from this information we build the Cancer data warehouse to integrate between the operational data base and medical files and therefore the analysis on data makes easy by using OLAP cubes and viewing multilevel of details from the data. Then we can analyses the cancer diseases, the cost of treatment for these diseases, Death rate in specific type of cancer and the impact of a particular drug on the disease.

During the building data warehouse we are encounter a several challenges such as the following:

- Data warehouse development requires specialized skills that are very different from a typical database development.
- Data integration plays the most critical role in a data warehouse Building.

Data should be extracted from physical medical files, such as patient medical records, blood tests, urine test results, x-ray results, CT scan results etc., or retrieved directly from the operational medical system.

FUTURE WORKS

We implemented this research to DSS for Health Insurance Organization – Elsharkiya Branch - Egypt which could be used by doctors, physicians and other health professionals to support the healthcare process as well as to formulate the appropriate model to improve the quality of diagnosis, treatment recommendation decision making, the impact of a particular drug on the disease this implementation contain ETL process and star schema with fact and dimension table and create data cube for multi view of data and finally create reports with charts and time series evaluation this all in one package using C# programing language.

REFERENCES

1. KFF. (2006). "Comparing Projected Growth in Health Care Expenditures and the Economy", Snapshots: Health Care Costs Retrieved 22.10.2007, from http://www.kff.org/insurance/snapshot/chcm050206oth2.cfm
2. Marleen de Mul, Peter Alons, Peter van der Velde, Ilse Konings, Jan Bakker, Jan Hazelzet, (2010) "Development of a clinical data warehouse from an intensive care clinical information system", CMPB, 2010.07.002
3. Web site, http://en.wikipedia.org/wiki/Cancer
4. Teh Ying Wah, Ong Suan Sim (2009) "Development of a Data Warehouse for Lymphoma Cancer Diagnosis and Treatment Decision Support".
5. W. H. Inmon, (2002) "Building The Data Warehouse", Wiley Computer Publishing
6. Ralph Kimball, Joe Casertam. (2004) "The Data Warehouse ETL Toolkit.
7. Laura Hadley, (2002) "Developing a Data Warehouse Architecture".
8. Surajit, Chaudhuri and Umeshwar, Dayal, (1996) "An Overview of Data Warehousing and OLAP Technology".
9. Paulraj Ponniah, (2010) "data warehousing fundamentals for it professionals", John Wiley & Sons.
10. Golfarelli, Matteo; Rizzi Stefano (2009). "Data Warehouse Design: Modern Principles and Methodologies.
11. Kimball, R, (1998) "The Data Warehouse Lifecycle Toolkit: Expert Methods for Designing, Developing, and Deploying Data Warehouses". New York: Wiley.
12. Kathleen B Hass, Richard Vander Horst (2008). "From Analyst to Leader: Elevating the Role of the Business Analyst".
13. Detailed Guide, (2007) "Lymphoma, Non-Hodgkin Type, How is Non-Hodgkins Lymphoma staged, American Cancer Society Inc", Retrieved from http://www.cancer.org/.
14. Mohamed Salah and Amine Farhat (2010) "Building A Data Warehouse National

Social Security Fund Of The Republic Of Tunisia " IJDMS, Vol2, No2.

15. Kimball, R. and M. Ross. (2002) "The Data Warehouse Toolkit: The Complete Guide to Dimensional Modeling. 2nd ed". New York: Wiley.

11
CHAPTER

OSTEOPOROSIS DATA WAREHOUSE IN THE OSTEOPOROSIS COMMUNITY HEALTH INFORMATION MANAGEMENT SYSTEM

Qiang Wang, Yingchao Shen

Keywords: Community Management; Data Warehouse, Information Management System, Osteoporosis, Remote Management of Osteoporosis

INTRODUCTION

Osteoporosis is a multifactorial bone disease in addition to being a noninfectious chronic disease (NCD) that is arousing increased attention-like diabetes mellitus and hypertension. Osteoporosis has definite pathophysiological and social psychological effects in addition to exerting economic consequences [1]. Osteoporosis can increase the incidence of fractures. Among osteoporosis patients, about 30% of females suffer fractures [2]. Osteoporosis has no obvious symptom, thus it is referred to as a "silent" disease. Patients tend not to properly understand treatment nor do they place a strong emphasis upon it. Most elderly osteoporosis patients have a low educational level and therefore do not fully use the services provided by health departments. Therefore, staff in community health centers needs to provide instruction, intervention, and appropriate management prior to disease attack.

Community intervention is an important aspect in promoting NCD management [3]. Active risk evaluation of the population at risk from osteoporosis and appropriate intervention at an early stage of the condition through the community health service are effective in reducing the incidence of osteoporosis and improving patients' quality of life [4]. Since osteoporosis is a multifactorial, chronic epidemic disease, informationization provides important technical support in real-time management and

Citation: Qiang Wang, Yingchao Shen, "Osteoporosis data warehouse in the osteoporosis community Health Information Management system," J. Biomedical Science and Engineering, 2013, 6, 1072-1076, http://dx.doi.org/10.4236/jbise.2013.611134.

efficient use of human resources [5]. Integration of all procedures is the most important factor in community intervention and management. It involves optimization and assembly of staff, equipment, and desktop application systems to pro-mote cooperation among application users, departments and staff in general hospitals, community health service centers, medical staff overall, community residents, medical institutions, and health administration officials. Most hospital information systems are used to manage the business side of proceedings, that is, one-time integration of information, and they are unable to support full data use.

Thus, there is a need to build a data warehouse that al-lows full analysis towards strategy development [6].

DATA ANALYSIS AND MODEL BUILDING

In cooperation with rural community health service centers, we analyzed data sources towards promoting com-munity health management for osteoporosis by means of a data warehouse.

Data Research

We invited staff from Yushan Xinglong Community Health Service Center, the Departments of Orthopedics, Gynecology and Obstetrics, and Endocrinology of Changshu Hospital of Traditional Chinese Medicine, Health Bureau of Changshu, and software engineers to compose the group for our data research. The outpatient clinic of Changshu Hospital of Traditional Chinese Medicine was responsible for the organization and communications related to this study, and the data warehouse was constructed for physicians from Yushan Xinglong Community Health Service Center and the indicated departments of Changshu Hospital of Traditional Chinese Medicine and health management institutions. The data warehouse users were provided with basic training with regards to the study concept and required levels of analysis.

Data Scope

Data source was divided according to subjects and data research to integrate information models of various business systems for macroscopic merge, abstraction, and da-ta scope to confirm that all required data were extracted from business systems and well organized. The data scope was defined as community residents with osteoporosis or at a high risk of osteoporosis; it mainly comprised post-menopausal females and elderly males (older than 60 years). The data of all residents in the data scope were used in the study except those of residents who moved out of the community or died.

Subject Elements of Community Management for Osteoporosis

The subject elements for community management of osteoporosis included dimension (content of business), subjects (includes data of subjects), particle size (dimension levels to extract data details), and storage limit (of data). Based on a comprehensive analysis of data conducted by physicians from community health service centers and the indicated departments of Changshu Hospital of Traditional Chinese Medicine, several dimensions were con-firmed; these included baseline information, osteoporosis-related high-risk factors, bone density, and assessments of interventions. Each dimension was divided into several levels, and particle size was used to confirm and elucidate the dimension levels. Osteoporosis-related high-risk factors are complex. Among males, 21 high-risk factors have been identified, whereas 26 have been identified among females [7]. We screened the high-risk factors and provided options for data entry, analysis, and mining. Evaluated osteoporosis-related high-risk factors comprised age, body mass, family history, and nutritional factors; intervention measurements included appropriate diet, exercise, sufficient calcium intake, vitamin D intake, and correction of poor life-style habits; bone density examination items included quantitative computed tomography, dual energy X-ray absorptiometry, and ultrasound bone intensity examination; treatment measurements included calcium agents, vitamin D, alendronate sodium tablets, calcitonin, Aclasta, and estrogen replacement therapy. The dose and duration of each intervention, examination, and treatment were recorded.

The snowflake model was used to summarize the above multidimensional data relationships; the model consisted of a fact table and a group of dimension tables. This al-lowed the dimension factors to be further divided; for example, intervention factors included sports, amount of sunlight, appropriate diet, and medication. The "intervention" dimension could be snow flaked, that is, the dimensions could be decomposed in terms of the attributes for sports, amount of sunlight, appropriate diet, and medication to form four-dimension tables. For the "female" dimension, time since menopause had to be recorded as the particle size.

Dynamic Loading

Community management needs to be continuously up-dated so as to provide dynamic data loading when constructing a database. Traditional data warehouses store diachronic, resting, and integrated business data, which initially load data and then support business searches. However, data loading with a dynamic data warehouse can load data while simultaneously allowing users to con-duct searches. Moreover, dynamic loading does not affect the use of the data warehouse, which allows the immediate analysis of loading data. The intervention measures and bone density measurements of subjects could be continuously recorded.

CONSTRUCTION OF DATABASE AND PHYSICAL ACHIEVEMENT

Fact Table of Data Warehouse

The fact table contains all the osteoporosis health data. The fact table was the largest table we constructed and its information was updated the fastest in the data ware-house. All attributes for each record depended on the primary key of the fact table, and a series of foreign keys was associated with each dimension table. With regard to the search function of the data warehouse, it is necessary to minimize connection operations among different tables. The fact table was designed as shown in **Table 1**.

DESIGN OF RELATED DIMENSION TABLES

For each attribute in the fact table, the dimension information was recorded using a special dimension table to confirm the values of some dimensions [4]. The design of the dimension tables was based on the table name (main key word coding, name), and content in parentheses in **Table 2** represents the field names. The main dimension tables are shown in **Table 2**.

The search function was improved by combining the small dimension tables. For example, the social dimension table is presented in **Table 3**.

Table 1. Design of the osteoporosis health file data fact table

Field name	Meaning
ID	File compile
Xingming	Name
Chusheng	Birth data
Shequ	Community
Xingbie	Sex
Juejing	Menopause time (female)
Jibing	History of disease
Jiazu	Family history
Gmdff	Measurement method of bone density
Gmdt	Measurement time of bone density
Gmdz	Bone density value
Gmdgk	Bone mineral density
Ganyuss	Intervention diet
Ganyush	Intervention life
Ganyuyd	Intervention exercise
Ganyuyw	Intervention drugs
Beizhu	Remarks
Lrname	Name of data entry staff
Lrrq	Date of data entry
Guidang	Filing or not (1: filing; 0: not)

Table 2. Design of the main dimension tables

Structure of dimension table	Instruction
BASIC (basic information)	Dimension table of basic information
FACTORS (risk factors with osteoporosis)	Dimension table of risk factors for osteoporosis
BMD (bone mineral density)	Dimension table of bone mineral density
IM (intervention measures)	Dimension table of intervention measures

Interactive Data Distributed Structure

System management was achieved through interactive management of physicians from the community health service center and general hospital and health administration departments. Therefore, we used an interactive data mart structure. Although different data marts were achieved in specific departments, they were integrated and interlinked to provide a comprehensive data view for business scope. The administrator assigned different per-missions for different grades of users. The user had to register the database for data entry, correction, export, and analysis, that is, the data warehouse for business scope. For example, the staff of different community health service centers could enter different data relating to their own communities.

User management is also a special dimension table. The user management was built as presented in **Table 4**.

PLATFORM DEVELOPMENT AND DATA WAREHOUSE

Hypertext Preprocessor was used to develop web application programs. The Linux operating system was employed as the server operating system, equipped with the Apache 2.0 operating platform. The MySQL 4.5 relational database was built and is accessible on the internet. The user can input http://www.cszlf.net/sycweb/ in the web browser, and the log-in page appears as seen in **Figure 1**.

The data entry interface appears after inputting the user name and password **Figure 2**.

The system provides online analysis for real-time and online analysis of data in the data warehouse, including individual case analysis, group analysis, and global analysis. For individual case analysis, the user can search the target records through a conditional search and click the "analyze" button on the interface to obtain the individual case analysis by system and primary diagnosis and treatment suggestions; these do, however, require the confirmation of clinical physicians. This process achieves computer-assisted diagnosis and treatment **Figure 3**.

Table 3. Social dimension table (expression of patients in the community)

Id	Community no.
Sqmc	Community name

Table 4. Users table (system administrator list)

Id	User encoding
Name	Logging name
Pass	Logging password
Xinming	Real name
Level	Management level (0: system administrator; 1: common administrator)
Last	Last logging time

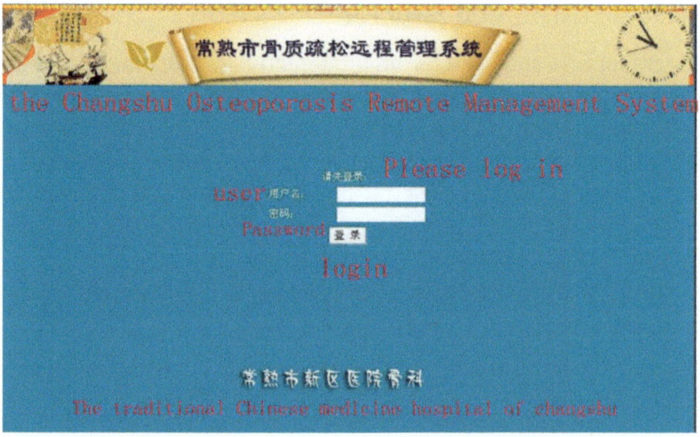

Figure 1. Log-in screen of Changshu osteoporosis remote management system.

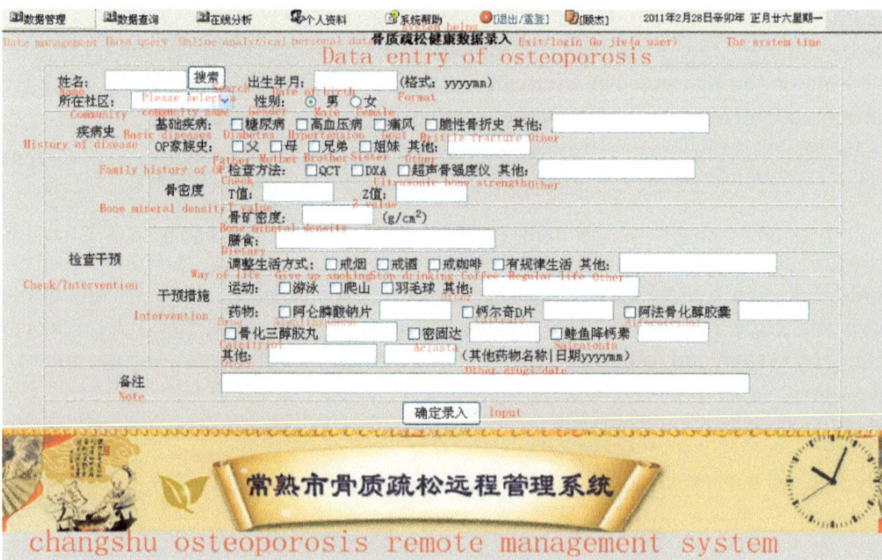

Figure 2. Data entry interface of the Changshu osteoporosis remote management system.

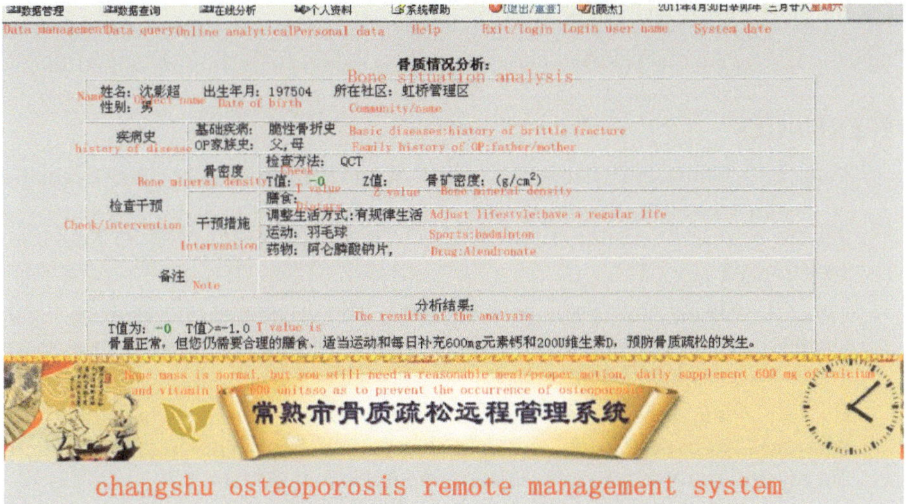

Figure 3. Online analysis interface of the Changshu osteoporosis remote management system.

DISCUSSION

There is a common lack of appropriate tool software and unified ordered organization in community public health service management, [8] and it is difficult to analyze daily working data or to further community health management. Although some information management systems for osteoporosis have been developed and used, most of them use databases rather than data warehouses; thus, they do not support data analysis functions or data mining [9]. We have been collecting data since 2010, and we have combined basic principles and methods for a data warehouse with community intervention in constructing such a warehouse that achieves dynamic loading. This data warehouse has several positive features: It effectively organizes data sources, and provides deep-level data mining and online analysis. In addition, users can include community health service centers, osteoporosis departments of hospitals, and health administration departments. In this way, it is possible to provide strategic evidence and support for health administration departments, provide complex computer-aided diagnosis and treatment for community health service centers, provide patients with follow-up data, and provide raw scientific research data and real -time health statistics for hospital-based physicians. The system can be used for data management, data query, online analysis, etc. for specialist out-patients for osteoporosis in community health service center and health administration sectors [10]. The web-based network environment eases data searches, and on-line analysis of the data warehouse in combination with data-mining techniques can analyze the data distribution and dynamic changes of each variable, support research and strategy, and provide evidence for clinical research and community NCD [11].

ACKNOWLEDGEMENTS

Thanks to Changshu audio-visual classroom Zhao Weifei for technical supporting.

REFERENCES

1. Yang, S.Q., Wang, H.P., Guan, L.Z., Qu, L.Y. and Li, M.Q. (2008) Effect evaluation on health education for the elderly with high-risk potential of osteoporosis in Zhong- guancun Community of Beijing. *Chinese Journal of Health Education*, **24**, 593-595.
2. Liu, Z.L., Huang, J.G. and Liu, Z.J. (2007) The discussion and analysis for the mechanism and prevention of osteoporosis in women after menopause. *China Medical Her*, **24**, 157-158.
3. Hu, R., Zhou, Z.M., Zhai, D.Y., Yue, X.Y., Xu, G.L. and Liu, X.F. (2010) Awareness of hypertension among is-chemic stroke survivors in the community: Survey and analysis. *Postgraduate Medical Journal*, **23**, 167-170.
4. Stolba, N. (2007) Towards a sustainable data warehouse approach for evidence-based heathcare. PhD Thesis, Vienna University of Technology, Vienna.
5. Wang, H.X., Wang, H.L. and Li, F.H. (2011) Application of nursing information system. *Postgraduate Medical Journal*, **24**, 72-74.
6. Zhang, J.X., Wang, X.L., Chang, S.F., Li, R., Wang, H.J. and Kan, X.L. (2010) Research and construction for data warehouse of TCM medical record in cold. *Jiangsu Journal of Traditional Chinese Medicine*, **42**, 66-68.
7. Yang, J.Q. and Jiang, X.Y. (2005) Risk factors and their assessment of osteoporosis. *Journal of Fujian Medicine University*, **39**, 237-239.
8. Chen, W.C., Han, Z.Z., Zhang, L. and Yang, J. (2008) Re-search on developing information system with new concept for community health services. *Journal of Chinese General Practice*, **11**, 1414-1416.
9. Zhao, L., Xin, Z.Q. and Yu, W.Z. (2009) Clinic use of in-formation management system of osteoporosis patient. *Modern Hospital*, **9**, 142-144.
10. Yu, J.F., Shen, Y.C., Zhou, B.K., Chen, X., Wang, Q. and Gu, Y.F. (2012) Remote management system of osteoporosis community intervention and design of data ware-house. *Journal of Chinese General Practice*, **15**, 26-28.
11. Pan, X.Y. (2010) Survey data analysis for health needs of urban community. *Chinese Communication Doctors*, **12**, 165.

12
CHAPTER

INTEGRATIVE GENOMIC AND PROTEOMIC DATA WAREHOUSE

Francesco Pessina, Marco Masseroli, Arif Canakoglu

Keywords: SQL Query Composition, Visual Interface, Integrated Data Extraction, Data Warehousing, Bioinformatics Database

INTRODUCTION

A great amount of valuable and heterogeneous biomedical molecular data and information is increasingly produced thanks to the modern high-throughput technologies. It is stored in publicly accessible molecular biology databases that are continuously increasing in number and coverage of the included biomolecular entities, as well as of their described structural and functional biomedical features and associated phenotypes [1]. Such databases provide extremely valuable information to infer new knowledge and potentially answer biomedical questions, which are generally complex. To obtain enough evidence to support such answers, several different structural, functional and phenotypic annotations must be collected and comprehensively evaluated. Yet, even the information about a single biomolecular entity is often scattered across many different sources.

Several approaches have been proposed to integrate data from multiple heterogeneous data sources and query them comprehensively. Data warehousing well supports off-line processing to mine the integrated data towards knowledge discovery. Yet, the global schemas for bio-logical data warehousing that have been proposed are quite complex [2-5]. Although they can support a complete representation of the underlying biological aspects described by the integrated data, they make it difficult to

Citation: Francesco Pessina, Marco Masseroli, Arif Canakoglu, "Integrative Genomic and Proteomic Data Warehouse," Engineering, 2013, 5, 94-98. http://dx.doi.org/10.4236/eng.2013.510B019.

face the integration challenges of evolving data. Difficulties arise in both maintaining updated the data warehouse that adopts one of such data schemas and in expanding it with other data and data types from new sources.

To overcome such difficulties, we created a Genomic and Proteomic Data Warehouse (GPDW) that adopts an original metadata-based modular global schema [6]. It supports integration of data sources that evolve in data content, structure (although limitedly) and number, as the biomedical molecular ones do. Thanks to the adopted data schema, we easily kept updated and extended progressively the numerous genomic, proteomic and phenotypic controlled annotation data of different species integrated in the GPDW. Here, we describe and discuss the original Web application that we developed to easily access and search such valuable integrated biomolecular knowledge. It leverages the GPDW metadata-based modular data schema to enable any user to visually perform queries, although complex, whose extracted data can support answering difficult biomedical questions.

GENOMIC AND PROTEOMIC DATA WAREHOUSE

Integrative Data Schema

To integrate heterogeneous data available from many different sources, abstraction and generalization of concepts to be integrated are paramount. As well, modularity and customizability of global data schema are vital to support easy integration, data schema extension with the inclusion of new data types and sources, and maintenance with respect to data, format and schema evolution of the integrated original data sources. With such aims and with the goal of creating the GPDW, as illustrated in [6], we focused on biomedical molecular entities and features described by data to be integrated, provided by distinct sources. Briefly, we abstracted and generalized such features and defined our integrated relational data schema as composed of multiple interconnected modules. Each module represents a single feature, whose data are provided by one or more of the integrated data sources, and it is composed by a number of data tables that de-pends on the integrated data. Such tables are hierarchically related as shown in the Directed Acyclic Graph (DAG) in **Figure 1**.

Feature modules can be pair wise associated; such associations represent the valuable association/annotation data provided by the integrated data sources, which are stored in hierarchically related association tables (**Figure 2**).

The feature modules and their associations contained in a specific instance/version of our generalized global data schema depend on the particular data sources and their provided data that are integrated in that specific data schema instance.

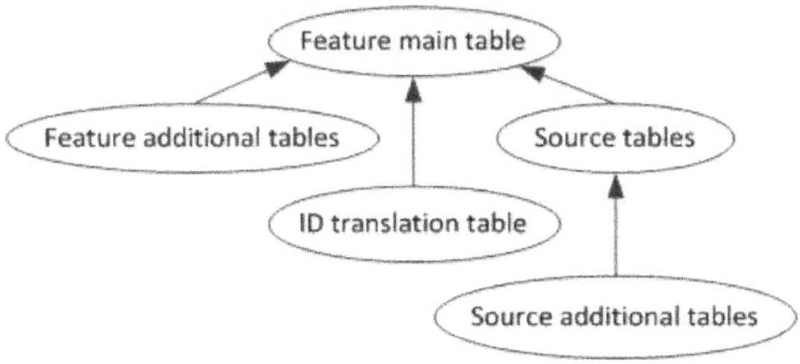

Figure 1. Directed acyclic graph of the tables in a GPDW feature module.

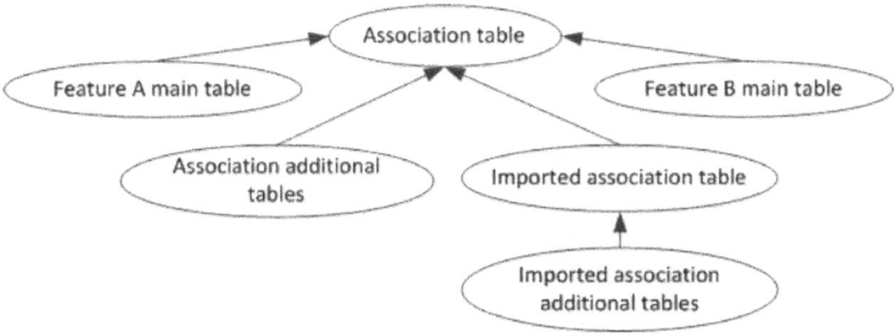

Figure 2. DAG of the association tables between two GPKB feature modules.

To support the automatic construction and updating of a database adopting such data schema, we defined a procedure to register the data sources and their feature data to be integrated, and to collect all the required metadata information about them and their associations. We store these metadata in a specific metadata schema, useful to seamlessly and transparently access all data in the database regardless the specific database version.

Data Integrated in the GPDW

The GPDW adopts our defined modular data schema to integrate data provided by several of the main bioinformatics databases, including Entrez Gene, Homologene, MINT, IntAct, Expasy Enzyme, GO, GOA, BioCyc, KEGG, Reactome, eVOC and OMIM. Currently, data in the GPDW regard several features, including DNA sequences, genes, transcripts, proteins, enzymes, protein domains, small molecules of biological interest, biological function features (*i.e.* Gene Ontology biological processes, molecular functions and cellular components), pathways, gene expression features, genetic disorders, clinical synopses and their association.

Among others, at time of writing the GPDW contains 9,537,645 genes of 9,631 organisms, 38,960,202 proteins of 338,004 species, 19,522 protein domains and 824,797 protein domains annotations, 28,889 biochemical path-ways and 171,372 pathway annotations (77,812 gene and 93,560 protein annotations), 35,252 Gene Ontology terms and 64,185,070 Gene Ontology annotations (1,272,168 gene and 62,912,902 protein annotations), 10,212 human genetic disorders and their 27,705 gene annotations. These figures demonstrate the valuable unique characteristics of the GPDW.

DYNAMIC COMPOSITION AND RESULT VISUALIZATION OF GPDW DATA EXTRACTION SQL QUERIES

To enable any user to easily compose queries, although complex, on all data integrated in the GPDW, we developed a Web application in Java programming language using Servlets and Java Server Pages (JSP) technology. It is publicly available at http://www.bioinformatics.dei.polimi.it/GPKB/. Through a visual interface (**Figure 3**), the user is only required to select, out of the features integrated in the GPDW, the ones and their attributes to be included in the query, together with the conditions on the data values to be retrieved. All information about the GPDW content required to build the visual interface is taken from the GPDW metadata. Thus, transparently to the user, the visualized features and their attributes automatically adapt to the content of the specific GPDW instance.

Interactive menus, present in the visual interface for each feature attribute, enable the user to define filtering conditions on the data values to be retrieved. The content of each of these menus depends on the data contained in the particular attribute to which the menu refers. Furthermore, the user can also select some general options (Search Options) for the query, e.g. make a "distinct" SQL query, set the conjunctive logical clause to use for the defined filtering conditions (AND/OR), select the result counting mode and define how many results per page to show.

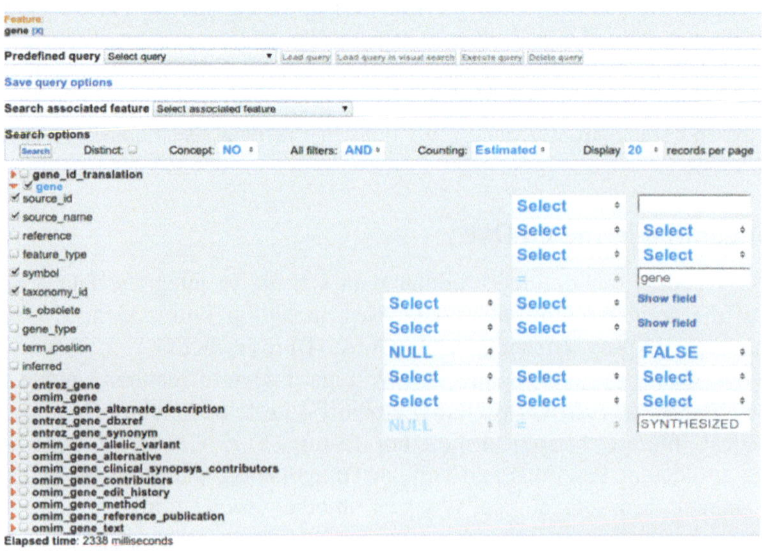

Figure 3. User interface for visual composition of a query on a single feature.

Query Composition Algorithm

We designed a specific algorithm to automatically com-pose a SQL query that can efficiently extract data from any instance of the GPDW, according to any combination of user selected feature attributes and filters. The core of the query composition algorithm leverages the metadata and modular structure of the GPDW. It is di-vided in two steps: 1) generation of a complete and ordered list of tables to be included in the query and 2) generation of the query FROM, JOIN and WHERE clauses.

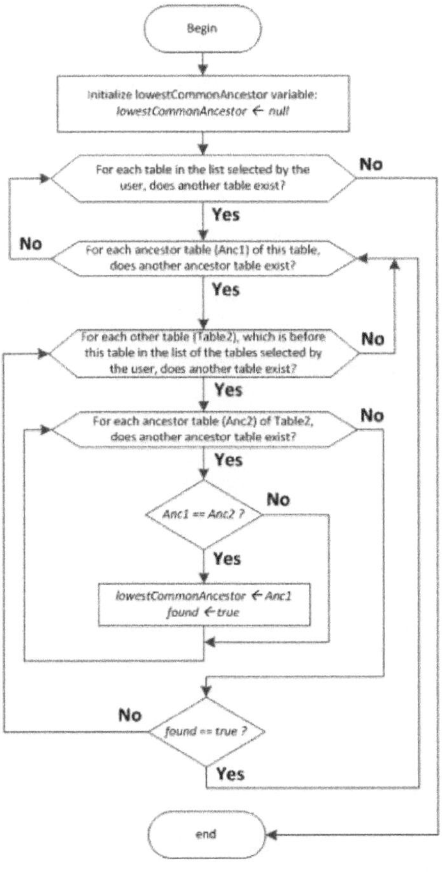

Figure 4. Flowchart of the lowest common ancestor search over the list of all ancestor tables of each GPDW table containing user selected attributes.

The first step starts with the identification of the lowest common ancestor (LCA) between all the tables that contain the attributes selected by the user to be included in the query. This is performed as shown in **Figure 4**, ac-cording to the DAG structure in **Figures 1** and **2**. Through a recursive function, all the ancestors of each table are calculated and the LCA table between all of them is found. It completes the list of all tables involved in the query, which also includes the tables that contain the attributes selected by the user. Then, the tables in the list are ordered based on the feature module, or feature association they belong to and the order in which the user selected the features to query. If the user selected first the feature A and then the feature B, the feature A tables will be at the top of the list, then the association tables be- tween feature A and feature B, and finally the feature B tables. In the list, the order of tables belonging to each feature module or association is then defined from top to bottom by the order of tables in the DAG of the feature module (**Figure 1**) or of the association (**Figure 2**).

In the second step, the query join generation is per-formed as follows. The first table of the list is the table inserted into the FROM clause of the query and set as reference table for the joins with the following tables in the list. Then, the ordered table list is scanned from top to bottom and each table in the list is evaluated. During this scan, when a feature or association table is found, it be-comes the reference table for the joins with the following tables in the list. If it is a feature table, no join is added into the query. If it is an association table, the two joins between this association table and each of the two feature tables (if present in the list) that it associates are added into the query. If the table is neither a feature nor an association table, the join between this table and the last reference table found is added into the query. Finally, all filters defined by the user are added to the WHERE clause of the query.

Query Result Visualization

The data extracted by the composed query are processed to be neatly visualized to the user. Furthermore, ID data are enriched with hyperlinks to external resources with more detailed information over the entity identified by the ID. Each of these hyperlinks is composed of the ID itself and a base URL stored in the GPDW metadata.

Counting of the extracted data is also provided. Since the counting query is generally much slower than the main data extraction query, initially an approximate count is shown to the user. It is obtained by the SQL EXPLAIN command, quickly executed over the main query, while the real counting query is executed in back-ground. When this query ends, in the user interface the approximate count is refreshed with the exact one.

SYSTEM PERFORMANCE

Performance of the created Web application was tested while running on a TomCat 6.0 Web Server installed on a computer with two Intel XEON CPU E5320 1.86 GHz, 32 GB RAM, and connected to the described GPDW instance implemented in a PostgreSQL DBMS. Generation of the visual user interface for query composition, execution of the composed queries and query result visualization processing were evaluated.

Visual User Interface for Query Composition

The loading times of the visual interface for query com-position on a single feature are shown in **Table 1**. The "Servlet Execution Times" are those of a servlet created to retrieve from the GPDW metadata schema all the table names of the feature selected by the user and to create a Web page where showing them. The "JavaScript Execution

Times" refer to the tasks performed by some created AJAX calls to the server or client-side JavaScript routines. This JavaScript processing shows the table field names in the user interface and populates their interactive menus for the definition of the query filtering conditions. In the default visualization, only the fields of the feature main table (and association table(s) in case of a search on more features) are immediately shown. The other table fields can be interactively opened by the user. This penalizes slightly the total loading time of the query composition Web page for a single feature with few tables. Yet, it makes the total loading time of the query composition Web page much lower in the case of more features, which involves many tables. The total loading times are always lower than 1 second, which represents an immediate response to the user according to [7], and show a very good performance.

Table 1. Loading times of the visual user interface for single feature query composition

Feature	Servlet Execution Time (ms)	JavaScript Generation Time (ms)	Total Time (ms)
Biological Function Feature	517	416	933
Clinical Synopsis	155	423	578
DNA Sequence	65	324	389
Enzyme	134	351	485
Gene	334	400	734
Gene Expression Feature	405	352	757
Genetic Disorder	226	491	717
Pathway	114	558	672
Protein	97	324	421
Protein Family & Domain	60	589	649
Small Molecule	69	294	363
Transcript	58	329	387
Mean	186.17	404.25	590.42
Standard Deviation	153.74	96.23	182.52

Query Execution Performance

Execution performance of the composed queries was tested on a single, two and multiple features. All queries got a low execution time, also in the cases where several tables were involved and millions of tuples were found. For example, a query over the "gene" and "biological function feature" associated features, which involved 3 tables, found 10,647,473 tuples in an execution time of 753 ms. Besides to the good GPDW data structure and indexing, this performance is also due to the created query composition algorithm, which generates queries with an optimized number of joins. By taking advantage of the modular structure of the GPDW, in the generated query the algorithm tends not to include all the tables and joins which would be required by following the foreign key path among the tables that contain all user selected feature attributes. Instead, it only includes the minimum number of tables and joins needed to return the same results. In so doing, the algorithm generates efficient and neat queries.

Result Processing and Visualization

Processing times to visualize enriched the results re-turned by a query on the "transcript" feature, which selects all, or only the default, feature attributes, are re-ported in **Table 2**. As expected, the processing time is proportional to the number of attributes requested and result rows visualized. For all attributes, until 300 rows, the processing time stays under 10 seconds, which is an acceptable loading time according to [7] if a feedback to the user is shown (as it is). For more rows the time is greater, but still under a minute. In any case, the benefit of an enriched visualization of result data is much more worthy than the time the user has to wait to see the results.

USABILITY TESTING

Usability of the created Web application was tested by 9 users with 3 different profiles: 4 computer scientists who knew the GPDW, 4 computer scientists who did not know before the GPDW and 1 biologist. All users were observed while doing some significant tasks over the Web application and were interviewed about their user experience. In the evaluation, for each task, the metrics used were the success rate, the time, the number of un-do/errors and the time perceived by each user. All users completed all tasks, some with assistance (success rate 80%). This is a strong indication that the Web application does not present any critical issue. The number of undo/errors was very low (in few tasks the users did more than 1 undo/error). The perceived time, evaluated from 1 to 5, got a mean of 3, demonstrating the intuitiveness of the interface despite of the complexity of some tasks. Overall, all users showed satisfaction for their user experience. Observing them to perform the tasks pointed out some little usability issues, mainly about navigation of query composition Web pages and results visualization that will be tackled in future work.

Table 2. Visualization processing time of data extracted with a query on the "transcript" feature

Visualized Rows	All Attribute Visualization Time (ms)	All Default Attribute[a] Visualization Time (ms)
20	855	356
30	1101	506
50	1682	841
100	3504	1585
300	9731	4386
500	16,473	7263
1000	32,179	14,002

[a]Default attributes for Transcript feature are source_id, source_name, symbol and taxonomy_id.

REFERENCES

1. M. Y. Galperin and X. M. Fernández-Suárez, "The 2012 Nucleic Acids Research Database Issue and the Online Molecular Biology Database Collection," *Nucleic Acids Research*, Vol. 40, Database Issue, 2012, pp. D1-D8. http://dx.doi.

org/10.1093/nar/gkr1196

2. N. W. Paton, S. A. Khan, A. Hayes, F. Moussouni, A. Brass, K. Eilbeck, C. A. Goble, S. J. Hubbard and S. G. Oliver, "Conceptual Modeling of Genomic Information," *Bioinformatics*, Vol. 16, No. 6, 2000, pp. 548-557. http://dx.doi.org/10.1093/bioinformatics/16.6.548
3. E. Bornberg-Bauer and N. W. Paton, "Conceptual Data Modelling for Bioinformatics," *Briefings in Bioinformat-ics*, Vol. 3, No. 2, 2002, pp. 166-180. http://dx.doi.org/10.1093/bib/3.2.166
4. M. Masseroli, D. Martucci and F. Pinciroli, "GFINDer: Genome Function INtegrated Discoverer through Dyna-mic Annotation, Statistical Analysis, and Mining," *Nu-cleic Acids Research*, Vol. 32, 2004, pp. W293-W300. http://dx.doi.org/10.1093/nar/gkh432
5. M. Masseroli, O. Galati and F. Pinciroli, "GFINDer: Ge-netic Disease and Phenotype Location Statistical Analysis and Mining of Dynamically Annotated Gene Lists," *Nu-cleic Acids Research*, Vol. 33, 2005, pp. W717-W723. http://dx.doi.org/10.1093/nar/gki454
6. Canakoglu, G. Ghisalberti and M. Masseroli "Integra-tion of Biomolecular Interaction Data in a Genomic and Proteomic Data Warehouse to Support Biomedical Know-ledge Discovery," In: E. Biganzoli, A. Vellido, F. Am-brogi and R. Tagliaferri, Eds., *Computational Intelligence Methods for Bioinformatics and Biostatistics*, Springer, Heidelberg, 2012, pp. 112-126. http://dx.doi.org/10.1007/978-3-642-35686-5_10
7. J. Nielsen, "Usability Engineering," Morgan Kaufmann, San Francisco, 1993.

13
CHAPTER

TRUNCATULIX – A DATA WAREHOUSE FOR THE LEGUME COMMUNITY

Kolja Henckel, Kai J Runte, Thomas Bekel, Michael Dondrup, Tobias Jakobi, Helge Küster and Alexander Goesmann

BACKGROUND

Medicago truncatula is a model plant for studying legume biology. Legumes are mainly characterized by their ability to interact with beneficial microbial organisms, leading to the formation of nitrogen-fixing root nodules and to phosphate-acquiring arbuscular mycorriza. Various international research projects are investigating these different symbioses of *Medicago truncatula*. The arbuscular mycorrhiza (AM) interaction between the host root and the fungal partner is an interesting field of research because more than 80% of land plants depend on an efficient AM for the uptake of nutrients, primarily phosphate. Apart from AM, *Medicago truncatula* is capable of entering a nitrogen-fixing symbiosis with the soil bacterium *Sinorhizobium meliloti*. The capacity for symbiotic nitrogen fixation allows legumes such as *Medicago truncatula* to grow on nitrogen-depleted soils and to develop protein-rich seeds, which are properties exploited in sustainable agriculture [1,2, 3, 4, 5].

In recent years, more and more databases for the storage of microarray expression data (Arrayexpress [6], PEPR [7], The Stanford MicroArray Database [8], PlexDB [9]), and data from different sequencing projects (EST sequencing (dbEST [10]), BAC sequencing (GenMapDB [11]), ultrafast sequencing (Short Read Archive [12])), have been developed to store the exponentially growing amount of data. However, scientists have to search for the specific information in each and every database separately.

Directly adressing this issue, data warehouses, specially designed databases, offer an approach to store different aspects of a certain data object in an optimized data schema. This provides fast data access and enables return of query results in minimal time [13, 14].

Citation: Kolja Henckel, Kai J Runte, Thomas Bekel, Michael Dondrup, Tobias Jakobi, Helge Küster and Alexander Goesmann, "TRUNCATULIX – a Data Warehouse for the Legume community," DOI: 10.1186/1471-2229-9-19.

To overcome the problem of distributed data sources in the field of *Medicago truncatula* research, we created TRUNCATULIX, a data warehouse storing sequence data, annotations, and expression experiments of the model legume *Medicago truncatula*.

CONSTRUCTION AND CONTENT

The construction of the TRUNCATULIX data warehouse is divided in three main parts: 1) the database schema, 2) the data integration, 3) and the source data. The following sections outline these three aspects in detail.

Database Schema

The intention of the TRUNCATULIX data warehouse is to store information on gene sequences, functional annotations, and expression data. Thus, we created a relational data schema (see Figure 1), containing all these aspects. The different tables that store the information are linked via unique keys.

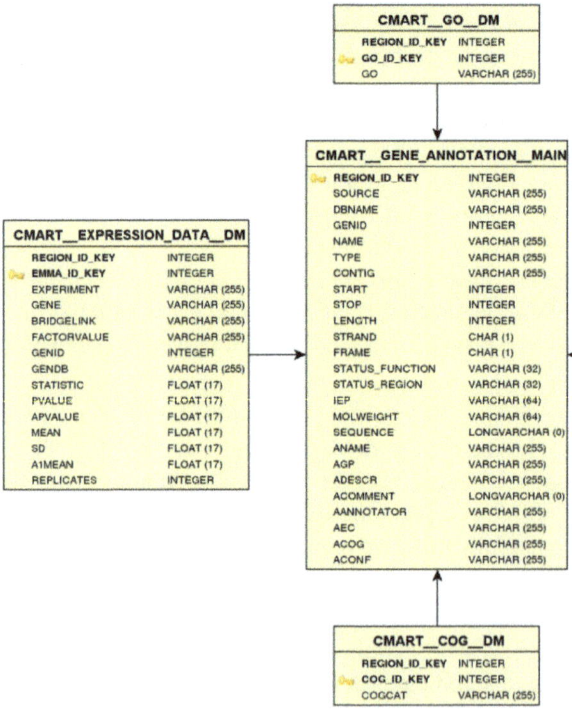

Figure 1: The TRUNCATULIX database schema. The TRUNCATULIX database schema. The main table stores the sequence data. All other information is stored in different tables refering to the main table.

The TRUNCATULIX data warehouse is based on the IGetDB data warehouse engine [15] using Java [16]. It uses MySQL [17] as the database management system and is based on the Biomart API [18], while providing additional functionality such as full-text searches and direct access to SQL-functions (e.g. SUM, AVG, ROUND). The primary gene information such as sequence data, start codon, stop codon, length of the encoded open reading frame, name, or gene_id are stored in the main table, whereas data such as gene expression values from different experiments, GO numbers, or KOG categories are stored in extra tables refering to the main table.

Data Integration

High throughput technologies yield vast amounts of data. However, in order to investigate, for example, regulatory pathways, further standard genetics approaches are yet most effective. High throughput data provide an excellent means to reduce the number of possible mutation targets. Such data is found, in general, in different sources and the screening of (most likely) thousands of candidates is, when performed manually, a rather tedious task. On the other hand, if the data was integrated and preprocessed for querying, such a task can be performed in a matter of minutes. As has been shown recently, such data integration strategies saves both time and money [19].

For the integration and import of data we use the extract, transform and load (ETL) approach commonly used in data warehousing [20]. Sequence and annotation data are extracted from SAMS (cf. next section), and are subsequently transformed and loaded into the TRUNCATULIX database. Expression data is exported from EMMA (cf. Section “Expression data”) via an export script that can be initiated by a human curator within the EMMA web interface. During the transformation step, the expression data are linked to the sequence data. This enables the user of TRUNCATULIX to conveniently search across annotation and expression data.

Data Sources

Sequence Data

- *Medicago truncatula* Gene Index 8.0

The Institute for Genomic Research (TIGR – J. Craig Venter Institute since October 2006) clustered and assembled 226,923 high-quality ESTs from over 60 different *Medicago truncatula* EST-libraries sequenced in laboratories all over the world. Using the clustering software *tgicl* [21], the *Medicago truncatula* Gene Index (MtGI, hosted at the Dana-Farber Cancer Institute – DFCI), was built. The MtGI 8.0 contains 18,612 Tentative Consensus sequences (TCs) and 18,238 singletons (Jan. 2005) [22]. The sequences were imported into the Sequence Analysis and Management System (SAMS) [23], an annotation software created at the Center for Biotechnology (CeBiTec) in Bielefeld. The SAMS system contains an automatic annotation pipeline (Metanor), which runs several bioinformatics tools for gene annotation (Blast, Interpro, TMHMM) [24, 25, 26]. A high quality consensus annotation is created, covering EC numbers [27], KEGG functions [27], GO numbers [28], KOG numbers [29], putative gene functions, and gene names.

- *Medicago truncatula* Gene Index 9.0

Recently, the J. Craig Venter Institute released a new version of the *Medicago truncatula* Gene Index, now covering over 70 EST-libraries. The assembly of the 259,642 ESTs led to 29,273 TCs, while 26,696 ESTs remained as singletons. In addition to the previous Gene Index 8.0, TIGR used 25,600 mature transcripts (ETs) from the qcGene Database [30] for the EST assembly, whereof 11,494 ETs remained as singletons. The new sequences were downloaded from the DFCI websites and imported into SAMS, where a complete automatic annotation was performed.

- *Medicago* genome project

The *Medicago* Genome Sequence Consortium (MGSC) sequenced the *Medicago truncatula* genome using a classical BAC sequencing approach [31, 32]. Starting in 2005, they released a assembly of the sequences in October 2007 (release 2.0). This release contains 38,759 coding sequences (CDS) and the same number of translated protein sequences. The CDS›s were downloaded from the project website and afterwards imported into SAMS. Using SAMS, a complete automatic annotation was performed.

- Affymetrix *Medicago* GeneChip® probes

Affymetrix [33] offers a GeneChip® microarray holding probes primarily for genes of *Medicago truncatula*, but also for the related legume *Medicago sativa* and their symbiontic *Sinorhizobium meliloti*. The sequences used by Affymetrix to construct the *Medicago* Genome GeneChip® were downloaded from the Affymetrix website and imported into SAMS. That way, 61,103 sequences containing the Affymetrix annotations were integrated into SAMS and were automatically re-annotated using the Metanor pipeline.

- *Medicago truncatula* 454 sequencing project

In 2006, Cheung *et al.* used the pyrosequencing approach to generate 292,465 cDNA reads of *Medicago truncatula* using a GS20 sequencer [34]. The reads were assembled forming 3,619 sequences. These sequences were downloaded from the project website and imported into SAMS. Using SAMS, a complete automatic annotation was performed.

Using Blast homology search, the sequences of all five projects were compared against the sequences of the other projects (one-by-one). This way, the sequences corresponding to each other in the different datasets could be found (using an e-value cutoff of e^{-5}). The complete sequence and annotation data from all five projects was integrated into the TRUNCATULIX data warehouse. Table 1 presents the number of sequences imported into TRUNCATULIX from the five projects, giving additional information about the automatic annotation.

Table 1: Sequence data integrated into TRUNCATULIX

Project	Sequences	EC numbers	KOG numbers	GO numbers
MtGI 8.0 TCs & Singletons	36,878	6,174 (16.74%)	12,746 (34.56%)	10,268 (27.84%)
MtGI 9.0 TCs & Singletons	67,463	11,253 (16.68%)	20,570 (30.49%)	19,008 (28.18%)
Mt Genome 2.0	38,759	5,938 (15.32%)	3,434 (8.85%)	10,444 (26.95%)
Affymetrix Medicago				
GeneChip® probes	61,103	12,044 (19.71%)	18,731 (30.65%)	19,775 (32.36%)
Medicago 454 sequencing project	3,619	911 (25.17%)	1,798 (49.68%)	519 (14.34%)
Total	**207,822**	**36,320 (17.48%)**	**57,278 (27.56%)**	**60,014 (28.88%)**

The table shows the number of sequences integrated in TRUNCATULIX via the SAMS software. The annotation information was calculated using various bioinformatic tools.

Expression Data

- Oligo-microarray expression data

In recent years, almost 1,000 oligo-microarrays studying *Medicago truncatula* gene expression in different conditions were hybridized in the framework of various international projects [35]. These microarrays used two chip layouts designated Mt16kOLI1 [5] and Mt16kOLI1Plus [36] (Arrayexpress ID: A-MEXP-85/A-MEXP-138). These arrays are associated to more than 50 different expression profiling experiments that were analyzed via the EMMA [37, 38] software. EMMA is a tool that analyses microarray expression data and stores it in a MIAME compliant way [39]. It is also MAGE compliant [40] and the analysis pipelines used are well documented and evaluated. EMMA supports various image analyses software, such as ImaGene [41] and GenePix [42]. Within EMMA it is possible to group different mircoarrays into experiments. The user can decide to filter the differentially expressed genes using different significance tests. Some of the results of these analyses can be found in [1, 2, 3, 35]. Table 2 lists the currently available *Medicago truncatula* oligo-microarray experiments, as well as the number of microarrays and the number of transformed datasets integrated into TRUNCATULIX via EMMA. Some of the integrated data is already published in [43, 44, 45], some more is unpublished data by H. Küster(*), M. Hahn, N. Hohnjec, H. Küster(**), D. Hinse, A. Becker, H. Küster(***), C. Hogekamp, H. Küster(****) and F. Frugier(*****). More microarray experiments will be integrated as soon as the researchers in charge have approved their integration into the data warehouse.

Table 2: Microarray expression data imported from EMMA into TRUNCATULIX

Experiment	**Number of micro-arrays**	**Number of transformed datasets**
Nitrogen-fixing root nodules in *Medicago truncatula**	4	10
Nod-Factor response in *Medicago truncatula* roots [43]	9	13
Root endosymbiosis in *Medicago truncatula* [5]	10	23
Uromyces pathogenesis in *Medicago truncatula***	3	4
AHL treatment of *Medicago truncatula roots****	11	17
LMW EPS I treatment of *Medicago truncatula* roots I****	6	8
LMW EPS I treatment of *Medicago truncatula* roots II****	6	8
LMW EPS I treatment of *Medicago truncatula* roots III****	24	32
Nod-factor treatment of *Medicago truncatula* roots I****	6	8
Nod-factor treatment of *Medicago truncatula* roots II****	18	24
Seed development in *Medicago truncatula* [44]	22	51
Early Salt Stress in *Medicago truncatula* [45]	4	5
Cold stress in *Medicago truncatula******	8	11
Medicago truncatula wild type roots vs. TN1_11 mutant roots after 1 h of salt stress*****	16	20
Response to phosphate in *Medicago truncatula* roots [5]	3	4
Total	**150**	**248**

The table shows the amount of microarray expression data integrated into TRUNCATULIX via EMMA. Currently there are 15 different experiments with a total of 150 microarrays (248 transformed datasets) integrated. Some of the integrated data is unpublised: H. Küster(*), M. Hahn, N. Hohnjec, H. Küster(**), D. Hinse, A. Becker, H. Küster(***), C. Hogekamp, H. Küster(****) and F. Frugier(*****). Abbreviations: AHL: acetylhomoserine lactone, LMW: low molecular weight, EPS: exopolysaccharide, Nod-factor: Nodulation factor.

- GeneChips® expression data

In 2008, Benedito *et al.* hybridized more than 50 Affymetrix *Medicago truncatula* GeneChip arays® [46], addressing three major topics: mature organs covering the whole plant, nodule development, and seed development. For each of these topics, four to eight experiments were perfomed in three replicates each (see Table 3). The expression data of the GeneChip arrays was downloaded and directly migrated into the TRUNCATULIX data warehouse.

Table 3: GeneChip data integrated into TRUNCATULIX

Experiment	Number of GeneChip arrays
Mature organs series	**24**
Leaf: 4-week old trifolia were harvest without their petioles (but with their petiolule) [46]	3
Petiole: Petioles from 4-week old plant [46]	3
Stem: Stems of 4-week old plants (without vegetative buds) [46]	3
Vegetative Bud: Vegetative buds of 4-week old plants [46]	3
Root: 4-week old non-inoculated roots [46]	3
Nodule: Nodules from 4-week old plants [46]	3
Flower: Fully open flowers were harvest at the day of anthesis [46]	3
Pod: Mix of small, medium and physiologically mature pods [46]	3
Nodulation development series	**12**
Root-0d: Roots at 0 dpi (control for nodule developmental series) [46]	3
Nod4d: Nodules at 4 dpi (root lumps with residual roots) [46]	3

Nod10d: Developing nodules at 10 dpi [46]	3
Nod14d: Mature nodules at 14 dpi [46]	3
Seed development series	**18**
Seed10d: Developing seeds at early embryogenesis – 10 dap [46]	3
Seed12d: Developing seeds at 12 dap (transition between embryogenesis and seed filling) [46]	3
Seed16d: Developing seeds at 16 dap (accumulation of storage proteins) [46]	3
Seed20d: Developing seeds at 20 dap (seed filling) [46]	3
Seed24d: Developing seeds at 24 dap (maturation phase) [46]	3
Seed36d: Developing seeds at 36 dap (physiologically mature seeds, desiccation) [46]	3
Total	**54**

The table shows the experiments and number of GeneChip arrays® directly imported into TRUNCATULIX. The three experiments address major topics: Mature organs covering the whole plant, nodulation development, and seed development.

The integrated data (sequence and expression data) is curated before it is imported into TRUNCATULIX. No user is allowed to import any datasets, this is reserved to the curators, but can be done upon request. In case of an update of one of the source databases the integrated data are updated by the curators.

UTILITY AND DISCUSSION

TRUNCATULIX is a relational, integrated database of sequence data, annotation information and microarray expression data, which is specially created to store data of the model legume *Medicago truncatula*.

Web Interface

The interface for the TRUNCATULIX data warehouse can be accessed via a web browser. It provides a user-friendly interface built with Echo2 [47].

Case Study

Consider a query for genes concerning GRAS transcription factors, suggesting that these genes are activated during nodulation [48, 49]. As an example, we search for genes annotated as GRAS transcription factors in microarray experiments covering nodulation with three or more replicates.

To calculate this query, a user first specifies the standard search dialog on the left (see Figure 2). The user is guided through the different filter steps with an indicator bar on the top of the web pages. Help texts give examples and describe the options given by the different filters. Because some filters are more commonly used than others, the most commonly selected filters are highlighted in red.

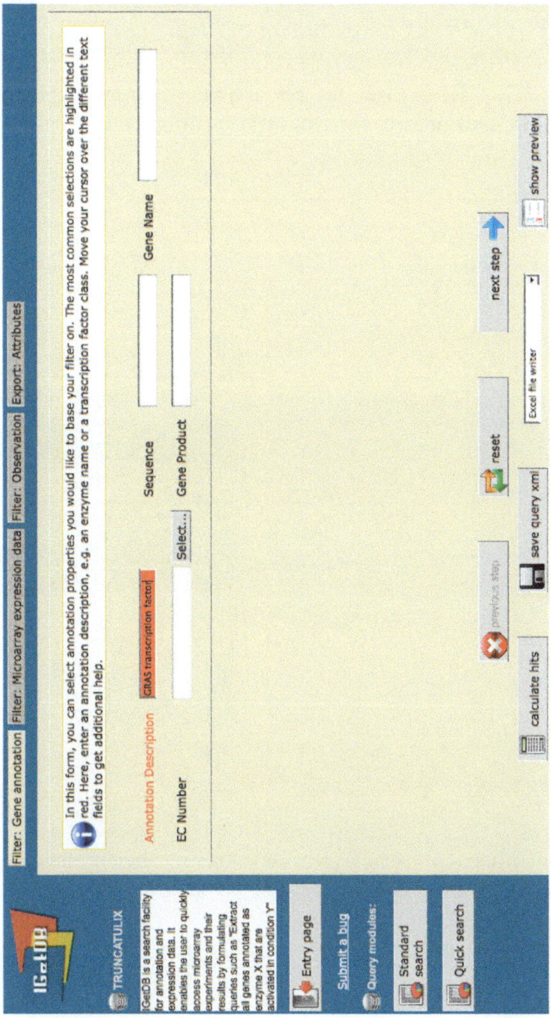

Figure 2: The first filterstep – gene annotation. The screenshot shows the filter page for the gene annotation data. The annotation descriptions can be queried, as well as the gene names, sequences and EC numbers.

For our example, the Annotation Description field is set to “GRAS transcription factor”, due to our interest in GRAS genes. This way only genes that are annotated as GRAS transcription factor genes remain for the next filterstep.

The next page directly informs the user that only 222 entries passed the first filterstep and asks for a filtering concerning microarray expression data. The user now selects all nodulation related experiments ("Nitrogen-fixing root nodules in *Medicago truncatula*", "Nod-factor response in *Medicago truncatula* roots", "Root endosymbiosis in *Medicago truncatula*", "AHL treatment of *Medicago truncatula* roots", "LMW EPS I treatment of *Medicago truncatula* roots I", "LMW EPS I treatment of *Medicago truncatula roots* II", "LMW EPS I treatment of *Medicago truncatula* roots III", "Nod-factor treatment of *Medicago truncatula* roots I", "Nod-factor treatment of *Medicago truncatula* roots II", "Response to phosphate in *Medicago truncatula* roots", "Nodulation development series, Mt oligo-dT primed») as Experiments and sets the No. of Replicates (>) to «2» (Figure 3).

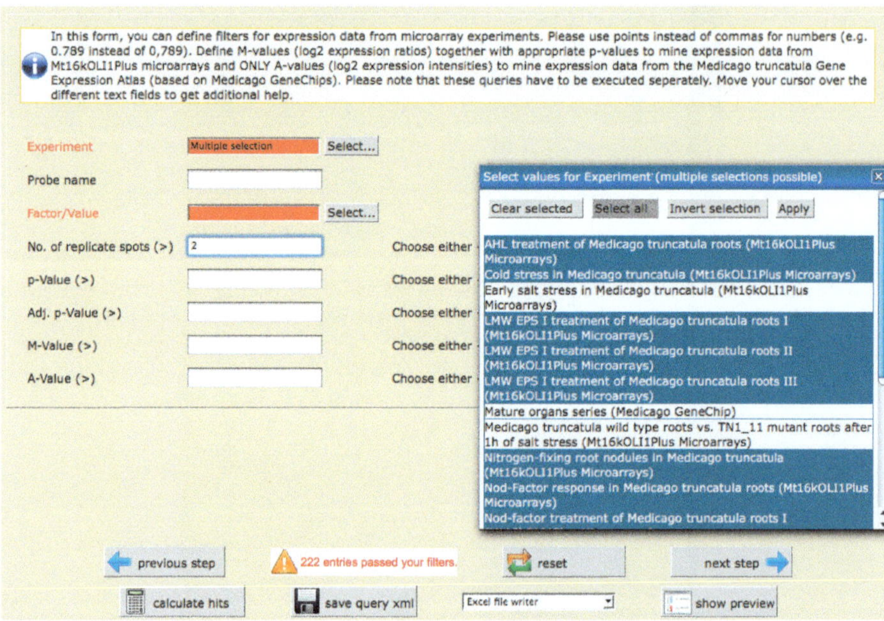

Figure 3: The second filterstep – gene expression. This screenshot shows the filter page for the expression data. The different integrated experiments can be selected, as well as different expression values and the number of replicates.

In the next step, the user can specify results for the different functional annotation tools, as well as for KOG Categories and Gene Ontology numbers. They remain unused in our example, but more complex queries could use these to filter for specific KOG categories or GO numbers.

The last page shows the possible export options that can be selected for the remaining 35 entries. The previously selected filter criteria are preselected for the export.

In this case, the export covers Database, Gene Name, Region Type, EC Number, and Annotation Description for the gene annotation; the Experiment name, Factor/Value, Probe name, p-Value, Adj. p-Value, M-Value, and no. of Replicates for the gene expression data from EMMA; the GO Number and the KOG Category, as well as the annotation Observations made by different Tools (Figure 4). Hitting the "calculate hits" button shows the number of datasets to be exported. This number may differ from the number of hits calculated previously based on sequence information because the new value is based on both sequence and expression information. To sneak a peek at the data, the user can use the preview option and browse through the first 100 results, or export the data as Excel, HTML, or csv file. A quick search – a more simple search interface found on the left side of the navigation panel – offers options to search for gene names, gene annotations, gene products, and repoter names using a google-like search interface (Figure 5).

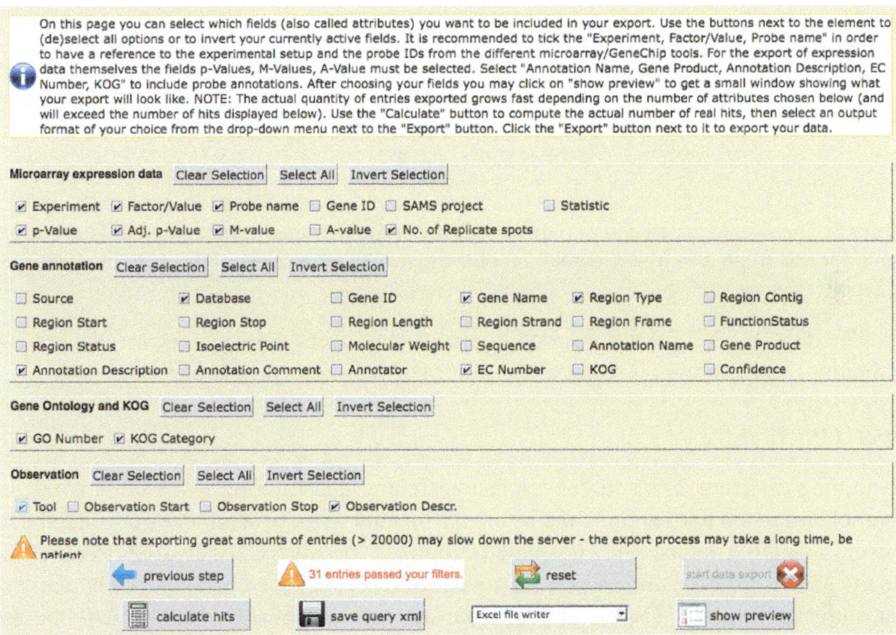

Figure 4: Export options of TRUNCATULIX. The screenshot shows the last page of the query dialog. The user can select which data and details should be exported, receiving an Excel, HTML, or csv file as result.

After sumbitting the query, the details of the export can be selected as shown before using the complete query dialog (see Figure 4).

With the TRUNCATULIX data warehouse, it is now possible to have a look at the specific gene expressions for the different experiments and to find possibly interesting candidates for further experiments. Our example covers GRAS transcription factors. Some of them having already been reported to be key components of symbiotic signal transduction during nodulation [48, 50, 51].

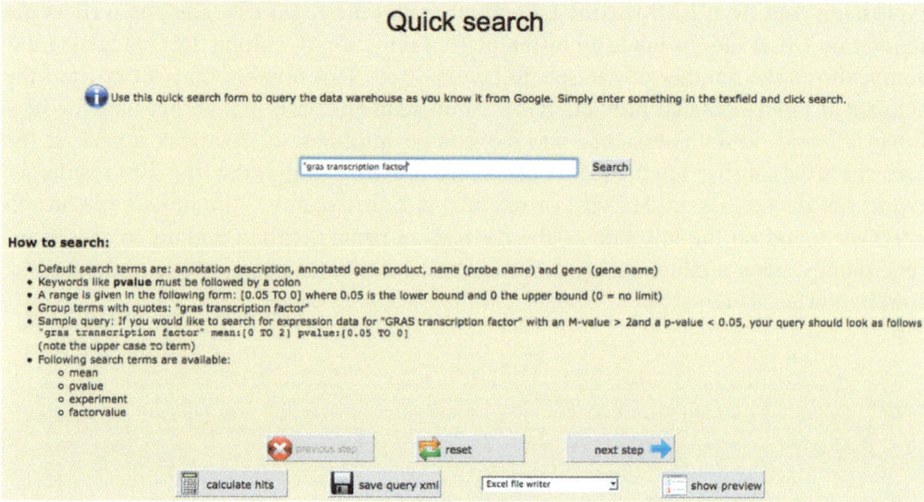

Figure 5: The simple search dialog. The screenshot shows the simple search dialog. The user can search for text fragments in the annotation of the genes, the gene names, the gene products, and the reporter names.

The TRUNCATULIX data warehouse allows users easy access to sequencing, annotation, and expression research done at many laboratories worldwide.

DISCUSSION

Combining different data sources for fast searching and filtering is a widely used and common approach to overcome the immense manual work of searching for related data in every available database [52]. Related examples for this technique are **GeWare** [13] and the *Medicago truncatula* **Gene Expression Atlas** [46]. GeWare is a data warehouse that stores Affymetrix GeneChip® microarray data combined with manually added annotations and data from public databases like GO, Ensembl, LocusLink and NetAffx [28, 53, 54, 55]. The GeWare data warehouse focuses on the processing and analysis of microarrays, mostly containing clinical data. Various filter and export options are implemented.

The *Medicago truncatula* Gene Expression Atlas stores previously processed and analyzed gene expression and annotation data from Affymetrix GeneChip® experiments. The data published is also available on ArrayExpress. The annotation data from Affymetrix is integrated into the data warehouse, but it can only be used for queries, it cannot be exported or viewed. In the same way, the GO numbers, KEGG functions, and the annotations of the genes can be queries. A homology search using Blast offers the opportunity to find genes according to their similarity to the Affymetrix GeneChip® reporter or consensus sequences. The results of a query can be downloaded, but only the names of the reporters and the expression values are listed, the annotations are not shown and cannot be extracted.

In contrast to the other data warehouses, TRUNCATLIX not only stores the sequence and annotation data of the Affymetrix GeneChip arrays, but also sequence data from other genetic projects and institutes. The annotations that are provided are calculated using a well evaluated pipeline, offering KEGG, KOG, and GO numbers, if found in the annotations of homologues. TRUNCATULIX offers the option to export the results of a query, but in contrast to the the export of the *Medicago truncatula* Gene Expresison Atlas, not only the gene names and the expression values are exported, but (on request) also any other information that is integrated into the data warehouse. Table 4 compares the main features of the three data warehouses. The immense amount of intergrated sequence, annotation, and expression information makes the TRUNCATULIX data warehouse a very convenient resource in the field of *Medicago truncatula* research. TRUNCATULIX is freely available to the research community and additional expression data can be integrated upon request.

Table 4: A comparison of TRUNCATULIX to other data warehouses

Data Warehouse feature	**GeWare**	***Medicago truncatula* Gene Expression Atlas**	**TRUNCATULIX**
Target organism	*homo sapiens*	*Medicago truncatula*	*Medicago truncatula*
static/dynamic data	dynamic	Static	static
number of microarray experiments	unknown	18	18
number of microarrays mircoarrays	unknown	54	204
automatic annotation information	yes	searchable, but not visible	yes
KEGG-mapping	no	yes	yes
GO-numbers	no	yes	yes
search	yes	yes	yes
blast homology search	no	yes	no, planned
export options	yes	yes	yes
free use	yes	yes	yes
free access	no	yes	yes

The table shows a comparison of the three data warhouses GeWare, the *Medicago truncatula* Gene Expression Atlas, and TRUNCATULIX.

FUTURE DEVELOPMENT

As more *Medicago trunculata* data becomes available from oligo-microarray and Affymetrix GeneChip®experiments, it will be integrated into TRUNCATULIX. Additionally, a homology search using Blast will be implemetend.

CONCLUSION

We created TRUNCATULIX, a data warehouse that combines data from microarray experiments with sequence data and high quality annotations in the area of *Medicago truncatula*. TRUNCATULIX is the first data warehouse in the field or *Medicago truncatula* research that offers the opportunity to search in all publicly available *Medicago truncatula* sequence data and expression data for different criteria and as a result to get a complete list of sequences, expression data, and annotations. Thus, a researcher can save much time and work finding interesting genes and results of previously conducted expression experiments. As the application uses an AJAX-based web interface, it can be used via a web browser and is platform independent. The results can be exported as Excel, HTML, or as csv files.

ACKNOWLEDGEMENTS

KH thanks the International NRW Graduate School in Bioinformatics and Genome Research for funding the project. We thank Florian Frugier (ISV, Gif-sur-Yvette) for making available data prior to publication.

AUTHORS' CONTRIBUTIONS

KH initialized the project, computed the annotations for the sequence data and is the main author of the manuscript. KR was responsible for the data schema, the data warehouse backend, and supervised the design of the web interface. TB helped on annotating the sequence data using SAMS. MD contributed in extracting of the microarray data from EMMA. TJ designed the web interface. HK analyzed some of the microarray data and supervised the export. AG supervised the integration of the different data sources. All authors revised and approved the final manuscript.

REFERENCES

1. Baier M, Barsch A, Küster H, N H: Antisense repression of the Medicago truncatula nodule-enhanced sucrose synthase leads to a handicapped nitrogen fixation mirrored by specific alterations in the symbiotic transcriptome and metabolome. Plant Physiol. 2007, 145 (4): 1600-1618.
2. Gallardo K, Firnhaber C, Zuber H, Héricher D, Belghazi H, Henry C, Küster H, R T: A combined proteome and transcriptome analysis of developing Medicago truncatula seeds: Evidence for metabolic specialization of maternal and filial tissues. Mol Cell Proteomics. 2007, 6 (12): 2165-2179.
3. Hohnjec N, Henckel K, Bekel T, Gouzy J, Dondrup M, Goesmann A, Küster H: Transcriptional snapshots provide insights into the molecular basis of arbuscular mycorrhiza in the model legume Medicago truncatula. Functional Plant Biology. 2006, 33 (8): 737-748.
4. Barsch A, Tellström V, Patschkowski T, Küster H, K N: Metabolite profiles of nodulated alfalfa plants indicate that distinct stages of nodule organogenesis are accompanied by global physiological adaptations. Mol Plant-Microbe Interact.

2006, 19 (9): 998-1013.

5. Hohnjec N, Vieweg M, Pühler A, Becker A, Küster H: Overlaps in the transcriptional profiles of Medicago truncatula roots inoculated with two different Glomus fungi provide insights into the genetic program activated during arbuscular mycorrhiza. Plant Physiol. 2005, 137: 1283-1301.
6. Parkinson H, Kapushesky M, Shojatalab M, Abeygunawardena N, Coulson R, Farne A, Holloway E, Kolesnykov N, Lilja P, Lukk M, Mani R, Rayner T, Sharma A, William E, Sarkans U, Brazma A: ArrayExpress-a public database of microarray experiments and gene expression profiles. Nucleic Acids Res. 2007, 35 (Database issue): D747-D750.
7. Chen J, Zhao P, Massaro D, Clerch L, Almon R, DuBois D, Jusko W, Hoffman E: The PEPR GeneChip data warehouse, and implementation of a dynamic time series query tool (SGQT) with graphical interface. Nucleic Acids Res. 32 (Database issue)2004:578-581.
8. Sherlock G, Hernandez-Boussard T, Kasarskis A, Binkley G, Matese J, Dwight S, Kaloper M, Weng S, Jin H, Ball C, Eisen M, Spellman P, Brown P, Botstein D, Cherry J: The Stanford Microarray Database. Nucleic Acids Res. 2001, 29 (1): 152-155.
9. Wise RP, Caldo RA, Hong L, Shen L, Cannon E, Dickerson JA: BarleyBase/PLEXdb. Methods Mol Biol. 2007, 406: 347-363.
10. Boguski M, Lowe T, CM T: dbEST-database for "expressed sequence tags". Nat Genet. 1993, 4 (4): 332-3.
11. Morley M, Arcaro M, Burdick J, Yonescu R, Reid T, Kirsch IR, Cheung VG: GenMapDB: a database of mapped human BAC clones. Nucleic Acids Res. 2001, 29: 144-147.
12. Short Read Archive. [http://www.ncbi.nlm.nih.gov/Traces/sra/sra.cgi].
13. Rahm E, Kirsten T, Lange J: The GeWare data warehouse platform for the analysis of molecular-biological and clinical data. Journal of Integrative Bioinformatics. 2007, 4: 47
14. Hu H, Brzeski H, Hutchins J, Ramaraj M, Qu L, Xiong R, Kalathil S, Kato R, Tenkillaya S, Carney J, Redd R, Arkalgudvenkata S, Shahzad K, Scott R, Cheng H, Meadow S, McMichael J, Sheu SL, Rosendale D, Kvecher L, Ahern S, Yang S, Zhang Y, Jordan R, Somiari SB, Hooke J, Shriver CD, Somiari RI, Liebman MN: Biomedical informatics: development of a comprehensive data warehouse for clinical and genomic breast cancer research. Pharmacogenomics. 2004, 5 (7): 933-941.
15. IGetDB. [http://www.cebitec.uni-bielefeld.de/groups/brf/software/igetdb_info/].
16. Java. [http://java.sun.com/].
17. MySQL. [http://www.mysql.com/].
18. Durinck S, Moreau Y, Kasprzyk A, Davis S, Moor BD, Brazma A, Huber W: BioMart and Bioconductor: a powerful link between biological databases and microarray data analysis. Bioinformatics. 2005, 21 (16): 3439-40.

19. Zimmermann P, Hennig L, Gruissem W: Gene expression analysis and network discovery using Genevestigator. Trends Plant Sci. 2005, 9 (10): 407-409.

20. Kimball R, Caserta J: Data Warehouse ETL Toolkit: Practical Techniques for Extracting, Cleaning, Conforming.

21. Pertea G, Huang X, Liang F, Antonescu V, Sultana R, Karamycheva S, Lee Y, White J, Cheung F, Parvizi B, Tsai J, Quackenbush J: TIGR Gene Indices clustering tools (TGICL): a software system for fast clustering of large EST datasets. Bioinformatics. 2003, 19 (5): 651-652.

22. Quackenbush J, Cho J, Lee D, Liang F, Holt I, Karamycheva S, Parvizi B, Pertea G, Sultana R, White J: The TIGR Gene Indices: analysis of gene transcript sequences in highly sampled eukaryotic species. Nucleic Acids Res. 2001, 29: 159-164.

23. Bekel T, Henckel K, Dondrup M, Küster H, Meyer F, Mittard-Runte V, Neuweger H, Paarmann D, Rupp O, Zakrzewski M, Pühler A, Stoye J, Goesmann A: The Sequence Analysis and Management System-SAMS-2.0: Data management and sequence analysis adapted to changing requirements from traditional sanger sequencing to ultrafast sequencing technologies. J Biotechnol.

24. Altschul S, Gish W, Miller W, Myers E, Lipman D: Basic Local Alignment Search Tool. J Mol Biol. 1990, 215 (3): 402-410.

25. Mulder N, Apweiler R: InterPro and InterProScan: tools for protein sequence classification and comparison. Methods Mol Biol. 2007, 396: 59-70.

26. Sonnhammer E, von Heijne G, Krogh A: A hidden Markov model for predicting transmembrane helices in protein sequences. Proc Int Conf Intell Syst Mol Biol. 1998, 6: 175-82.

27. Kanehisa M, Goto S: KEGG: kyoto encyclopedia of genes and genomes. Nucleic Acids Res. 2000, 28: 27-30.

28. Ashburner M, Ball CA, Blake JA, Botstein D, Butler H, Cherry JM, Davis AP, Dolinski K, Dwight SS, Eppig JT, Harris MA, Hill DP, Issel-Tarver L, Kasarskis A, Lewis S, Matese JC, Richardson JE, Ringwald M, Rubin GM, Sherlock G: Gene ontology: tool for the unification of biology. The Gene Ontology Consortium. Nat Genet. 2000, 25: 25-29.

29. Tatusov R, Fedorova N, Jackson J, Jacobs A, Kiryutin B, Koonin E, Krylov D, Mazumder R, Mekhedov S, Nikolskaya A, Rao B, Smirnov S, Sverdlov A, Vasudevan S, Wolf Y, Yin J, Natale D: The COG database: an updated version includes eukaryotes. BMC Bioinformatics. 2003, 11 (4): 41

30. The qcGene Database. [http://compbio.dfci.harvard.edu/tgi/qcGene.html].

31. Cannon SB, Sterck L, Rombauts S, Sato S, Cheung F, Gouzy J, Wang X, Mudge J, Vasdewani J, Schiex T, Spannagl M, Monaghan E, Nicholson C, Humphray SJ, Schoof H, Mayer KFX, Rogers J, Quetier F, Oldroyd GE, Debelle F, Cook DR, Retzel EF, Roe BA, Town CD, Tabata S, Peer Van de Y, Young ND: Legume genome evolution viewed through the Medicago truncatula and Lotus japonicus genomes. Proc Natl Acad Sci USA. 2006, 103 (40): 14959-14964.

32. Young ND, Cannon SB, Sato S, Kim D, Cook DR, Town CD, Roe BA, Tabata S: Sequencing the genespaces of Medicago truncatula and Lotus japonicus. Plant Physiol. 2005, 137 (4): 1174-1181.

33. Affymetrix. [http://www.affymetrix.com/].

34. Cheung F, Haas B, Goldberg S, May G, Xiao Y, Town C: Sequencing Medicago truncatula expressed sequenced tags using 454 Life Sciences technology. BMC Genomics. 2006, 7: 272

35. Küster H, Becker A, Firnhaber C, Hohnjec N, Manthey K, Perlick A, Bekel T, Dondrup M, Henckel K, Goesmann A, Meyer F, Wipf D, Requena N, Hildebrandt U, Hampp R, Nehls U, Krajinski F, Franken P, Pühler A: Development of bioinformatic tools to support EST-sequencing, in silico- and microarray-based transcriptome profiling in mycorrhizal symbioses. Phytochemistry. 2007, 68: 19-32.

36. Thompson R, Ratet P, Küster H: Identification of gene functions by applying TILLING and insertional mutagenesis strategies on microarray-based expression data. Grain Legumes. 2005, 41: 20-22.

37. Dondrup M, Goesmann A, Bartels D, Kalinowski J, Krause L, Linke B, Rupp O, Sczyrba A, Pühler A, Meyer F: EMMA: a platform for consistent storage and efficient analysis of microarray data. J Biotechnol. 2003, 106 (2–3): 135-46.

38. Dondrup M, Albaum S, Griebel T, Henckel K, Jünemann S, Kahlke T, Kleindt C, Küster H, Linke B, Mertens D, Mittard-Runte V, Neuweger H, Runte K, Tauch A, Tille F, Pühler A, Goesmann A: EMMA 2 – A MAGE-compliant system for the collaborative analysis and integration of microarray data. BMC Bioinformatics.

39. Brazma A, Hingamp P, Quackenbush J, Sherlock G, Spellman P, Stoeckert C, Aach J, Ansorge W, Ball H, Causton C, Gaasterland T, Glenisson P, Holstege F, Kim I, Markowitz V, Matese J, Parkinson H, Robinson A, Sarkans U, Schulze-Kremer S, Stewart J, Taylor R, Vilo J, Vingron M: Minimum information about a microarray experiment (MIAME) – toward standards for microarray data. Nature Genetics. 2001, 29: 365-371.

40. Spellman P, Miller M, Stewart J, Troup C, Sarkans U, Chervitz S, Bernhart D, Sherlock G, Ball C, Lepage M, Swiatek M, Marks W, Goncalves J, Markel S, Iordan D, Shojatalab M, Pizarro A, White J, Hubley R, Deutsch E, Senger M, Aronow B, Robinson A, Bassett D, Stoeckert C, Brazma A: Design and implementation of microarray gene expression markup language (MAGE-ML). Genome Biology. 2002, 3: research0046.1-0046.9.

41. Biodiscovery. [http://www.biodiscovery.com/].

42. MDS Analytical Technologies. [http://www.moleculardevices.com/].

43. Combier JP, Kuster H, Journet EP, Hohnjec N, Gamas P, Niebel A: Evidence for the involvement in nodulation of the two small putative regulatory peptide-encoding genes MtRALFL1 and MtDVL1. Mol Plant Microbe Interact. 2008, 21 (8): 1118-1127.

44. Gallardo K, Firnhaber C, Zuber H, Héricher D, Belghazi M, Henry C, Küster H,

Thompson R: A combined proteome and transcriptome analysis of developing Medicago truncatula seeds: Evidence for metabolic specialization of maternal and filial tissues. Mol Cell Proteomics. 2007, 6 (12): 2165-2179.

45. Gruber V, Blanchet S, Diet A, Zahaf O, Boualem A, Kakar K, Alunni B, Udvardi M, Frugier F, Crespi M: Identification of transcription factors involved in root apex responses to salt stress in Medicago truncatula. Mol Genet Genomics. 2009, 281: 55-66.

46. Benedito V, Torres-Jerez I, Murray J, Andriankaja A, Allen S, Kakar K, Wandrey M, Verdier J, Zuber H, Ott T, Moreau S, Niebel A, Frickey T, Weiller G, He J, Dai X, Zhao P, Tang Y, Udvardi M: A gene expression atlas of the model legume Medicago truncatula. Plant J. 2008, 55 (3): 504-513.

47. Echo Web Framework. [http://echo.nextapp.com/site/].

48. Kaló P, Gleason C, Edwards A, Marsh J, Mitra R, Hirsch S, Jakab J, Sims S, Long S, Rogers J, Kiss G, Downie J, Oldroyd G: Nodulation signaling in legumes requires NSP2, a member of the GRAS family of transcriptional regulators. Science. 2005, 308: 1786-1789.

49. Smit P, Raedts J, Portyanko V, Debelle F, Gough C, Bisseling T, Geurts R: NSP1 of the GRAS protein family is essential for rhizobial Nod factor-induced transcription. Science. 2005, 308: 1789-1791.

50. Heckmann A, Lombardo F, Miwa H, Perry J, Bunnewell S, Parniske M, Wang T, Downie J: Lotus japonicus Nodulation Requires Two GRAS Domain Regulators, One of Which Is Functionally Conserved in a Non-Legume. Plant Physiol. 2006, 142 (4): 1739-1750.

51. Limpens E, Bisseling T: Signaling in symbiosis. Current Opinion in Plant Biology. 2003, 6 (4): 343-350.

52. Kimball R, Margy R: The Data Warehouse Toolkit: The Complete Guide to Dimensional Modeling. ISBN 0471200247. John Wiley & Sons Inc; 2002.

53. Liu G, Loraine A, Shigeta R, Cline M, Cheng J, Valmeekam V, Sun S, Kulp D, Siani-Rose M: NetAffx: Affymetrix probesets and annotations. Nucleic Acids Res. 2003, 31 (1): 82-86.

54. Birney E, Andrews T, Bevan P, Caccamo M, Chen Y, Clarke L, Coates G, Cuff J, Curwen V, Cutts T, Down T, Eyras E, Fernandez-Suarez X, Gane P, Gibbins B, Gilbert J, Hammond M, Hotz H, Iyer V, Jekosch K, Kahari A, Kasprzyk A, Keefe D, Keenan S, Lehvaslaiho H, McVicker G, Melsopp C, Meidl P, Mongin E, Pettett R, Potter S, Proctor G, Rae M, Searle S, Slater G, Smedley D, Smith J, Spooner W, Stabenau A, Stalker J, Storey R, Ureta-Vidal A, Woodwark K, Cameron G, Durbin R, Cox A, Hubbard T, Clamp M: An Overview of Ensembl. Genome Res. 2004, 14: 925-928.

55. Pruitt K, Maglott D: RefSeq and LocusLink: NCBI gene-centered resources. Nucleic Acids Research. 2001, 29: 137-140.

14
CHAPTER

APPROACHES TO ACCESS BIOLOGICAL DATA SOURCES

Assia Rharbi, Khadija Amine, Zohra Bakkoury, Afaf Mikou, Anass Kettani and Abdelkader Betari

INTRODUCTION

In recent years, technological revolutions in genomics and proteomics have revolutionized the work of researchers in molecular biology. Through various techniques of data generation, they have at their hand in the web a very large amount of information contained in public and heterogeneous data sources. Each source has content organized around a particular data type like sequences in Uniprot (for proteins) and Genbank (for gene and mRNA), protein structure in PDB (Protein Data Bank) and publications in biomedical Medline. Their content is heterogeneous in the sense that a similar data can be represented differently in two data sources (e.g. different names for the same gene). More data sources have a variety in terms of structure, and there are sources of structured data, such as relational databases or semi-structured sources like XML and unstructured sources such as databases composed of flat files. That is to say that a biologist who wishes to obtain information from these sources have to question these one by one, then copy and analyze the data collected, and manage redundancy, complementarities of the information and inconsistencies. Today, one of the greatest challenges of bioinformatics is to enable biologists to effectively access multiple data sources, each with a different pattern. Various approaches have been adopted to unify access to various data sources given a query. Several systems have been produced from data warehouses, a federation of databases or mediators.

In this work, we are interested in mediation systems. Such systems offer to the user a uniform and centralized view of distributed data, this view may also reflect a more abstract, condensed, qualitative data and therefore more meaningful to the user. These mediation systems are also very useful in the presence of heterogeneous data, because

Citation: Assia Rharbi, Khadija Amine, Zohra Bakkoury, Afaf Mikou, Anass Kettani andAbdelkader Betari (2012). Approaches to Access Biological Data Sources, Lipoproteins - Role in Health and Diseases, Prof. Gerhard Kostner (Ed.), InTech, DOI: 10.5772/48740.

they seem to use a homogeneous system. We aim to assist biologists in their research through the development of a generic tool for the integration of heterogeneous genomic data distributed over the web, and we are placed in a very particular context that is the study of cardiovascular disease and especially familial hypercholesterolemia. This is a disorder of high LDL ("bad") cholesterol that is passed down through families, which means it is inherited. This disease is caused by a genetic mutation of certain lipoproteins. Indeed, these lipoproteins (called LDL) carry the 2/3 of cholesterol circulating in the blood; they deliver cholesterol to tissues by a system of recognition between Apo lipoprotein Band a receiver: the LDL receptor (lock and key system) that allows the entry of LDL and their cholesterol content in cells. When the LDL receptor (LDL-R) is weak (about one mutation), LDL accumulates in the blood and artery walls causing familial hypercholesterolemia (HF). So knowing these different mutations by biologists, can greatly facilitate the molecular screening of the disease and therefore to find the proper treatment. However, to answer such a query: "What are the mutations that cause familial hypercholesterolemia (HF)?" The biologist hasto make a fastidious search in disparate and heterogeneous databases which requires a considerable investment time.

This chapter is structured as following:

- First we present the background of the project
- Second we focus on the problem of heterogeneity of data sources and biological characteristics of these sources.
- Third we present the state of the art of data integration, problems and constraints of this integration and the various existing approaches to solve this problem.
- And fourth we expose studied scenario, the realization and perspectives.

GENERAL CONTEXT

Since the completion of the human genome sequencing in April 2003, we observe the accumulation of an outsize amounts of genomic and proteomic data on the web often syntactically and semantically heterogeneous and difficult to capitalize.

Information about genes provides access to their corresponding proteins. In addition, all diseases are associated with alterations in the structure or function of such proteins. A good knowledge of protein structure provides insight into their function.

Bioinformatics has become an important tool to explore genomic data by relying heavily on computer systems. It suggests methods and software's for biological data storage and processing. Actually, it is acquiring and organizing data, developing software for the analysis, comparison and modeling of these data and analysis results produced by bioinformatics software to infer new biological knowledge, in collaboration with biologists.

This work contributes to facilitate to biologists searching among heterogeneous and distributed data in public and / or private data sources on the web. In particular, it helps them to analyze proteins, by building a platform for integrating biological data.

This will provide a tracking system to target special proteins involved in a disease known as familial hypercholesterolemia and thus, to better understand the biological activity of these macromolecules.

Familial hypercholesterolemia disease results from mutations in the LDLR gene. The LDLR gene provides instructions for making a protein called a low-density lipoprotein receptor. This type of receptor binds to particles called low-density lipoproteins (LDLs), commonly known as bad cholesterol. By removing low-density lipoproteins from the bloodstream, these receptors play a critical role in regulating cholesterol levels. When the LDL receptor (LDL-R) is deficient, LDL accumulated in arteries induces the familial hypercholesterolemia (HF) pathology. So, in biology knowing these different mutations can greatly facilitate the molecular screening of the disease and thus find appropriate treatment.

BIOLOGICAL DATA SOURCES

Number of data sources and tools available to biologists on the web has grown dramatically in recent years. This huge number of available data along with heterogeneous information generated wide variety of access interfaces, and also a profound heterogeneity.

Genomic Databases

There are two types of databanks, those that correspond to a set of heterogeneous data so-called "databases" and those more homogeneous established around a specific theme.

Also, to avoid confusion we will distinguish between semantic databases, general [2] and specialized [3] databases.

For specific requirements related to the activity of a group, or to bibliographic compilations, many specific databases were created in laboratories. In some cases, these databases have been developed continuously; others have not been updated and disappeared as they represented a specific need. Still others are unknown or poorly known and are waiting for further investigation.

All these specialized databases of interest may vary considerably from one base to another according to their size. In most of the case, these bases correspond to a combination compared of generalist databases such as: Swiss-Prot, GenBank. DDBJ (DNA Data Bank of Japan), EMBL (European Molecular Biology Laboratory) which are used very often. It is important to know, that according to the field of activity or the genomics research, the surveyed banks are not necessarily the same. The genomic libraries contain various information that may include:

- Characteristics of proteins or genes such as localization of the gene in the cell: LocusLink5, the 3D structure of protein: Protein Data Bank (GDP) and Molecular Modeling Database (MMDB) or its biological function. More specifically, some databases contain information about a specific family of protein such as "Enzyme8" which include exclusively enzyme type proteins.

- Some phenotypes (specific genes, morphological feature, clinical syndrome...) or more specifically some genetic diseases: Online Mendelian Inheritance in Man (OMIM);
- Specific species or families of species: FlyBase, Reptilia, Saccharomyces Genome Database (SGD), Mouse Genome Database (MGD);
- The medical literature (banks abstracts): Medline, PubMed.

Table1 and Table 2 give two examples of genomic databases along with protein database.

Characteristics of Biological Data Sources

The diversity of information distributed sources and their heterogeneity are the one of the main problem that the web users have to face. This heterogeneity may result from the size or structure of the sources (structured sources: relational databases, partially structured sources: XML documents, or unstructured: texts), the access mode and query, or semantic heterogeneity: between concept maps, and implicit or explicit underlying ontology's.

Table 1. Genomic databases

Designation	**Location**	**Roles**	**Comments**	**Web sites and references**
Nucleic bases				
EMBL	European Bioinformatics Institute (EBI) Europe	More than 1 million records (January 1998) for more than 15,500 species. The predominant species: Homo sapien, Caenorhabditis elegans, Saccharomyces cerevvisae ...	Information's search tools: SRS, System Retrieval System and via a web interface on EBI, through BLAST et FASTA software	Accessible via the web site: http://www.ebi.ac.uk/ebi_docs/embl_db/ebi/topembl.html
Specific genomic resources				
SGD Saccharomyces Genome Database	Works of Cherry and al, 1998.	Online resources on molecular biology and S.cerevisiae genetic	Numerous research help functions on line	Accessible via the web site: http://genome-www.stanford.edu/Saccharomyces/

Table 2. Protein databases

Designation	**Location**	**Roles**	**Comments**	**Web sites and references**
Primary databases				

PIR Protein Information Resource	National Biomedical Research Foundation	Sequences collecting to detect evolutionary relationship between proteins	The current structure includes 4 compartments : PIR1, PIR2, PIR3 and PIR4	Accessible via the web site
Composite databases				
NRDB Non-redundant Database	National Center Biotechnology Information USA	Composed of GenPept (derived from GenBank), PDB sequences, SWISS-PROT, SPupdate, PIR, and GenPeptupdate (update of GenPept). NRDB is the default database of BLAST and NCBI service	Accessible via the web site:	NRDB Non-redundant Database

Biological sources have a large heterogeneity at different levels:

- Syntactic: because of the different formats for describing the content sources usually ASN.1 (formal notation for describing data transmitted via exchange protocols), (e.g. Enter), but also more standard formats such as XML (e.g. GenBank).

- Semantic which covers several aspects. First, it concerns the focus. However, each base focuses on a type of biological object (e.g., the focus of Swiss-Prot is the protein, the focus of GenBank is gene, and the PDB is the 3D protein structure).

- Then, according to the base, the same information is not represented with the same level of detail: some bases are generalists (e.g. Swiss-Prot in general on proteins) while others are more specialized (eg SGD (Saccharomyces Genome Database) on yeast proteins).

- The final aspect of semantic heterogeneity is related to the diversity of nomenclature modes. Different vocabularies are used to annotate the sequences and the reliance on such annotations is seldom complete. Moreover, within a same database, there are a several names for each single entity (protein, gene). The name of an entity may depend on the disease to which it is linked or to its inventor.

- Source query language: another form of heterogeneity comes from query languages. Languages are often simple forms (combinations of words to search in a text), in the case of portals or simple databases. But one can also find structured languages such as SQL or OQL.

- Protocols for collecting data that are different such as CGI / HTTP or FTP. Access to web sources is limited to the entry forms and their underlying programs

- The tools offered by the Web: there are many tools for text searching and sequence comparison algorithms such as BLAST (Basic Local Alignment Search Tool), FASTA15 or LASSAP16.

STATE OF THE ART OF APPROACHES TO INTEGRATION

A data integration system remedies to the problems associated with the expansion of public data sources by giving the possibility to have a unified view of them. Such a system is the interface between user and data sources simplifying requests to perform (a request to query all sources covered by the system). The user is not obliged to know where the data are and how they are structured.

Current Integration Approaches

There are two major approaches for integration of information: (1) the data warehouse (DW) or materialized approach and (2) virtual approach (mediator based).In DW approach, huge amount of historic data is stored in the DW. In the virtual approach, on the other hand, the data is not materialized, but rather is globally manipulated using views. Each of these approaches is suitable in some kinds of applications.

Data Warehouse

DW is a powerful tool for decision support and querying the data because it explicitly stores information from heterogeneous sources locally. However, some external data, such as new product announcements from opponents and currency exchange rates, may be needed to support the accuracy of the business decisions. We should not neglect the importance of such data to avoid the problems of incompleteness, inexact, or sometimes wrong results. Warehousing huge and frequently changed information is a big challenge for the following reasons.

Firstly, since the data in the DW is loaded in snapshots and the DW is a huge information repository. Secondly, as the data sources change frequently, the maintenance becomes a complicated and costly issue

Here are two examples of using data warehouses:

- Genomics Unified Schema, GUS [4] is a system for creating a data warehouse focused on molecular biology;
- Gene Expression Data Warehouse, GEDAW [5] is a warehouse dedicated to the analysis of the transcriptome of human liver.

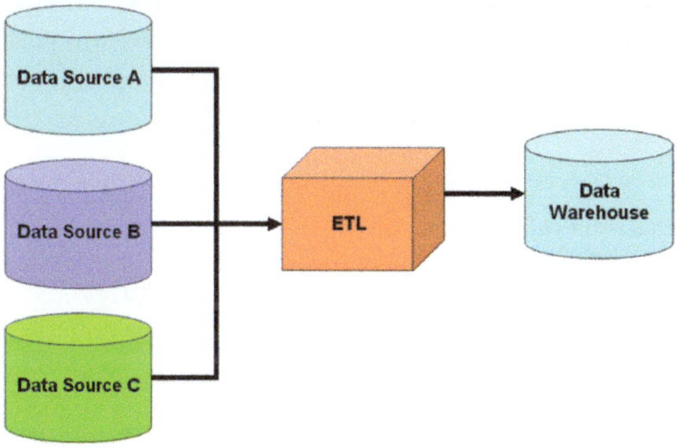

Figure 1. Simple schematic for a data warehouse.

The. Virtual Approach (Mediator Based)

In this approach, the actual data resides in the sources, and queries against the integrated 'virtual' view will be decomposed into sub queries and posed to the sources. This approach is preferred over the materialized approach DW when the information sources change very often. On the other hand, the DW approach may be desired when a quick query answer is required and the information sources change rarely.

The most important step in the construction of a mediator is the creation of the global schema. The mapping consists on the relations between the global schema and local sources. Specification of this mapping, depending on the method, determines the difficulty of query reformulation and the facility of adding or removing sources within the system. Two methods are commonly used to determine the global schema

- GAV (Global As View) approach: In this approach, each concept of the global schema is mapped to a query over data sources. In other words, when the user presents his/her query over the integrated schema, the data corresponds to a concept in the integrated schema, which can actually be answered from the data sources through a specific query. The query processing in GAV is easy, since it just unfold each concept in the integrated schema in the user query with the associated query over the sources, but this approach does not help much when the sources change or grow very often, since these factors affect the mappings and require restricting the integrated schema.

- LAV (Local As View) approach: LAV approach defines the mapping in the other way around; each concept in the data sources is defined in terms of a query over the integrated schema. This makes query processing more difficult, since in this case, the system does not know explicitly how to reformulate the concepts in the integrated view expressed in the user query in terms of the data sources. On the other hand, changes or incremental growth in the sources will not lead to reconstruction of the integrated schema, and need only to modify the mappings

In fact, these two approaches are not opposite, but complementary; depending on the problem to be solved. To integrate a few sources, most of which are stable, better to use the GAV method. By cons, as part of a large-scale integration, the LAV method is preferable as a material change at a local source with little or no impact on the global schema.

Two examples of systems integration based mediator:

- *Tambis (Transparent Access To Multiple Bioinformatics Information Sources) [6]* is an integration system coupled to an ontology that allows for better interoperability between sources;
- K2/BioKleisli [7] is a system based on CPL (Collection Programming Language) is a query language for high-level querying multiple sources.

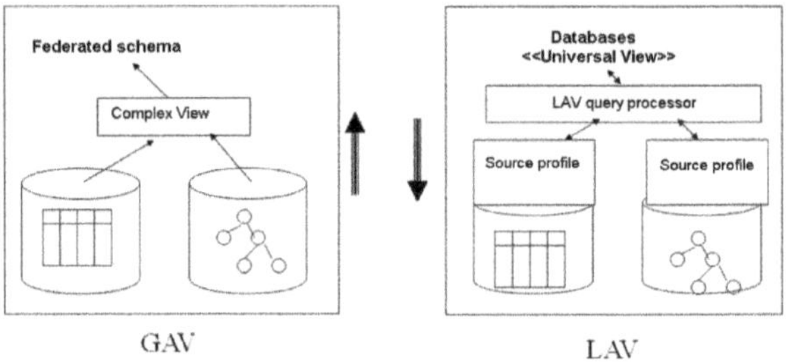

Figure 2. GAV vs. LAV.

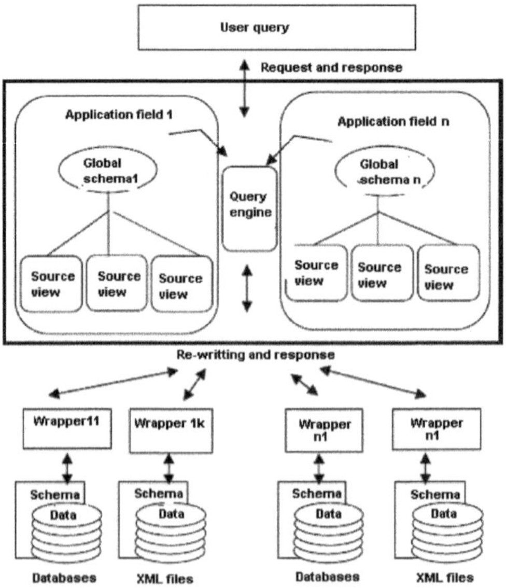

Figure 3. Architecture of a mediator.

The Multi Agents Approach

This approach was used in GID-IGC (Integrated Genomic Database - Genome Information System) project. The proposed architecture uses a network of agents communicating each with other via CORBA and KQML. All have a specific function, such as EIA (External Interface Agent)that manages the user interface, or SCA (Dial Selector

Agent) witch decompose the global query into sub-queries for local data sources. This approach is very modular and easily extensible.

Navigating. Between sources

This approach is based on what users usually do when searching for information on the web, which involves a search page to page by clicking the mouse. In practice, queries generated for this type of tool are converted into path expressions. The data banks are then integrated based on their cross-references. These expressions can answer the query of the user according to different levels of satisfaction.

A reference is a link between two data sources (Figure 4), a bridge between the information relating on the same object or the same concept. It can be done through an identifier of an external source or a URL (Unified Resource Locator). If the link can be browsed in both directions it is a cross-reference (“cross-reference”).

Adopted Approach

In this work, we are interested in mediation systems. Such systems offer a uniform and centralized view of distributed data. This view may also reflect a more abstract, condensed, qualitative data and therefore more meaningful to the user. These mediation systems are also very useful in the presence of heterogeneous data, because they seem to use a homogeneous system.

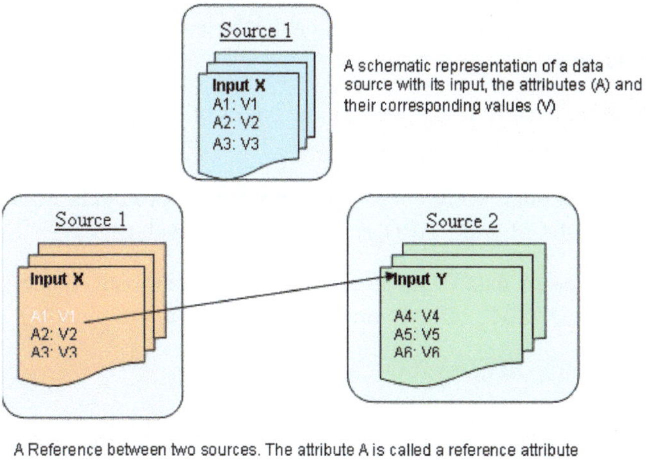

Figure 4. Navigating between sources.

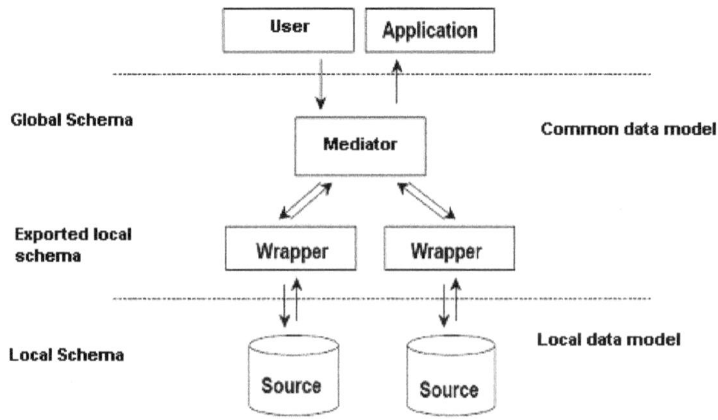

Figure 5. Adopted approach.

In this architecture, each component provides a set of features, which, together will help to satisfy the user request at the end.

- The mediator is a software module that directly receives the user's request. It has to locate the necessary information to answer the query, resolve schematic and semantic conflicts, query different sources and integrate the partial results in a consistent and coherent response. This is the most complex component but only one instance of it is necessary (unlike multiple adapters). It provides access to multiple data sources as if it was a single one and offers this consultation through multiple languages and ontologies.

This is a crucial component that allows a local system to distribute its information to a community of users.

- The adapter allows the presentation of data in the mediation's syntactic format. So it's an interface for querying a database using a standardized language (pivot language).
- Data source: Represent the sources and banks of biological information. A data source can be described by its:
    - Location: Reference, communication protocol, access technique (JDBC, ODBC API), support (DBMS, web pages)
    - Type of data it manages: structured (relational, object), semi-structured (XML, OEM), unstructured (image, multimedia)
    - Ability to query: SQL, OQL, search
    - Results Format: XML, HTML, relationships, texts

STUDIED SCENARIO

After exploring the different integration systems that solve the problem of heterogeneous biological data sources, this section describes the scenario we have chosen to work on.

Biologist's. Need

The objective of our work is to develop an integration system for biological data with an application on familial hypercholesterolemia. Such system should facilitate access to multiple data sources available on the Web, in a transparent and uniform way by giving biologists a single virtual source that summarizes the sites of interest to the application.

In order to satisfy this biologist's need we studied their current way to work. We first focused on existing tools, data sources they use and their functional specifications.

Tools: they use, mainly:

- CHARMM (Chemistry at Harvard Macromolecular Mechanics) [8]: This program offers a wide choice for the production and analysis of molecular simulations. It simulates the standard energy minimization of a given structure and the production of a molecular dynamics trajectory.

- VMD (Visual Molecular Dynamic) [9]: This software is used to visualize the molecules available on the web.

Data sources: The focus was mainly on the following sources:

- PDB (Protein Data Bank) [10] : It's a worldwide collection of data on three-dimensional structure of biological macromolecules: Proteins and nucleic acids. The PDB is the primary source of structural biological data. It allows access to 3D structures of pharmaceutical interest proteins.

- PubMed [11]: it's a free search engine giving access to the MEDLINE bibliographic database, gathering citations and abstracts of biomedical research.

Adopted Scenario

The adopted scenario consists on building a local database "homemade" that would include unorganized data already available in the biologist's laboratory and for our particular case data related to LDL receptor mutations. This goes along with the research we're going to do on the Web using the mediation system:

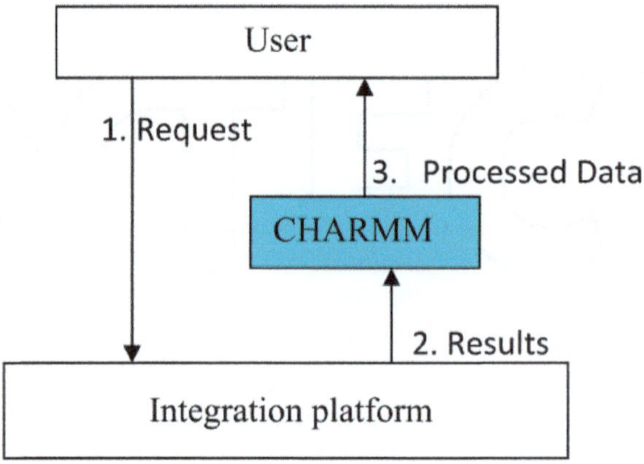

Figure 6. The adopted scenario.

The integration platform is the mediation system. It will query data sources related to cardiovascular diseases especially familial hypercholesterolemia namely: PDB and PubMed. The results of the query will be processed by the tool CHARMM before being presented to the user [12, 13].

Selected Data Sources

PubMed [8]: Is the leading bibliographic data search engine of all fields of biology and especially medicine. It was developed by the National Center for Biotechnology Information (NCBI), and is hosted by the National Library of Medicine U.S. National Institutes of Health. PubMed is a free search engine giving access to the MEDLINE bibliographic database, gathering citations and abstracts of biomedical research.

The MEDLINE database in April 2007 had more than 15 million citations from 1950 published in 5000 biomedical journals (journals in biology and medicine) distinct. It is the database of reference for biomedical sciences. As with other indexes, including a citation in PubMed has no content. In addition to MEDLINE, PubMed also provides access to:

- OldMedline for articles before 1966
- Citations of all articles, even "irrelevant" (that is to say, covering topics such as plate tectonics or astrophysics) from certain MEDLINE journals, primarily those published in major newspapers of general science or biochemical (such as Science and Nature, for example).
- Citations being listed before indexing in MEDLINE or MeSH, or passage or status "off topic"
- Older citations selected for MEDLINE journal from which they arise (when they are supplied electronically by the publisher)

- Articles submitted to PubMed Central for free

Most citations include a link to the full article when it is available (e.g. PubMed Central). PubMed is a search engine that allows users to search in the MEDLINE database; this information is also available from private organizations such as Ovid and Silver platter, among others. Pubmed is free since the mid-1990s. For optimal use of PubMed, it is necessary to have an understanding of his core, MEDLINE, and especially the MeSH vocabulary used for indexing articles in MEDLINE.

We can also find in PubMed information about the log, which can search by title, subject, short title, NLM ID, ISO abbreviation, and ISSN (International Standard Serial Number) written and electronic. The database "newspaper" includes all newspapers Enter Base.

The major interest of these bibliographic databases is that:

- Their bodies are used to identify recent publications in scientific journals.
- They help to establish bibliographies (lists of relevant articles) on a subject or author.
- They are portals to access full text documents available on the Internet.
- The bibliographic databases used to find references to documents, select, print or export them to other software. They may also propose to order documents or provide access to full text.

PDB (Protein Data Bank): The databank on proteins of Research Collaborator for Structural Bioinformatics, more commonly known as Protein Data Bank or PDB is a worldwide collection of data on the three-dimensional (or 3D structure) of biological macromolecules : protein essentially, and nucleic.

Founded in 1971 by Brookhaven National Laboratory, the Protein Data Bank was transferred in 1998 to the Research Collaborator for Structural Bioinformatics (RCSB), which consists of Rutgers University, the University of Wisconsin at Madison, National Institute of Standards and Technology (NIST) and the "San Diego Supercomputer Centre." The PDB originally contained (in 1971) 7 structures. The number of structures deposited has grown since the 1980s. Indeed, at that time, the crystallographic techniques have improved, the structures determined by NMR have been added, and the scientific community has changed its view on data sharing.

The PDB containedon 28-04-2008, 50480 structures. The data are from the original pdb format, and in recent years are also mmCif format, specifically developed for structural data from the PDB. From 2000 to 3000 structures are added each year. The bank contains files for each molecular model. These files describe the exact location of each atom of the macromolecule studied, that is to say, the Cartesian coordinates of the atom in a three-dimensional coordinate.

Each model is referenced in the bank by a unique identifier to 4 characters, the first is always a numeric character, the next three being alphanumeric characters. This identifier is called "pdb code".

Several formats exist for PDB files:

The PDB format: it is the original format. The guide of this format has been revised several times; the current version is version 2.2[14], which has existed since 1996. Originally pdb format was dictated by the width and the use of punch cards for computers. Consequently, each line contains exactly 80 characters.

Pdb file format is a text file where each column has its meaning: Each parameter is positioned so immutable. Thus, the first 6 columns, that is to say the first 6 characters for a given line, determine the scope of the file. Found for example in the fields "TITLE_ "(That is to say, the title of the macromolecule of interest)," KEYWDS "(The keywords of the entry)," EXPDTA "Which provides information on the experimental method used," SEQRES "(The sequence of the protein under study)," ATOM_ "Or" HETATM "Fields containing all information related to a particular atom.

Pdb format limitations: Format in 80 columns pdb files is relatively restrictive. The maximum number of atoms in a pdb file is 99999, since there are only 5 columns allocated for the numbers of atoms. Similarly the number of residues per chain is at most 9999: There are only 4 columns allowed for this figure. The number of channels is limited to 62 : A single column is available, and possible values are one of the 26 letters of the alphabet in upper or lower case, or one of the digits 0 through 9. As this format has been defined, these limitations did not seem restrictive, but they have been taken several times during the deposition of extremely large structures, such as viruses, ribosome, and multienzyme complexes.

MmCIF format:The growing interest in the development of database and electronic publications in the late 1980s has created the need for a more structured, standardized, open-ended and high quality data from the PDB. In 1990, the International Union of Crystallography IUCr extended to macromolecules data representation used to describe crystal structures of molecules of low molecular weight. This representation is called CIF, for Crystallographic Information File. The dictionary mmCIF (macromolecular Crystallographic Information File) published in 1996, was then developed.

In MmCIF format, each field of each section of a pdb file is represented by a description of a characteristic of an object, which includes both the name of the characteristic (eg _struct.entry_id), and the content of the description (pdb code : 1cbn). Which we can call " name-value ". It is easy to convert, without loss of information, an mmCIF file format pdb, since all information is directly analyzed. It is not possible, however, to completely automate the conversion of a pdb file format mmCIF, since many mmCIF descriptors are either absent from the PDB file, either in this field " REMARK "Who can not always be analyzed. The contents of fields " REMARK " is indeed separated according to different mmCIF dictionary entries, in order to preserve the completeness of the information contained in such Materials and Methods section (crystal characteristics, refinement method...) or in the description of the biologically active molecule or other molecules (substrate, inhibitor,...)

The mmCIF dictionary contains over 1700 entries, which are much safer not all used in a single PDB file. All field names are preceded by the character " underscore "(_), In order to differentiate the values themselves. Each name corresponds to an mmCIF dictionary entry, where the characteristics of the object are exactly defined. Pdbml format: This format is pdbml adaptation to XML data format bps and contains the entries described in the dictionary "PDB Exchange Dictionary".This dictionary contains the same entries as the mmCIF dictionary, in order to take into account all data managed and distributed by the PDB. This format can store much more information on models than pdb format.

Data retrieval : The files describing molecular models can be downloaded from the website of the PDB and visualized using various software such as Rasmol [15], Jmol [16], chime [17] or an extension VRML [18] (plugin) a browser. The website of the PDB also contains resources for teaching, on structural genomics and other useful software.

The Global Schema

By studying and exploring the previous sources and by combining data from genome sources, we have identified all data that define the dictionary related to familial hypercholesterolemia disease (Table 3). From this data dictionary and business rules (as defined and established by experts in the field of biology), we extracted the major biological entities useful for our study. These entities are not independent and form a semantic graph with nodes reflecting relationships between these entities.

Table 3. Data Dictionaries

Property	**Description**
code_biblio	Library code
auteur_biblio	Author of publication
date_biblio	Date of publication
volume_biblio	Volume of structure
langue_biblio	Language
contribution_biblio	Contribution
journal_biblio	Newspaper
revue_scint_biblio	Journal
livre_biblio	Book
Cd_proceeding_biblio	CD procedure
nom_recepteur	Name of receiver
nom_mutation	Name of mutation
classe_mutation	Class of mutation
nom_proteine	Name of the protein
longueur_proteine	Length of the protein
type_proteine	Protein type
structure_summary	Summary of the structure

structure_title	Under the structure
nom_molecule	Name of the molecule
author_name	Name of author
date_depot	Date Filed
date_release	Date of publication
derniere_release	Last update
Resolution	Resolution
Compound	Compound
Classification	Classification
molecule_chain_type	Channel Type
experimental_methode	Experimental method of resolution (RX, NMR)

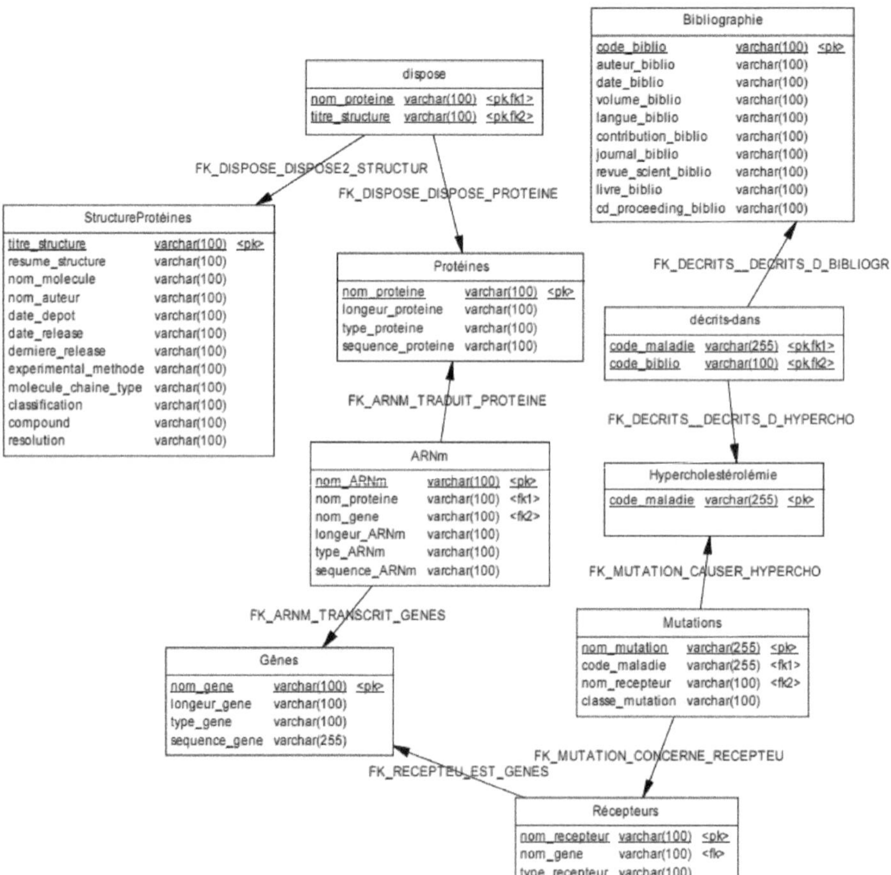

Figure 7. Global Schema.

From the global schema, it is possible to make our request and submit it to SQL mediator for treatment. For example, the query that gives the associated protein mutated gene and publications on familial hypercholesterolemia is expressed as follows in SQL:

```
Select nom_proteine, journal_biblio, auteur_biblio, date_biblio, langue_biblio
From mRNA, gene g, b bibliography
Where a.nom_gene = g.nom_gene
And g.nom_gene in (select nom_gene from recepteurs r, mutation m
                   Where r.nom_recepteur = m.nom_recepteur)
```

For its execution, the query is first submitted to the mediator which is responsible for locating sources and queries them through the wrapper or the associated adapter. It should be noted that the only access point to our sources for interrogation is a web form that, once processed through a wrapper, gives us the local sources that we describe below.

Analysis of the Query

In the global query, 6 attributes are involved: Nom_proteine, nom_gene, journal_biblio, auteur_biblio, date_biblio, langue_biblio shown in the following table along with the sources (PubMed (S1), and PDB (S2).

Table 4. Identification of sources

Attributes	Lists of sources
journal_biblio, auteur_biblio, date_biblio,langue_biblio	S1
nom_proteine	S2
nom_gene	S2, S1

From these sources, we can extract a local schema, for example:

S1_L (journal_biblio, auteur_biblio, date_biblio, langue_biblio, nom_gene),

S2_L (nom_proteine, nom_gene)

From a programming point of view, S1_L and S2_L represent wrapper sources.

Next section describes the realization in which we develop wrappers, submit queries to the mediator, and combine the final result to be presented to the user.

REALIZATION

We define four steps in the realization:

- The development of wrapper
- Definition of "global schema"

- Correspondence between local tables and global schema
- Results analysis

Step 1: Development of Wrappers

A wrapper is a program that envelops the execution of another program in the way that the environment can be more suitable. The mediator requests the various databases via wrappers that will extract information from websites of interest. It is necessary to create a wrapper for each specific database.

The sources that we identified in section 4 will be integrated through wrappers. There are different types of wrappers depending on the type of pages they incorporate. These can be either text files or XML files (Extensible Mark-up Language). It is necessary to know the structure of these files and know where the information is located (after any tag, for example). Developing wrappers is linked to functional specifications of the sources presented earlier.

Wrappers allow therefore the extraction of data to be represented in tables. Indeed, we declare the objects and their attributes for each site based on data provided. From all this information, local schemas (relational) for each of these databases are established.

Various programs were written in java. Even if a wrapper has been created for each database, they all have the same main structure. To fill out the fields of tables, the wrapper accesses the Web site to integrate the page and look for keywords behind which is the value to extract. Wrappers are of two types depending on the format of the sources: Either text wrappers or XML wrappers (Figure 8).

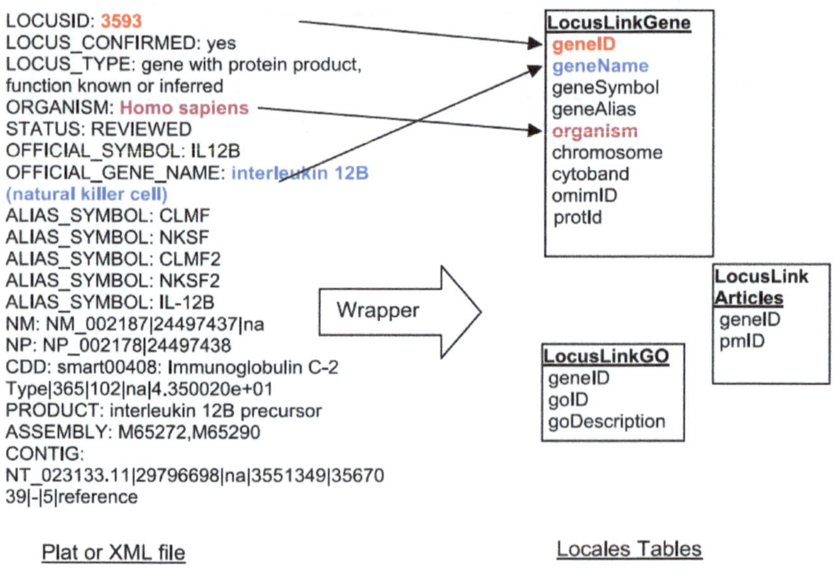

Figure 8. Presentation of a wrapper.

Finally, a program that generates and initializes (gives the starting values for all wrappers) is created to coordinate everything. This program is also written in Java and integrates all the wrappers and their relationships. We thus obtain a set of local tables (Provisional) performed by the wrappers.

Step 2: Definition of "Globalschema"

It is therefore necessary to build the global schema that will be the only interface for user. Indeed, the user does not know absolutely how the data are integrated. The global schema is a set of relational tables that are defined using local tables (for information). This schema was introduced in the previous section.

Step 3: Matches between Local Tables and Global Schema

As the various local tables have been filled by the wrappers and the global schema has been established, we should now define the correspondence rules between them in order to implement global schema with the extracted information from local schemas. The problem is that several sources may correspond to a business table (we must then join conditions on these tables) or otherwise a source may have several tables trades. For this, we use the Medience server tool.

Medience Server (Figure 5.2) is a complete environment that treats all matching problems (different formats, different representation of business information, dispersal of information described in a single business table). It is a "virtual database", because it does not store information but analyze the user needs. This tool will serve as a mediator that is to say that it will be the unique interface for the user as it will both integrate databases, present data and also offers possibility to loop and see only some information tables of interest to the user. The use of this tool goes in three steps:

1. The first step consists on recording data sources and creating associated source tables using source files provided by wrappers. The global schema is also implemented by local tables. We define the attributes of all tables.

2. In the second part we define the correspondence rules from source tables to the global schema tables. The supply of each table in the global database is defined from the records of source tables. It is thus possible to standardize results coming from various sources by the definition of a standard type.

3. The final step is the verification of all components and installation of all matching rules to make it operational (Figure 9).

Step. 4: Data Analysis

It is therefore possible through a platform like Medience to integrate data sources (BD, Excel files, and text files) and view the results in a tabular form. Now, we can process to the analysis of the results. For this, the definition of demand in terms of mining must be decided: How can we use the data provided. Medience offers the possibility to ask tables on the global schema in SQL way. It also offers the ability to define views on these tables and keep a small part that is particularly interesting. It is possible to use our tool to answer the question like what is the protein associated with the mutated gene responsible for familial hypercholesterolemia and related publications.

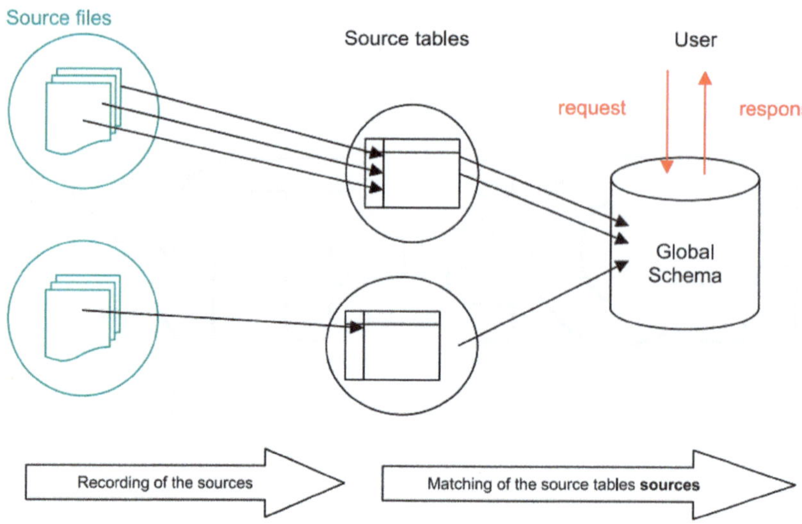

Figure 9. Architecture of Medience.

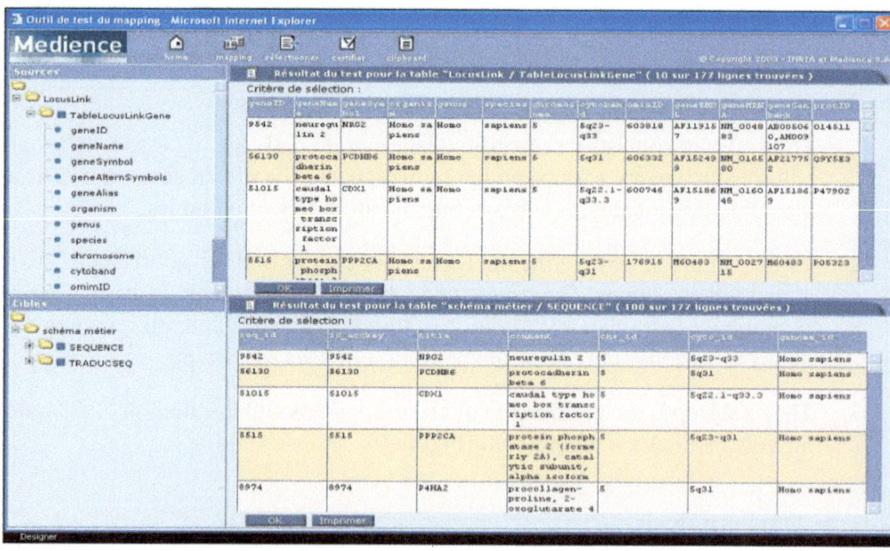

Figure 10. An example of Medience interface [19]

CONCLUSION

The objective of this work was to develop a system for integrating biological data with an application on familial hypercholesterolemia disease. Such a system should facilitate access to multiple data sources available on the Web, in a transparent and uniform way, giving biologists a single virtual source that summarizes all relevant data sources for the application.

This chapter describes the solution adopted to achieve such a system, where the main elements have been identified, and a computer deployment scenario developed. Among different existing integration approaches, we adopted the mediator approach to integrate data sources. In this approach the most important step is the construction of the global schema as the mediator has to process queries at runtime in order to integrate data sources. We first studied the biologists' needs by exploring different scenarios and we identified with their help various data sources involved.

A study of these sources was necessary in order to build our global schema. From the diagram established, we formulated our SQLquery as we built various adapters associated with different sources and at the end we have submitted this request to the mediator for treatment.

As prospects, we have to implement and test this solution and combine the final result of the mediator and that of the tool CHARMM before presenting to the user.

We are currently expanding the platform by integrating other proteins involved in cardiovascular diseases which are the main cause of mortality in the world. In particular, we are investigating a protein called paraoxonase-1 (PON1) which plays an important role in the cardiovascular diseases prevention.

PON1 is an HDL associated enzyme synthesized in the liver and distributed in the blood. It catalyzes the hydrolysis of modified lipids in both HDL (known as good cholesterol) and LDL (known as bad cholesterol) particles and protects them from oxidative modifications, and subsequently reducing the risk of atherosclerosis.

Further bioinformatics analysis including molecular simulations are performed on the PON1 enzyme to better understand the structure activity relationship and also to explore the mutated proteins (genetic polymorphism associated with heart disease) responsible for the weak activity revealed trough the clinical study in both diabetic and coronary patients from Morocco.

REFERENCES

1. . M. El Messal, K. Aït, R. Chihab, J. C. Chater, F. Vallvé, A. Bennis, J. Hafidi, M. Ribalta, M. Varret, J. P. Loutfi, A. Rabès, C. Kettani, L. Boileau, A. Masana, Adlouni, Approaches to Access Biological Data Sources J Hum 48 (4):199 EOF203 EOF , 2003
2. http://www.dsi.univ-paris5.fr/bio2/autof2/cha2_1.htm : Bases de données biologiques / Banques généralistes
3. http://www.dsi.univ-paris5.fr/bio2/autof2/cha2_2.htm : Bases de données biologiques / Banques spécialisées

4. www.gusdb.org : Genomics Unified Schema (GUS)
5. Emilie Guérin, Gwenaëlle Marquet, Anita Burgun, Olivier Loréal et Fouzia Moussouni, GEDAW : un environnement intégré pour l'analyse du Transcriptome, JOBIM 2005
6. http://www.cs.man.ac.uk/~stevensr/tambis/ : TAMBIS
7. Thomas Hernandez, Subbarao Kambhampati, Integration of Biological Sources:
8. Current Systems and Challenges Ahead, SIGMOD september 2004
9. http://www.charmm.org/ : CHARMM (Chemistry at HARvard Macromolecular Mechanics)
10. http://www.ks.uiuc.edu/Research/vmd/ : VMD (Visual Molecular Dyamic)
11. www.rcsb.org/pdb/
12. http://www.ncbi.nlm.nih.gov/sites/entrez?db=PubMed&itool=toolbar
13. Assia Rharbi, Zohra Bakkoury, Afaf Mikou, Anass Kettani, Abdelkader Betari, and Omar Boucelma, Intégration des données génomiques pour la maladie d'hypercholestérolémie familiale, Journées Scientifiques en Bio-informatique (JSB'2007)
14. Assia Rharbi, Zohra Bakkoury, Afaf Mikou, Anass Kettani, Abdelkader Betari, and Omar Boucelma, Intégration des données appliquée au domaine biologique, Cinquième Conférence sur les Systèmes Intelligents : Théories et Application (SITA'08)
15. http://www.rcsb.org/pdb/file_formats/pdb/pdbguide2.2/guide2.2_frame.html
16. http://rasmol.org/
17. http://jmol.sourceforge.net/
18. http://fr.wikipedia.org/w/index.php?title=Chime&action=edit&redlink=1
19. http://www.w3.org/MarkUp/VRML/
20. F.-M. Colonna, Thèse : "Intégration de données hétérogènes et distribuées sur le Web et applications à la biologie", Université Paul Cézanne (Aix-Marseille III), Décembre 2008

SECTION IV: DATA WAREHOUSE APPLICATIONS IN THE PUBLIC SECTOR

15
CHAPTER

DATA WAREHOUSE AND THE DEPLOYMENT OF DATA MINING PROCESS TO MAKE DECISION FOR LEISHMANIASIS IN MARRAKECH CITY

Habiba Mejhed, Samia Boussaa and Nour El Houda Mejhed

INTRODUCTION

In the last decade, the epidemiology applied more and more tools to help to make decision. The aim is to translate epidemic data using the modelling concepts of health information systems for the decision-making. The information is a value-increasing necessary to plan and control the activities of an organism with effectively. It is the raw material that will be transformed by information systems. Often, the availability of data makes it very difficult, if not impossible, to extrapolate the information that really matter. It is essential to have rapid and complete information needed for the decision-making process: the strategic indicators are extrapolated mainly operational data in a database, through a selection process or synthetic gradually. The widespread use of data analysis techniques has made the information system a strategic element and policy framework for achieving the business. Therefore, the decision-making systems have emerged in the 80s (decision support system) and offer techniques and means to extract information from a set of memorized data. As a result, the volume of information collected during an epidemiological case study enables the development of new observing systems to analyze and extract some indicators as appropriate clinical decision and public health.

The clinical decision support provided epidemiologist technologies necessary to facilitate this difficult task (Degoulet & Fieschi, 1998), (Gilbert, 2004), (Teh, 2009).

The data warehouse remains a valuable tool for storage and data accessibility, it is defined as a collection of information that integrates and reorganize the data from a variety of sources and make them available for analysis and assessment to scheduling and decision making. If the data warehouse used to store historical data, with the finality analysis, the data mining is defined as a process of exploration and modelling data

Citation: Habiba Mejhed, Samia Boussaa and Nour el houda Mejhed (2011). Data Warehouse and the Deployment of Data Mining Process to Make Decision for Leishmaniasis in Marrakech City, New Fundamental Technologies in Data Mining, Prof. Kimito Funatsu (Ed.), InTech, DOI: 10.5772/13384.

in order to discover new correlations, to find trends and stable patterns in the data. It proposes a number of tools from different disciplines, in particular, to decision making in epidemiology [Daniel, 2005), [René & Gilles, 2001), (Pascal et all, 2007), (Stéphane, 2007), (Egmont et all, 2002), (Hang & Xiubin, 2008). Data mining combines between various sciences domains (Databases, Statistics, Artificial Intelligence) to construct models from the data, and under the criteria fixed in advance and make a maximum of knowledge useful to make decision.

In Morocco, leishmaniasis remains a severe public health problem. Many foci were described in rural areas of Ouarzazate (Rioux et all 1986), Essaouira (Pratlong et all, 1991), Azilal (Rhajaoui et all, 2004), Chichaoua (Guernaoui et all 2005) and Al Haouz (Boussaa et all, 2009), (Rioux et all, 1986) but also in suburban areas, in Taza (Guessous et all, 1997) and Fez (Rhajaoui et all, 2004) Marrakesh is an interesting study site because it lies close to the focus of cutaneous leishmaniasis in the south of Morocco (Ouarzazate, Chichaoua and Al Haouz), and current studies have classified the area of Marrakesh as being at risk of cutaneous leishmaniasis (Boussaa et all, 2005), (Boussaa et all, 2007). As the best choice of a vector-control strategy is dictated by sandfly ecology, we try to simplify this complex of diseases and quantify the climatic factors which can determine the distribution and activity of sandflies vectors in Marrakesh city. According to the WHO (2005), the activity of sandfly fauna is affected by many climatic factors as temperature, humidity and wind, besides seasons and according to sandfly species.

In this chapter we present a simple contribution to the fight against leishmaniasis in Morocco. The idea is to propose to epidemiologists an application based on tools of data warehouse and data mining to help them to make decision. In the first time, we conceived and modelled our information system to establish the pattern of the database on which we are going to work. Then, we develop a data warehouse to store and extrapolate data collected in Marrakech city, and we used a data mining tools for Leishmaniasis data analysis to get a better decision-making. We studied three forms of leishmaniasis according to sandfly vectors collected in Marrakech city by (Boussaa et all, 2005), (Boussaa et all, 2007): Phlebotomus papatasi proven vector of zoonotic cutaneous leishmaniasis with Rodents as a reservoir; P. sergenti proven vector of anthroponotic cutaneous leishmaniasis and P. longicusis potential vector of visceral leishmaniasis with canine as reservoir hosts.

MATERIAL AND METHODS

Sandfly Collections

Specimens were collected in Marrakech city (31°36'N, 8°02'W, 471m a.s.l.) between October 2002 and September 2003 as described by (Boussaa et all, 2005). The specimens caught were preserved in 70% ethanol. They were cleared in potash 20% and Marc-Andre solution, then dehydrated and mounted in Canada balsam (Abonnenc, 1972). The identification was made by examining the morphology of male genitalia, female spermathecae and pharynges. For Larroussius species, we revised our specimens according to results of [Boussaa et all, 2008).

Data Analysis

We have a data file.xls containing all the information on the activity of sandflies P.Papatasi, P. Sergenti and P. Longicuspis based on climate change (date, temperature and density). We can present data from Excel files in the following diagrams:

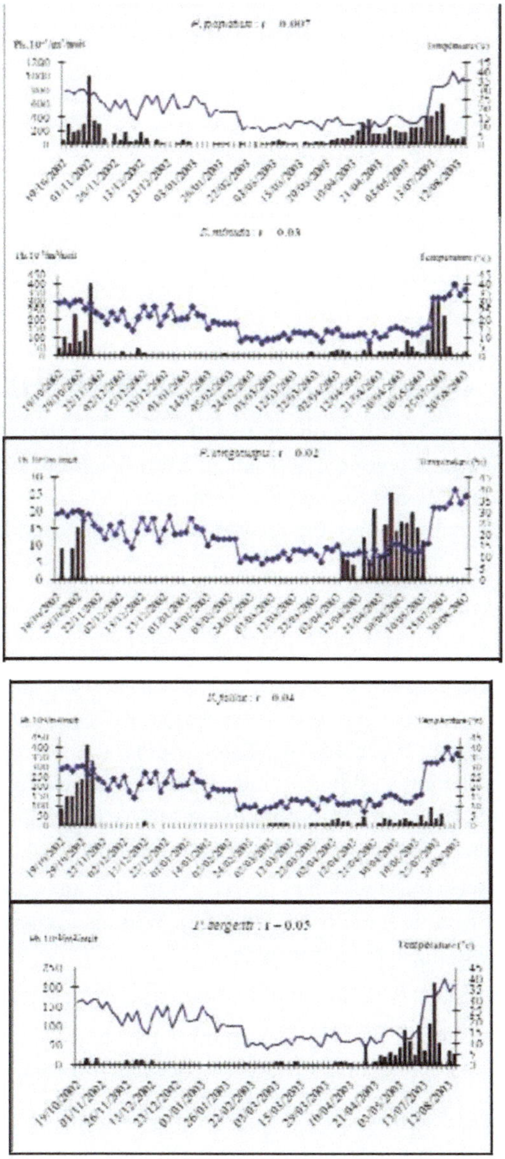

Figure 1. The activity of sandfly population in Marrakech area.

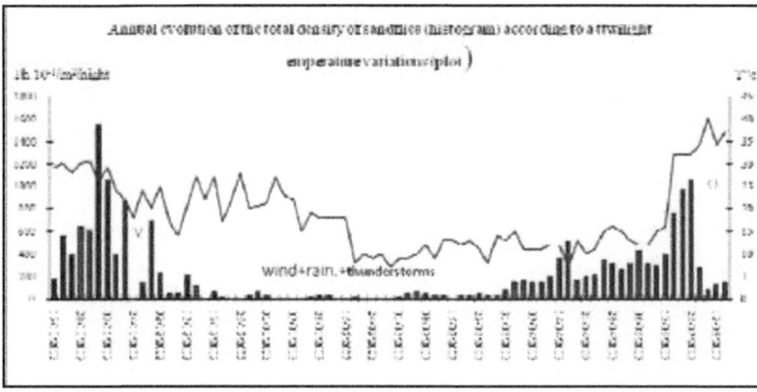

Figure 2. Annuel evolution of the global density of the sandflies vector according to the time and the climatic change.

DEVELOPMENT OF A DATA WAREHOUSE LEISHMANIASIS

In this section we proceed to the conception of our data scheme. Our investigations on the sandflies collections were carried out in Marrakech city. The goal is to design a database, to develop DW and to load this database, and then the relationships in the cube are built automatically to give the answer to question posed in this case.

BACKGROUND

The creation of a data warehouse involves several steps:

The conception: the implementation of a data warehouse usually begins by framing the project, define the needs and goals expressed by policymakers, modeling and designing a data structure. There are two data models, the star pattern, in this model, we must define one (or more) table (s) made with one or several measures (values of indicators). Both must have multiple dimension tables whose primary keys form the primary key tables done. Warning: The dimension tables are not linked.

Then the model snowflake which is derived from the star schema where the tables are standard size (of the table remains unchanged). With this scheme, each dimension is divided according to his (or her) hierarchy (s).

The acquisition of data: The data will be extracted from the sources.

a. The static extraction will be performed when the DW must be loaded for the first time and is conceptually a copy of operational data.

b. The incremental extraction, is used for the periodic updating of the DW, and captures just the changes in data sources at the last extraction.

The choice of extracting data is based mainly on their quality, selection of data from the database is not a simple task to do.

Data cleaning: This phase will improve the quality of duplicate data, inconsistencies between the values logically related, missing data, unexpected use of a field, impossible value or wrong ...

Loading DW: The loading of data in the DW is the process is to load the data cleaned and prepared in the DW.

Needs Specification

We have developed the analysis tools concerning, the population of sandflies, according to the various species listed in Marrakech city and their density, we considered the human population which may become affected after bites of infected sandflies.

These tools allow knowing the following information: (a) The density of each species of sandflies listed, (b) The period at risk for the spread of the disease, (c) The rate of infection of humans by infected sandflies, (d) The rate per unit time, which a man loses her immunity and becomes susceptible, (e) The rate of infected and susceptible in humans.

To meet the needs of decision makers, we implemented the DW with respect to the architecture described in the following section.

Data Warehouse Architecture

Schematic below shows the architecture of the data warehouse applied to Leishmaniasis data.

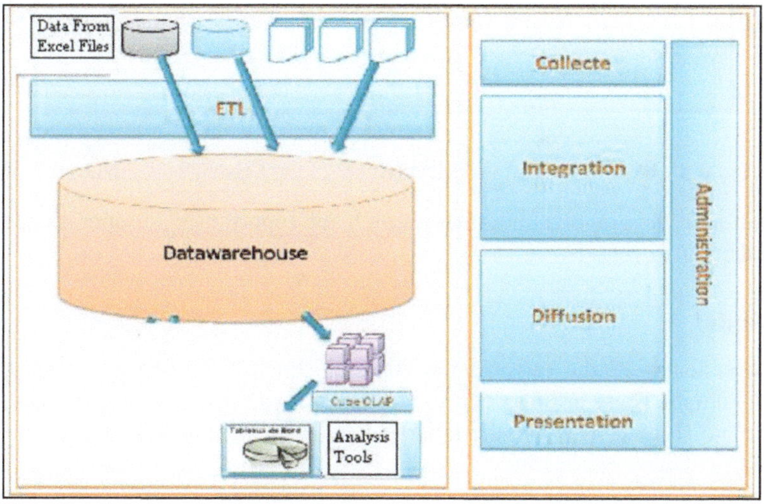

Figure 3. Data warehouse Architecture.

To ensure a robust, flexible and portable solution, we adopted a software architecture divided into several parts:

Collection of raw data files: the job of this module is periodically connected to all servers, to check the generation of new data files

Conversion of the Files: The application of this module is written in Java. This module convert the data files collected by the module above, and filter the information contained therein. It permits to leave only the information that will be used in the future treatments.

Loading data into the data warehouse: ETL process allows Extraction, Transformation and Loading of data from various sources (databases, files) into DW. ETL process is the most important module to design a Data warehouse with respecting two constraints: data sources and data types (data quality).

Building of multidimensionnel cubes:

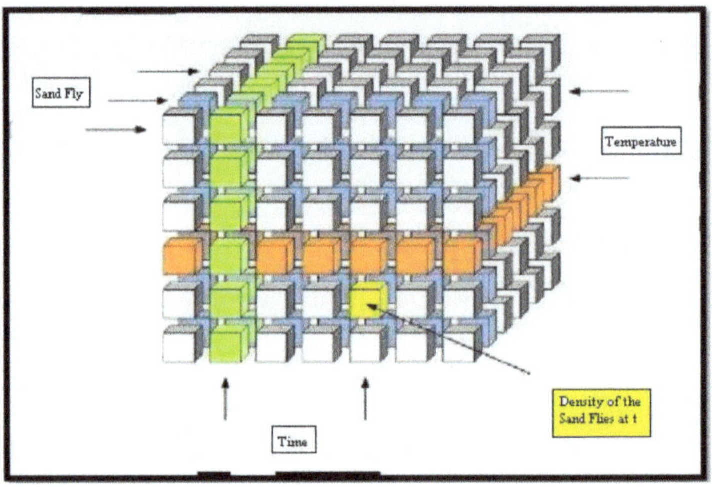

Figure 4. Example of multidimensional view (Cube) of the Leishmaniasis data.

Creation of the graphical interfaces, graph and report: used for operation, querying cubes and creating reports.

Data Model

This section deals with the transmission of the Leishmaniasis disease from the sandflies vector to human. There are four actors in this case, sandflies species, climatic change and Time and Human. The data dictionary given in the following table:

data	Description of data
Human	Sexe Age statut
sandflies	specie Name
Temperature	Degree
time	wear Month Day

The data layer architecture of Leishmaniasis is illustrated schematically by:

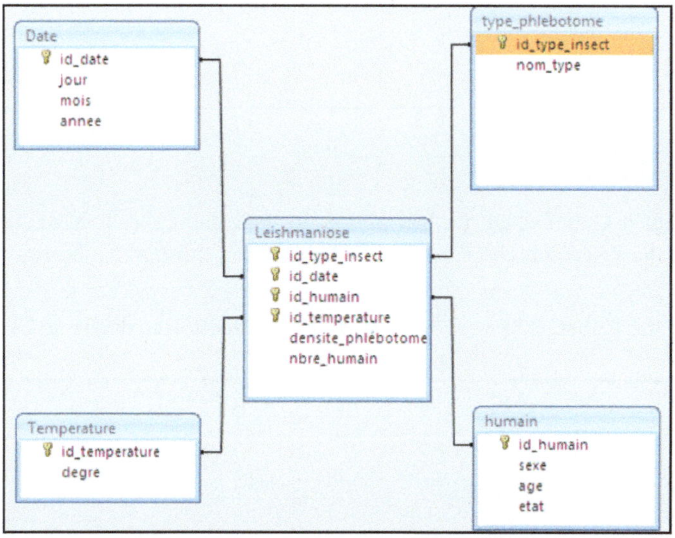

Figure 5. The model data warehouse diagram.

The model chosen must comply with the requirements and needs of use, in our case, we opted for a star pattern respecting the nature of the information we have.

Dimension Tables: Date, Temperature, Sandflies (P. Sergenti, S. Minuta, S. Fallax, P. Logicuspis, P. Papatasi), Human.

Fact Table: Leishmaniose.

Data is extracted from Excel files using java code. The program consists of two classes, one for extraction and one for export useful data to the database.

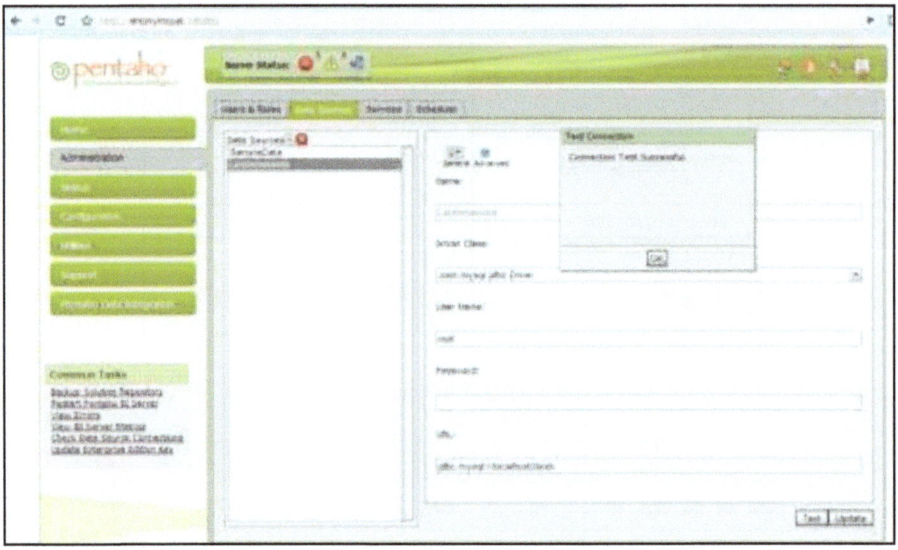

Dimensional Cube

Pentaho integr a CubeDesign tool, it allows to have the cube in XML format and to publish it in the User Pentaho Console. Cube creation through 5 steps as shown in the below:

Step 1. With the CubeDesigner we establish the connection to database Leishmaniose.

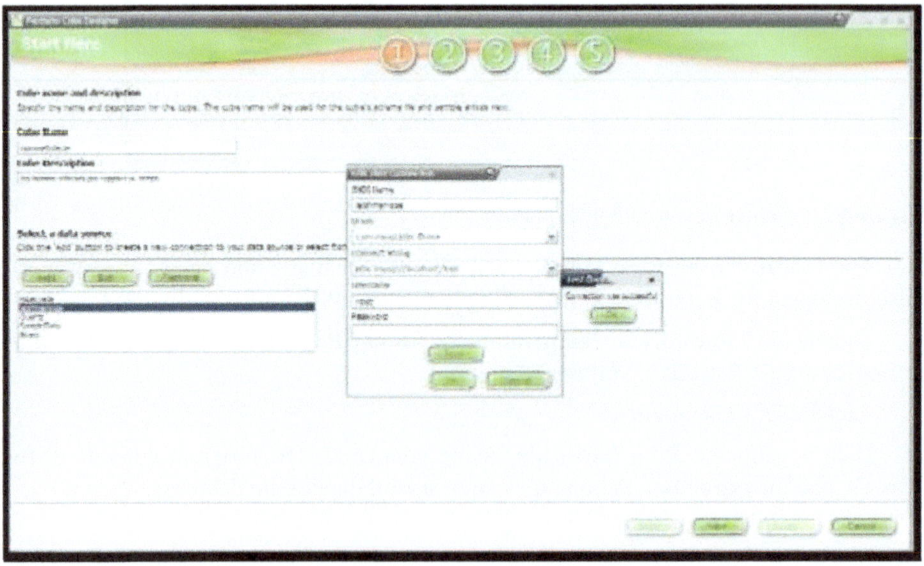

Step 2. Select tables and views useful to visualize the Cube. For example, to calculate the density of the P. Sergenti and the infected human in a fixed interval time.

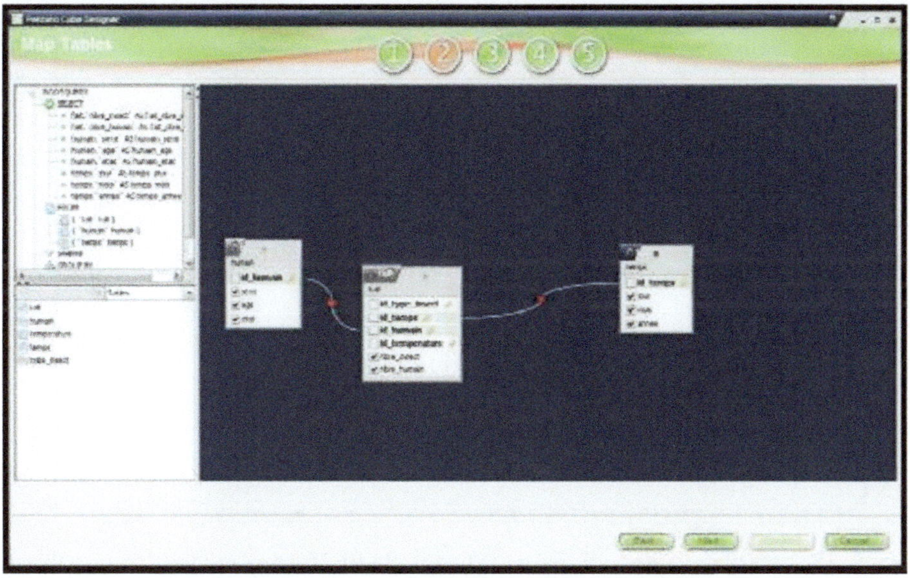

Step 3. Choose of the measures: Infected human

Step 4. All the dimensions and their aggregation will be specified via the interface below.

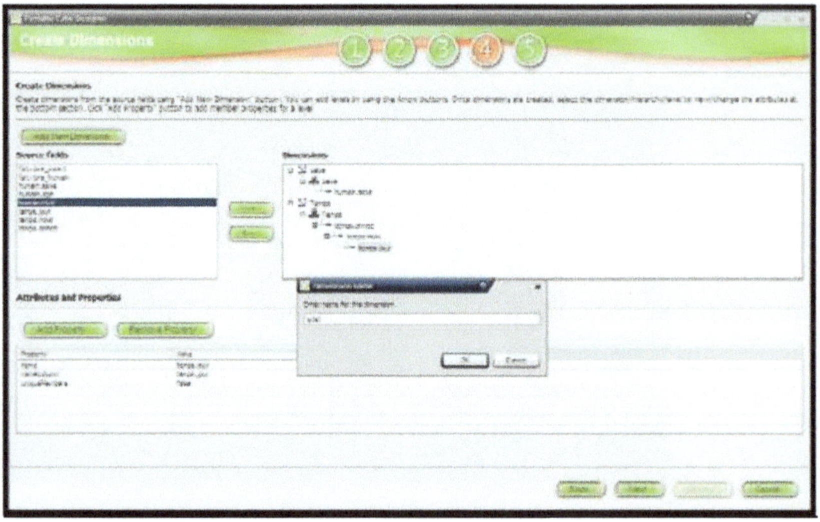

Step 5. The interface below allows us to view the file for the model; it's possible to update it as needed.

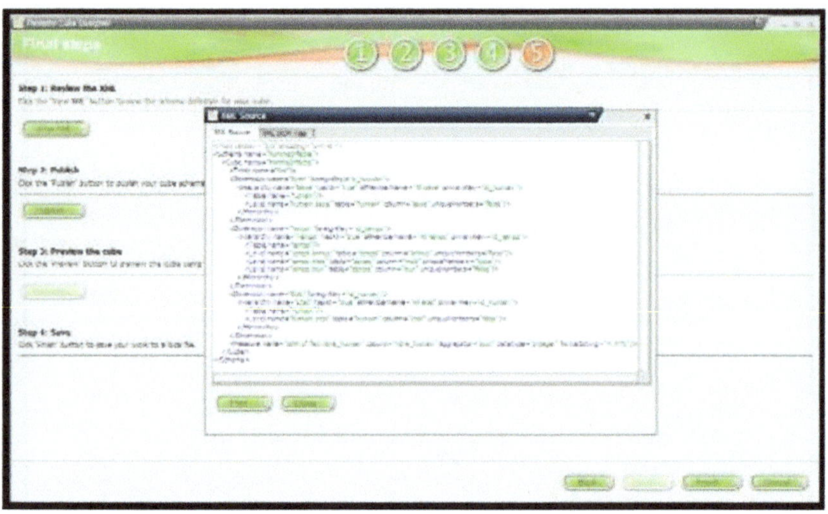

Finally, the pattern is saved.

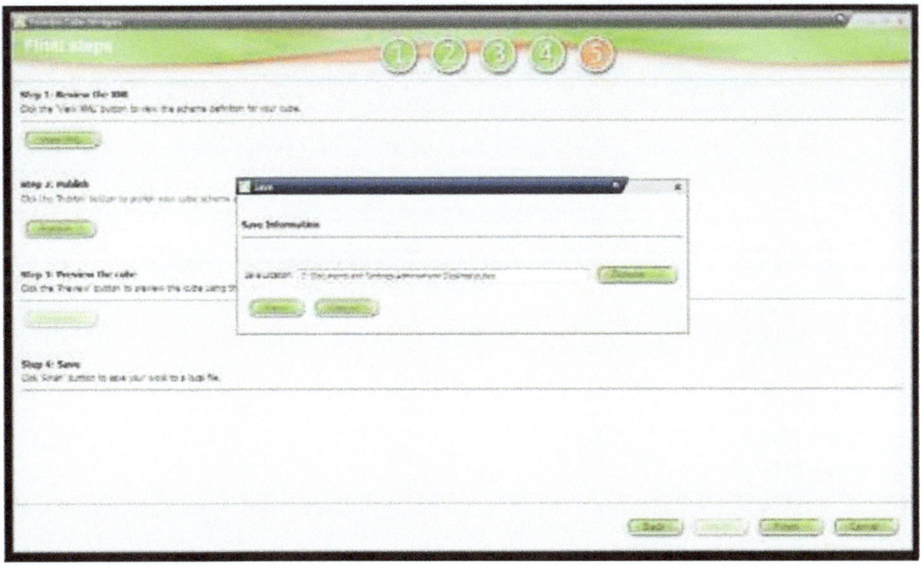

Tree files are generated : (a) Xml file to save the pattern produced by CubeDesigner. (b) Properties file : for the allocation of the database. (c) Xaction file : presents a set of all protocols to data access.

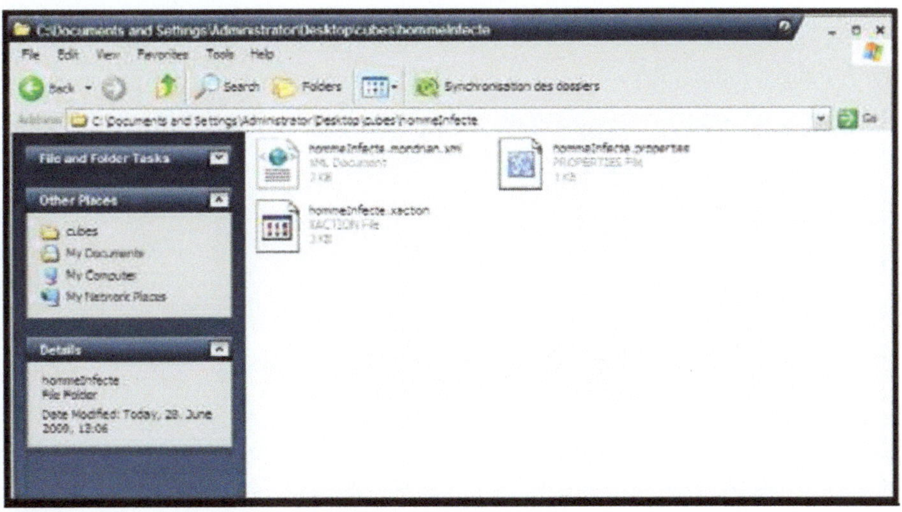

Pattern Publication with Workbench

Workben is a tool to create diagrams, for our case it is just used to refine and publish the pattern designed by CubeDesigner.

Step 1. Configuration of the Workbench references to establish connection to database.

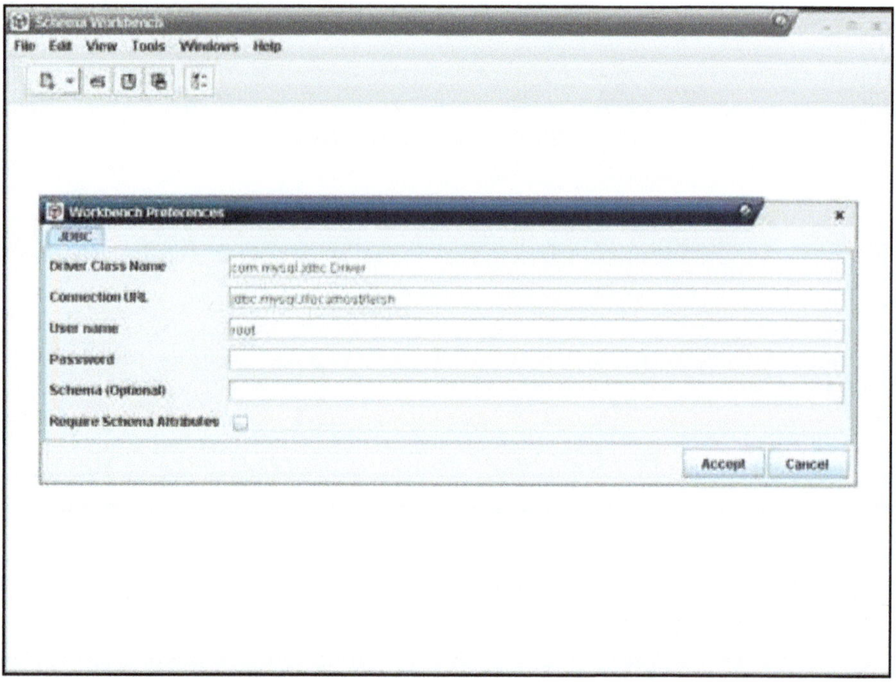

Step 2. Pattern raffinement.

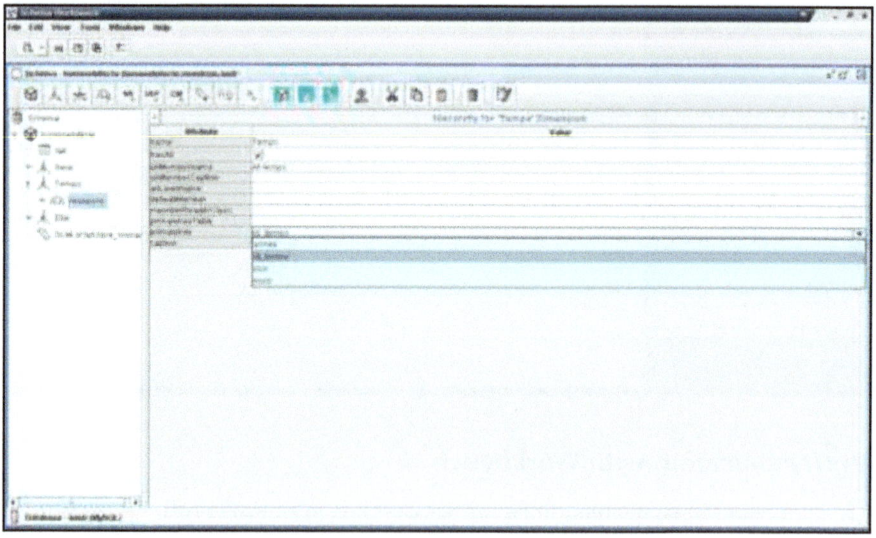

Step 3. Now, it is important to have URL for the host user, The password for the publisher and The login and password of the user server.

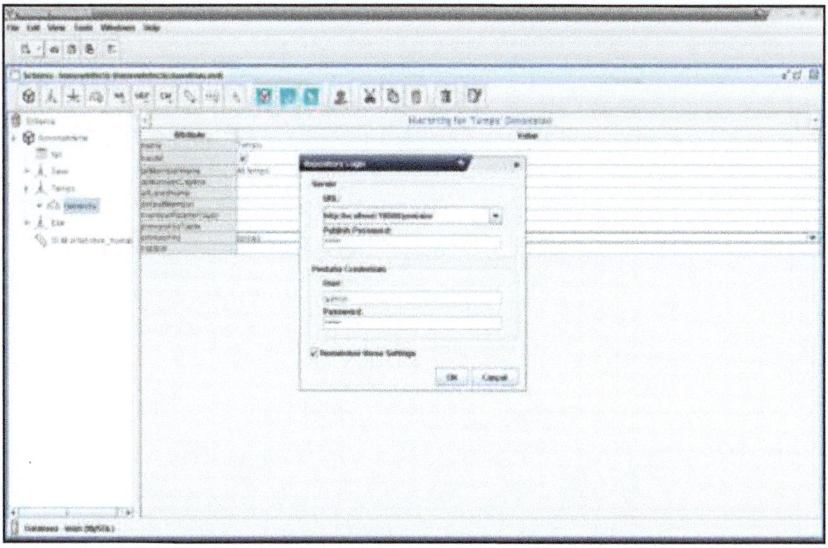

Visualization Phase

'User Console' tool gives different views of the pattern previously published.

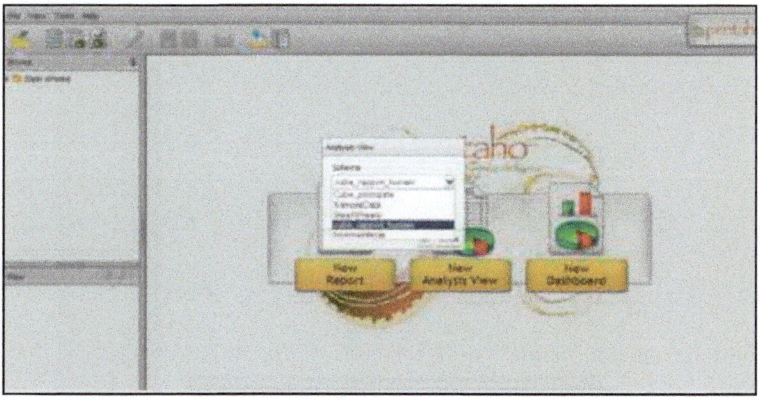

It's possible to have several modes to visualize data from database. As illustrated in the following figures.

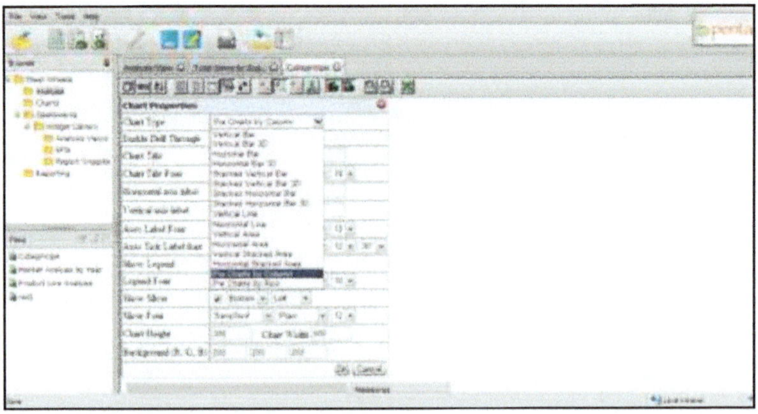

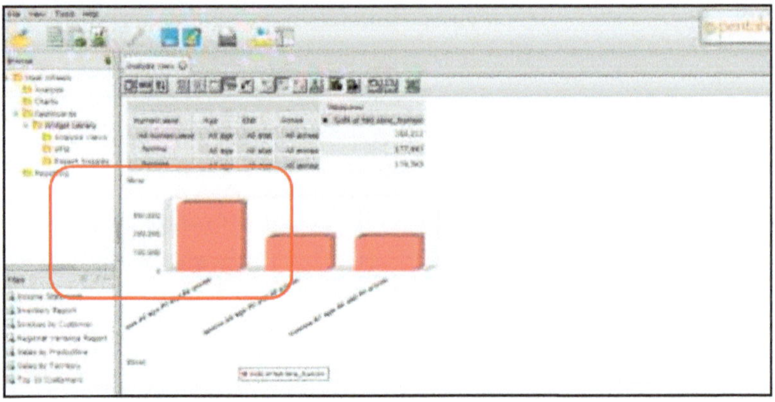

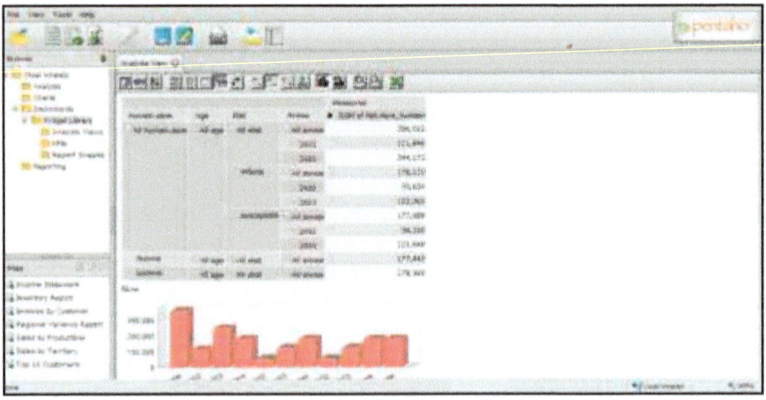

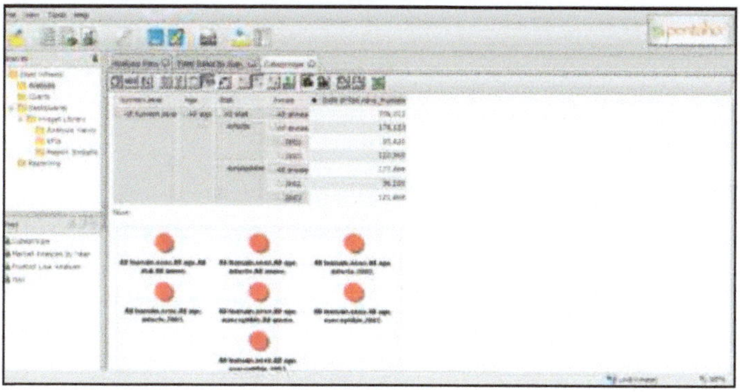

The hearlth professional may use OLAP concept to fialter and visualize other type of information.

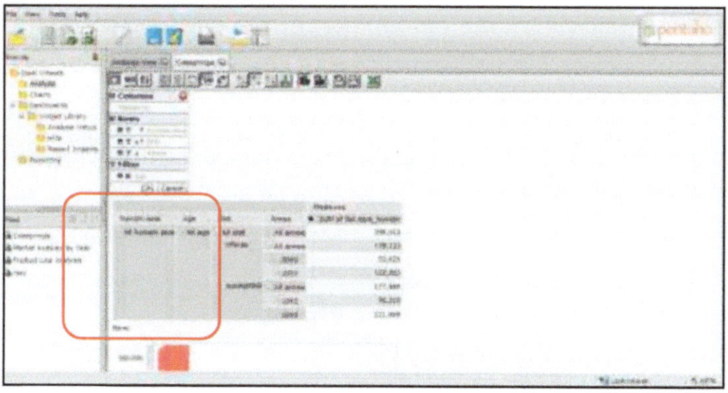

DATA MINING: APPLICATION TO THE LEISHMANIASIS

Given the seriousness of leishmaniasis in Morocco, it was essential to deploy easy methods to reduce its exploitable spread if not eradicate it completely. Our proposal aims to exploit tools of data mining process on this infectious disease. By definition, the data mining attempts to extract knowledge from vast volumes of data.

The wealth of information transmitted on vectors of disease allows us to apply these tools to identify methods and anticipate behavior, therefore, make a good decision.

K-Means and Deployment

The technologies that are on the market, offers comprehensive platforms and integrated data analysis to meet all requests of indicators developed in the industry. We are able to accede to any type of data stored in our data base, to implement operations to analyze the data and present results in a need predefined by the user. The software that we have developed our application offers a wide range of approaches ranging from methods of descriptive statistical analysis to predictive modeling methods. The first step is to create a new diagram and import the data as shown in the screenshot below.

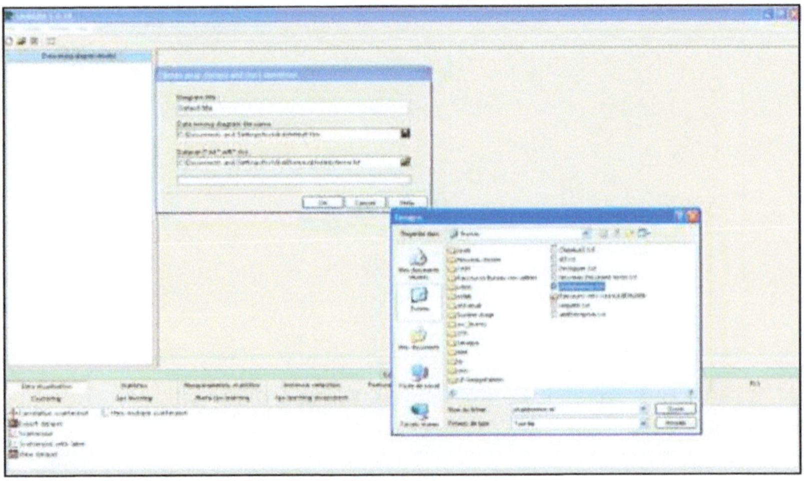

Descriptive Statistics

We can do descriptive statistics to variables. We calculate the frequency histograms on all columns to count the number of active and additional comments.

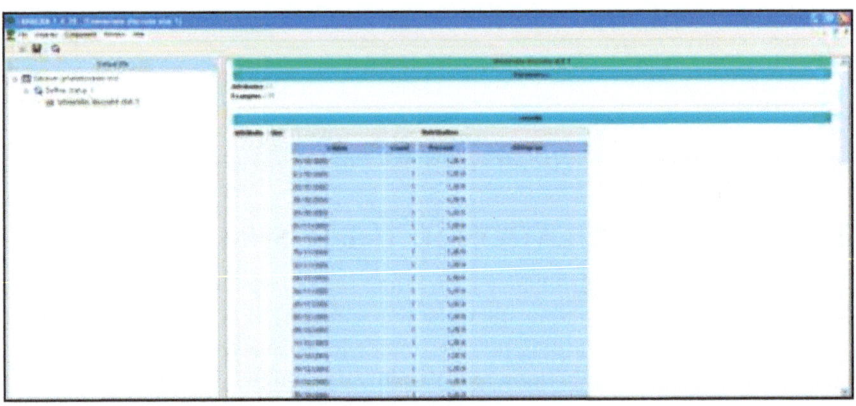

Method Principal Component Analysis (ACP)

They are three categories of data mining algorithms: supervised methods, unsupervised methods and methods of data reduction. Each category is based on a number of techniques. In this section, we chose the third type using the method of principal component analysis (ACP).

Given a set of observations described by variables exclusively digital (x1, x2, ..., xp), the APC aims to describe the same data set with new variables in reduced numbers. These new variables will be linear combinations of original variables. Principal component analysis can therefore be seen as a technique to reduce dimensionality.

Visualization of our Data

To implement the ACP method, we can see, for example, date and temperature data concerning P. longicuspis. After we define an analysis of the variables studied. The result is given in the following figure:

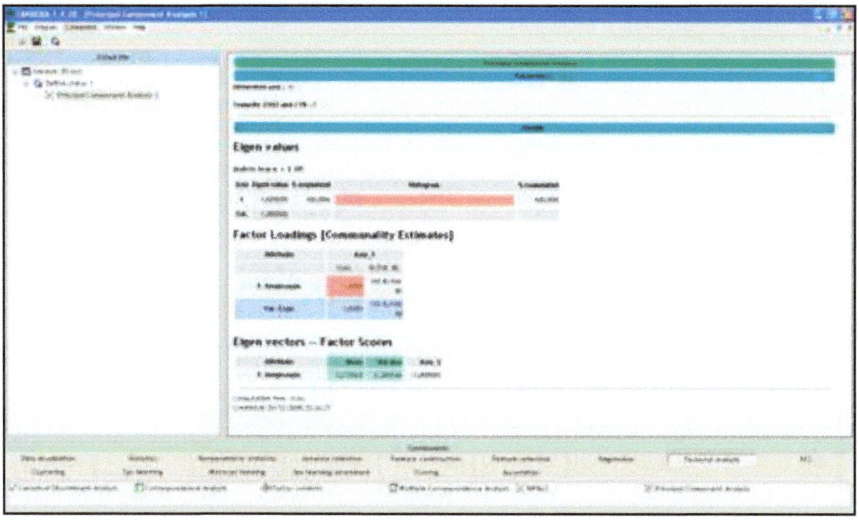

To better assess the relative positions to sandflies in the first factorial design, we add the component display. We put abscissa variable representing the first axis, calculated using the ACP, and ordered the second axis. We get the point cloud :

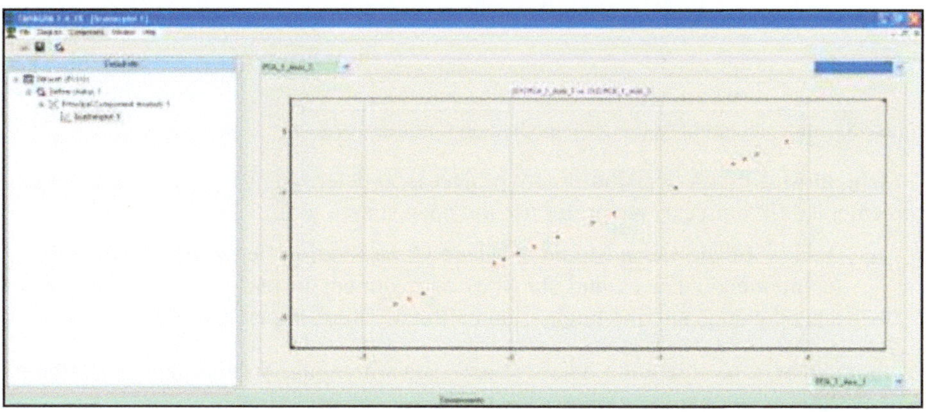

Figure 6. Point cloud data on (date, temperature, for P. longicuspis).

Among the variables are, we want to check the effect of the variable date that can distort our results. We will color the points according to this variable, we select as a variable component as is shown in this illustrative visualization.

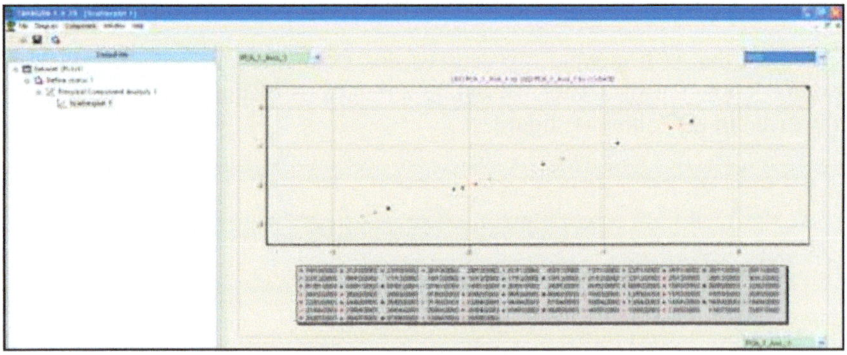

Figure 7. Using the date_format as illustrative variable.

Now we apply the ACP method on all data:

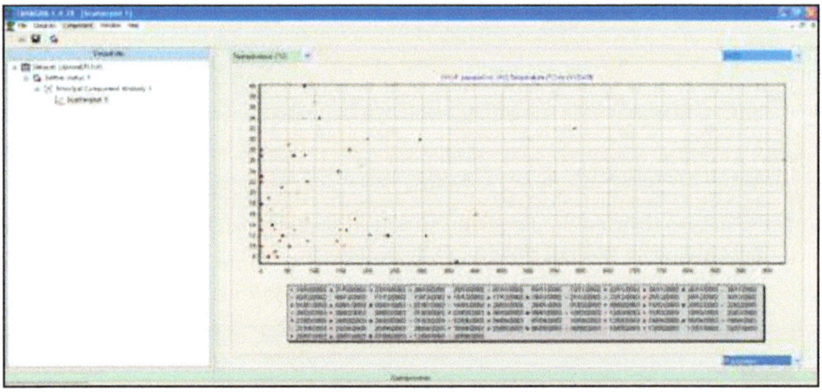

Figure 8. Implementation of the ACP method on sandflies data.

The most difficult decision in any project is to determine what method should be implemented. In our case, we prefer use the open source tools:

a. ETL « Talend Open Studio » Talend Open Studio offer: A complete range of components, Traces and statistics of treatment in real time, the addition of specific code and the integration on the decisional open source.

b. MySQL to create the database and data warehouse for the persistent storage area.

c. Pentaho BI Suite: cover many areas of Business intelligence through various software (owned by Pentaho or integrated into).

d. Pentaho Analysis (Mondrian + JPivot), Cube Designe, schema Workbench. For analysis OLAP

e. Open source data mining software Tanagra.

DISCUSSION

Our investigations were conducted in Akioud, an urban district in Marrakech city, during one-year-study. This site was selected, considering the presence, of all the sandfly species inventoried in the urban area of Marrakech (Boussaa et all, 2007).

According to the correlation between the weekly density of the three vectors (P. papatasi, P. sergenti and P. longicuspis) and the factor R0, we can prevent the risk of leishmaniasis in this area.

a. For P. papatasi population, R0 factor is superior to 1 during two periods of the year: November and May-June-July, which correspond to the periods of risk of zoonotic cutanous leishmaniais caused by L. major in this area.

b. For P. sergenti population, R0 is superior to 1 during the period of July–August and inferior to 1 in the rest of the year. So, this period corresponds to the phase of risk of anthroponotic cutanous leishmaniais caused by L. tropica in this area. We observe that R0 reaches its peak during the period of August when the temperature is very high.

c. For P. longicuspis, the results have shown two periods of risk of visceral leishmaniasis in this area: October and May-June.

(Boussaa et all, 2005) classified Marrakech area as being at risk of cutaneous leishmaniasis because of the high density of P. papatasi throughout the year, its position close to the cutaneous leishmaniasis foci in the arid region (Rioux et all, 1986) and the omnipresence of Meriones shawi, main L. major reservoir host in Morocco. In this work, we approve the conclusion of [Boussaa et all, 2005) and we exploit these data to assist in the decision on the issue of the fight against leishmaniasis in Morocco.

Indeed, these are spatio-temporal models which permit to follow and control the evolution of leishmaniasis in terms of time and region, and to find the appropriate threshold of the population of sandflies for stopping the multiplication of the disease. In Chichaoua (70 Km from Marrakech city), focus of anthroponotic cutanous leishmaniais, (Bacaër and Guernaoui, 2006) suggest that the epidemic could be stopped if the vector population were reduced by a factor (R0)2 = 3.76.

CONCLUSION

To fight against the spread of the cutaneous and visceral leishmaniasis and to address the need of the responsible for population health to set the policies that determine the nature of health care provided, and most importantly, for fast evaluation of the severity of the multiplication of the disease, we proposed to develop a model of data warehouse to storage appropriate data of the sandflies seasonality and the information about the susceptible human (patient with suspected Leishmania infection). Then, structural key and functional parameters will be measured to ensure the advanced treatment. By employing data mining process we have the ability to extract knowledge and to generate summaries for better health decision-making. Through this complete and operational platform, it will be easy to control the sandflies seasonality and the rate of the transmission disease.

REFERENCES

1. P. Degoulet et M. Fieschi (1998). *Informatique et santé Collection, Paris, Springer-Verlag*, Volume 10, Gilbert Saporta (2004). Data mining ou fouille de données, RST « Epidémiologie » *Data Mining.*
2. Daniel T. Larose (adaptation française T. Vallaud) (2005). Des données à la connaissance : Une introduction au data-mining (1Cédérom), *Vuibert.*
3. René Lefébure et Gilles Venturi (2001). Data Mining : Gestion de la relation client, personnalisations de site web, *Eyrolles*, mars 2001.
4. Pascal Poncelet, Florent Masseglia and Maguelonne Teisseire (Editors) (2007). Data Mining Patterns: New Methods and Applications, Information Science Reference, ISBN: 978-1599041629, October 2007.
5. Stéphane Tufféry (2007). Data Mining et Statistique Décisionnelle, Technip, nouvelle édition revue et enrichie, juin 2007.
6. Egmont-Petersen, M., de Ridder, D., Handels, H. (2002). Image processing with neural networks -a review. *Pattern Recognition 35*: pp. 2279–2301. doi: 10.1016/S0031-3203(01)00178-9. 2002.
7. Boussaa, S., Guernaoui, S., Pesson, B., Boumezzough, A. (2005). Seasonal fluctuations of phlebotomine sand fly populations (Diptera: Psychodidae) in the urban area of Marrakech, Morocco. pp. 86–91, *Acta Trop.* 95.
8. Boussaa, S., Pesson, B., Boumezzough, A. (2007). Phlebotomine sandflies (Diptera: Psychodidae) of Marrakech city, Morocco. pp. 715-724, *Ann. Trop. Med. Parasitol.* 101.
9. WHO (2005). Lutte contre les leishmanioses. *Série de Rapports Techniques.*
10. Rhajaoui, M., Fellah, H., Pratlong, F., Dedet, J.P., Lyagoubi, M. (2004). Leishmaniasis due to Leishmania tropica MON-102 in a new Moroccan focus. *Trans. R. Soc. Trop. Med. Hyg.* 98, pp. 299–301.
11. Teh and All (2009). Development of a Data warehouse for Lymphoma Cancer Diagnosis and Treatment Decision Support. *Proceedings of the 10th WSEAS International Conference on MATHEMATICS and COMPUTERS in BIOLOGY and CHEMISTRY,* Pp. 15 _24. ISSN: 1790-5125, ISBN: 978-960-474-062-8.
12. Abonnenc E. (1972). Les phlébotomes de la région éthiopienne (Diptera: Phlebotomidae). *Mémoire de l'ORSTOM.* 55, pp. 1–289.
13. Bacaër, N., Guernaoui, S. (2006). The epidemic threshold of a simple seasonal model of cutaneous leishmaniasis. *J. Math. Biol.* 53, pp. 421–436.
14. Boussaa, S., Boumezzough, A., Remy, P. E., Glasser, N., Pesson, B. (2008). Morphological and isoenzymatic differentiation of Phlebotomus perniciosus and Phlebotomus longicuspis (Diptera: Psychodidae) in Southern Morocco. *Acta*

Trop. 106, pp. 184– 189.

15. Boussaa, S., Pesson, B., Boumezzough, A. (2009). Faunistic study of the sandflies (Diptera: Psychodidae) in an emerging focus of cutaneous leishmaniasis in Al Haouz province, Morocco. *Ann. Trop. Med. Parasitol*. 103, pp. 73-83.
16. Guernaoui, S., Boumezzough, A., Pesson, B., Pichon, G. (2005). Entomological investigations in Chichaoua: an emerging epidemic focus of cutaneous leishmaniasis in Morocco. J. *Med. Entomol*. 42, pp. 697–701.
17. Guessous-Idrissi, N., Chiheb, S., Hamdani, A., Riyad, M., Bichichi, M., Hamdani, S.,
18. Krimech, A. (1997). Cutaneous leishmaniasis: an emerging epidemic focus of Leishmania tropica in north Morocco. *Trans. R. Soc. Trop. Med. Hyg*. 91, pp. 660–663.
19. Pratlong, F., Rioux, J.A., Dereure, J., Mahjour, J., Gallego, M., Guilvard, E., Lanotte, G., Périères, J., Martini, A., Saddiki, A. (1991). Leishmania tropica au Maroc. IV. *Diversité isozymique intrafocale. Ann. Parasitol. Hum. Comp. 66*, pp. 100–104.
20. Ramaoui, K., Guernaoui, S., Boumezzough, A. (2008). Entomological and epidemiological study of a new focus of cutaneous leishmaniasis in Morocco. *Parasitol.* Res. 103, pp. 859-863.
21. Rioux, J.A., et all (1986). Les leishmanioses cutanées du bassin méditerranéen occidental: del'identification enzymatique à l'analyse éco-épidemiologique, l'exemple de trois 'foyers', tunisien, marocain et français. Montpellier, France: *Institut Méditerranéen d'Etudes* Épidémiologiques *et Ecologiques*. pp. pp.365–395.
22. Hang Xaio, Xiubin Zhang (2008). Comparison Studies on Classification for Remote Sensing Image Based on Data Mining Method, *WSEAS TRANSACTIONS on COMPUTERS*. Volume 7, ISSN: 1109-2750, pp. 552 558.

16
CHAPTER

DATA WAREHOUSE TECHNOLOGY AND APPLICATION IN DATA CENTRE DESIGN FOR E-GOVERNMENT

Xuanzi Hu

INTRODUCTION

E-government allows governments to service citizens in a more timely, effective, and cost-efficient method. E- Government services focus on four main customers: citizens, the business community, government employees, and government agencies. E -government can provide four types of services, which are Government-to-Citizen (G2C), Government-to-Business (G2B), Government-to-Employee (G2E), and Government-to-Government (G2G). E-government system has already been very popular all over the world, because E-government helps to disseminate information. Further, it aids in the collection of information that helps decision makers serve citizens more effectively. E-Government allows government agencies to centralize decision making.

China have started first E-Government program in the late 1980s, in which the governments both at central and local levels built up office automation (OA) systems and established an intranet, subsequently the Central Government of China had formally launched five Golden Projects (Golden Bridge Project, Golden Customs Project, Golden Card Project, Golden Tax Project and Government online Project) aimed at building E-Government in China ever since 1990s. After realizing five Golden Projects, Chinese government has set ambitious visions in the implementation of E-Government: quicken the pace of change in government functions to suit the requirement of reform, opening up and modernization policies, improve the performance of government operation, introduce new government measures in a scientific manner and more effective mechanisms to monitor the economic activities, place a greater emphasis on central co-ordination and transparency of government work, carry out administrative

Citation: Xuanzi Hu (2010). Data Warehouse Technology and Application in Data Center Design for E-government, E-learning Experiences and Future, Safeeullah Soomro (Ed.), InTech, DOI: 10.5772/8800.

functions in accordance with law and provide better service for the public. To meet above ambitious visions, the Central Government of China have programmed to establish four governance information resource databases in next five years, governance information resource databases consist of four databases: population basic information database, judicial entity basic information database, natural resource and geography basic information database, and macroscopically economy database.

A data warehouse has been defined as a collection of data in support of management decisions which is: subject oriented, integrated, nonvolatile, time variant. Data warehouse, as a collection of database or data management technologies, emerged in the early 1990s. The data warehouse has now been more generally seen as a strategy to bring heterogeneous data together under a common conceptual and technical umbrella and to make the data available for new operation or decision support application. Three intrinsic features of data warehouse are data integration, data completeness and decision-making support. Management of government is from top to down, but collecting data of government is from down to top. To support construction of four databases, building data center is becoming an important project for E- government. Nanhai city of Guangdong province is a leading the way of E-government in China, this chapter put forward the design of data center based on data warehouse technology for Nanhai city, this solution not only consider to provide data for high level four databases, but also solve integration, share and exchange of data in various departments of Nanhai city, especially devised application database based on data warehouse technology for better utilizing accumulated data.

The remainder of this chapter is organized as follows. The section 2 provides an introduction to the basic technology of data warehouse for reader to understand explicitly data center design. In the following sections, data center design of Nanhai city is depicted. In section 3, we summarize requirement analysis of data center. In Section 4, we give the architecture of data center based on data warehouse technology. Section 5 gives some pivotal techniques of realizing data center. Finally, Section 6 gives the conclusion.

DATA WAREHOUSE TECHNOLOGY

Definition of Data Warehouse

A data warehouse is a subject oriented, integrated, non-volatile, and time-variant collection of data in support of management decisions. The goal of using a data warehouse is to allow businesses and organizations to make strategic decisions. According to the definition of a data warehouse, a data warehouse generally has following four characteristics.

a) Subject-Oriented

Subject-Oriented means that the main objective of data warehouse is to facilitate decision process of a company, and within any company data naturally concentrates around subject areas, so information gathering in data warehouse is aiming for a specific subject rather than for the functions of a company.

b) Integrated

Being integrated means that the data is collected within the data warehouse, that can come from different tables, databases or even servers, but can be combined into one unit that is relevant and logical for convenience of making strategic decision.

c) Non-volatile

Being the snapshot of operational data on a given specific time, the data in the data warehouses should be stable. The data in the data warehouse usually be added, but it should rarely be deleted.

d) Time-variant

Time-variant means that all the data within the data warehouse can be found with a given period of time.

Architecture of Data Warehouse

Data warehouses and their architectures vary depending upon the specifics of an organization's situation. Many architectures of data warehouse exists in the literature, According to study of Thilini Ariyachandra and Hugh J. Watson, Data Warehouse has five architectures: (1) independent data marts, (2) data mart bus architecture with linked dimensional data marts, (3) hub-and-spoke, (4) centralized data warehouse (no dependent data marts), and (5) federated. Other architectures tend to be variations on the five.

(1) Independent data marts

This architecture is common for organizational units to develop their own data marts. These marts are independent of other marts. These marts typically have inconsistent data definitions and use different dimensions and measures, so the architecture is difficult to analyze data across all the marts. Figure 1 shows the architecture for independent data marts.

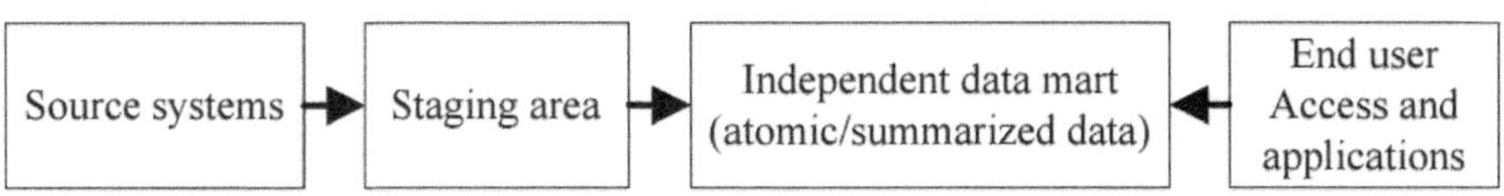

Figure 1. The independent data marts architecture.

(2) Data mart bus architecture with linked dimensional data marts

A business requirements analysis for a specific business process is the foundation for this architecture. The first mart is built for a single business process using dimensions and measures that will be used with other marts. Additional marts are developed using these dimensions and measures, which results in logically integrated marts and an enterprise view of the data. Atomic and summarized data are maintained in the marts and are organized in a star schema to provide a dimensional view of the data. This architecture is illustrated in Figure 2.

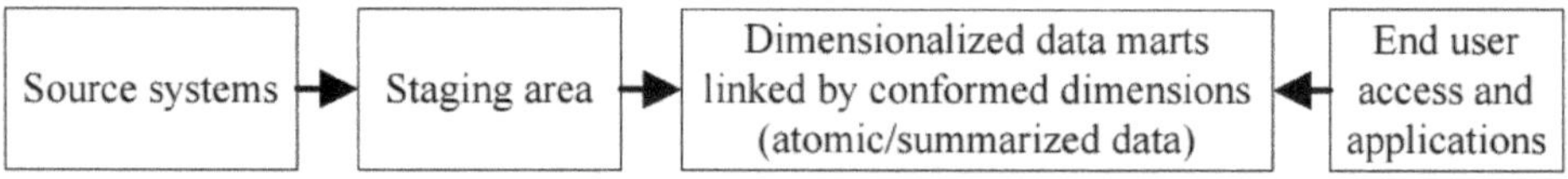

Figure 2. The data mart bus architecture with linked dimensional data marts.

(3) Hub-and-spoke

An extensive enterprise-level analysis of data requirements provides the basis for this architecture. Attention is also focused on building a scalable and maintainable infrastructure. Using the enterprise view of the data, the architecture is developed in an iterative manner, subject area by subject area. Atomic level data is maintained in the warehouse in third normal form. Dependent data marts are created that source data from the warehouse. The dependent data marts may be developed for departmental, functional area, or special purposes and may have normalized, de-normalized, or summarized/atomic dimensional data structures based on user needs. Most users query the dependent data marts. Figure 3 shows this architecture.

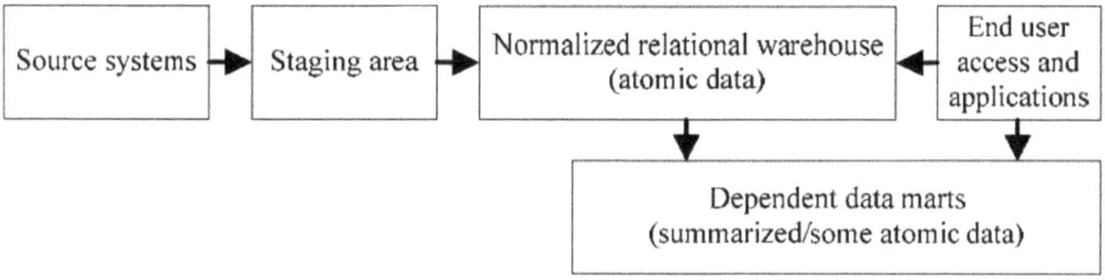

Figure 3. The hub and spoke architecture.

(4) Centralized data warehouse (no dependent data marts)

This architecture is similar to the hub and spoke architecture except that there are no dependent data marts. The warehouse contains atomic level data, some summarized data, and logical dimensional views of the data. Queries and applications access data from both the relational data and the dimensional views. This architecture is typically a logical rather than a physical implementation of the hub and spoke architecture. This architecture is shown in Figure 4.

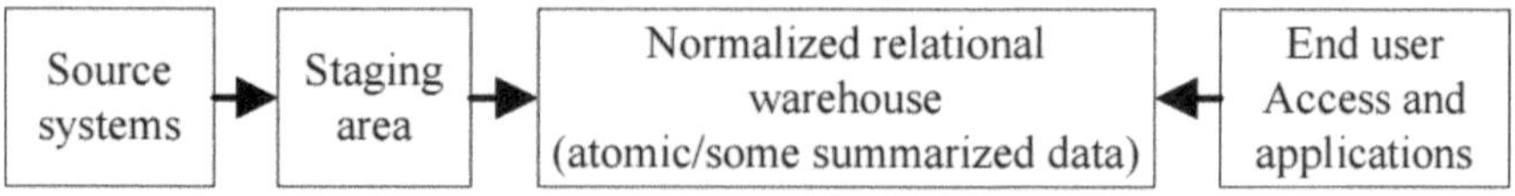

Figure 4. The centralized data warehouse architecture.

(5) Federated

This architecture is advocated as a practical solution for firms that have a pre -existing, complex decision support environment and do not want to rebuild. Based on business requirements, data is accessed from existing data warehouse, data marts, and legacy systems. The data is either logically or physically integrated using shared keys, global metadata, distributed queries or other methods. This architecture is shown in Figure 5.

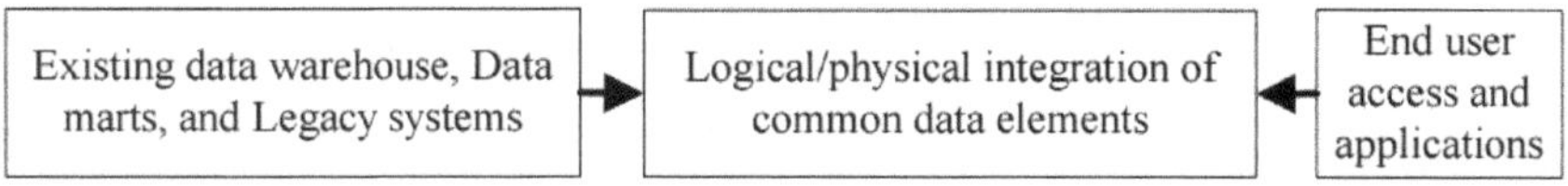

Figure 5. The Federated Architecture

Building of data warehouse

Building a data warehouse is only extracting the operational data and entering it into the data warehouse (Inmon, 2007), which sounds simple. However, creating a data warehouse is more than that. Extracting data, analysis data, and presentation result are a complex problem. The major steps of building data warehouse are described.

a) Data collection

The very first step before you start to build data warehouse, the data source will be identified. You need to figure out what are the data that are required to be put into your data warehouse. The data in the warehouse usually come from a number of source systems. Most of the data have been stored originally in transactional databases. External data may be stored in spreadsheets or personal databases. In some cases, source data may be collected automatically. If new data are required, a suitable system may need to be built to collect them. Otherwise, only minor changes should be needed to existing systems. In all cases, the owners of source data are responsible for maintaining quality, and this may require substantial effort.

b) Transformation & cleansing

This can be the most time consuming part where you need to grab the data from various data source and store it into the staging database. In this process, data are usually restructured to optimize subsequent use for querying, reporting and analysis. This is often done in stages, in a data staging area. These data feeds need to be run on a regular basis to keep the data warehouse up-to-date. To minimize disruption to other systems, and warehouse users, this often has to be completed within a tight overnight time window. Task of this stage is very hard and time-consuming, and usually can be done with the help of ETL tools.

c) Aggregation & analysis

Selected data are taken from the central warehouse using query tools and processed to produce useful results. Often, the most frequently accessed data are first summarized and stored in data marts to improve response times. Additional performance measures are typically derived at the same time. Analytic applications may also be developed to help users get useful information.

d) Presentation

Presentation is displaying results for end users, usually in the form of reports. Several different report types are normally needed to suit different types of user. The results might appear as text, tables or charts and could be viewed on-line, printed, published on a web server or distributed by email.

Tools of Data Warehouse

Developing data warehouse is a very complex and time-consuming task. In the process of building data warehouse, many tools can help developer to build data warehouse. According to purpose, data warehouse tools can be divided into ETL tools, OLAP tools, report tools, data mining tools, and database management systems (DBMS). These tools are introduced as following. Many materials get from official website of products.

ETL tools

IBM WebSphere DataStage delivers three key capabilities necessary for success in enterprise data integration: the most comprehensive connectivity to easily and quickly access any source or target system; advanced development and maintenance tools, which speed implementation and simplify administration; and a scalable platform that can easily handle today's massive volumes of corporate data. WebSphere DataStage is an industry-leading data integration and transformation product that provides advanced development and maintenance capabilities for virtually unsurpassed levels of productivity.

Teradata Parallel Transporter was designed for increased functionality and customer ease of use for faster, easier and deeper integration. The capabilities include: Simplified data transfer between one Teradata Database and another; Ability to load dozens of files using a single script makes development and maintenance of the data warehouse easier; Distribution of workloads across CPUs on the load server eliminates bottlenecks in the data load process.; The open database connectivity (ODBC) operator reads from the ODBC driver, which could pull data from any database; for example, DB2 or Oracle; Accessibility to myriad data sources via open standards is possible.

SAS ETL Studio is a visual design tool for building, implementing and managing ETL and data integration processes from source to destination, regardless of data sources or platforms. In-depth data transformations are provided to efficiently meet enterprise data integration requirements and support business and analytic intelligence. It also improves quality management by providing impact analysis of potential changes made throughout the data management life cycle. SQL Server Integration Services (SSIS) is a component of Microsoft SQL Server. SSIS is only available in the "Standard" and "Enterprise" editions. SSIS provides a platform to build data integration and workflow applications. The primary use for SSIS is data warehousing, as the product features a fast and flexible tool for data extraction, transformation, and loading (ETL). The tool may also be used to automate maintenance of SQL Server databases, update multidimensional cube data, and perform other functions. Informatica PowerCenter is a single, unified enterprise data integration platform for accessing, discovering, and integrating data from virtually any business system, in any format, and delivering that data throughout the enterprise at any speed.

OLAP tools

Oracle Discoverer is an ad hoc query tool that operates in the Caltech data warehouse environment. Discoverer's desktop-reporting features provide users the ability to generate financial reports and analyze financial information easily and quickly. Discoverer has three main components: User Edition (it provides the graphical interface utilized by users on a day-to-day basis to generate reports and analyze data), Administration Edition (it is the tool used to design and present the hierarchy of financial data) and End User Layer (it shields users from the complexity of the relational database from which Discoverer retrieves data).

SQL Server Analysis Services (SSAS) is a part of the Microsoft SQL Server platform. It adds OLAP and data mining capabilities for SQL Server databases. The OLAP engine supports MOLAP, ROLAP and HOLAP storage modes for data. Analysis Services supports the XML for Analysis standard as the underlying communication protocol. The cube data can be accessed using MDX queries. Data mining specific functionality is exposed via the DMX query language. Analysis Services includes various algorithms - Decision trees, clustering algorithm, Naive Bayes algorithm, time series analysis, sequence clustering algorithm, linear and logistic regression analysis, and neural networks - for use in data mining.

DB2 OLAP Server is a strategic member of IBM's Business Intelligence family. It integrates the powerful OLAP engine and the application programming interfaces of Hyperion Essbase with IBM's DB2® family of relational databases. It provides a fast path to turn user's warehouse data into business insight. It is built for e-business with tools to help you quickly deploy Web-based analytical applications.

SAS OLAP Server is a multidimensional data store designed from the outset to provide quick access to pre-summarized data generated from vast amounts of detailed data. Decision makers need quick access to summarized data so they can make timely decisions based on knowledge instead of gut feelings.

BusinessObjects OLAP Intelligence is an On Line Analytical Processing (OLAP) application for analysis business data. It was previously known as Crystal Analysis Professional, it is part of BusinessObjects Crystal Decisions.

report tools

Cognos ReportNet is the first all-in-one reporting software that lets user create, modify and distribute any report – invoices, statements, weekly sales and inventory reports to list a few. User can standardize all enterprise reports, not simply with one vendor – with one product and architecture.

Crystal Reports Server is software product of SAS. Crystal Reports Server provides a complete report management solution that enables IT professionals to securely share, schedule, and deliver interactive reports over the Web, in e-mail, and in Microsoft

Office documents. It empowers business users to view, print and share more compelling reports.

Oracle Reports is Oracle's award-winning, high-fidelity enterprise reporting tool. It enables businesses to give immediate access to information to all levels within and outside of the organization in an unrivaled scalable and secure environment. Oracle Reports consists of Oracle Reports Developer (a component of the Oracle Developer Suite) and Oracle Application Server Reports Services (a component of the Oracle Application Server).

SQL Server Reporting Services is a report generation environment for data gathered from SQL Server databases. It is administered via a web interface. Reporting services features a web services interface to support the development of custom reporting applications. Reports are created as RDL files. Once created, RDL files can be rendered in a variety of formats including Excel, PDF, CSV, XML, TIFF (and other image formats), and HTML Web Archive.

Data mining tools

IBM Intelligent Miner can help user detect fraud, segment your customers, and simplify market basket analysis. IBM's in-database mining capabilities integrate with existing systems to provide scalable, high performing predictive analysis without moving your data into proprietary data mining platforms. Use SQL, Web Services, or Java to access DB2's data mining capabilities from own applications or business intelligence tools from IBM's business partners.

Oracle Data Miner is the graphical user interface for Oracle Data Mining that helps data analysts mine their Oracle data to find valuable hidden information, patterns, and new insights. Data analysts can mine data with Oracle Data Miner's easy-to-use wizards that guide them through the data preparation, data mining, model evaluation, and model scoring process. Oracle Data Miner can automatically generate code needed to transform the data mining steps into an integrated data mining/BI application.

SAS Enterprise Miner streamlines the data mining process to create highly accurate predictive and descriptive models based on analysis of vast amounts of data from across the enterprise. Enterprise Miner Support the entire data mining process with a broad set of tools, for example, association, clustering, decision-tree, neural network, classical regression technology.

Teradata Warehouse Miner provides an array of data profiling and mining functions ranging from data exploration and transformation to analytic model development and deployment that are performed directly in Teradata Database. Teradata warehouse miner allows you to analyze detailed data without data movement, streamlining the data mining process.

Database management systems

Database management systems (DBMS) can be divided into two categories -- desktop databases and server databases. Generally speaking, Data warehouse applications adopt server database, such as Microsoft SQL Server, Oracle and IBM DB2, which offer organizations the ability to manage large amounts of data efficiently and in a manner that enables many users to access and update the data simultaneously.

Microsoft SQL Server is a relational model database server produced by Microsoft. Its primary query languages are T-SQL and ANSI SQL.

Oracle Database (commonly referred to as Oracle) consists of a relational database management system (RDBMS) produced and marketed by Oracle Corporation. Its primary query languages are Plus/SQL and ANSI SQL.

DB2 is a "Relational Database Management System" (RDBMS), DB2 is designed to make the storage and analysis of data easier. All access to and manipulation of data in DB2 is accomplished via SQL.

Sybase IQ is a highly optimized analytics server designed specifically to deliver faster results for mission-critical business intelligence, data warehouse and reporting solutions on any standard hardware and operating systems. It works with diverse data – including unstructured data – and diverse data sources to deliver unsurpassed query performance at the lowest price/performance available.

Teradata Database is a relational model database server produced by Teradata. Its data models are Relational, ANSI SQL Compatible, Full Query Parallelism and Balanced Performance.

REQUIREMENT ANALYSIS OF DATA CENTER

Nanhai city of Guangdong province is the state-level pilot city for information-based. Consequently Nanhai city is listed as the pilot cities for Model Project of China's E-government Application. Nanhai city has successfully programmed and developed a series of E-government projects, including village management, finance decision-making, education, irrigation management, soil management, police management, etc., which vigorously promoted information-based construction in such fields as governments, rural areas, education, culture. With many system applications in every department, data exchange among departments, data share among departments and data integration application are becoming a big demand for improving greatly management efficiency and service standards. The relations of data provider and user for population data and for judicial entity data are depicted in Figure 6 and Figure 7, respectively.

To solve data share and exchange among departments, establishing data center is a prime method. Main requirements of data center are summarized as following:

Realizing data share and exchange in the various departments, supplying data collecting, processing and loading from data sources to data center, achieving centralized storage of government information resource, in favor of the higher level construction of four databases, offering integration application service for government, enterprises and citizens, Offering integration management for population information.

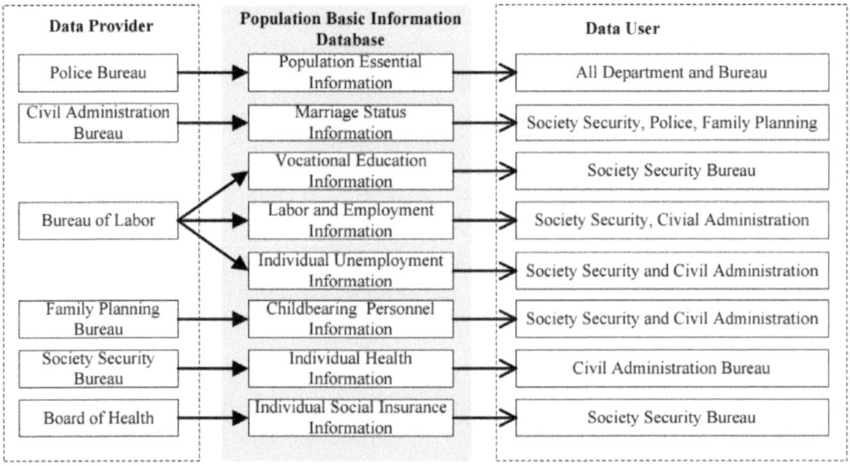

Figure 6. Relation of provider and user for population data.

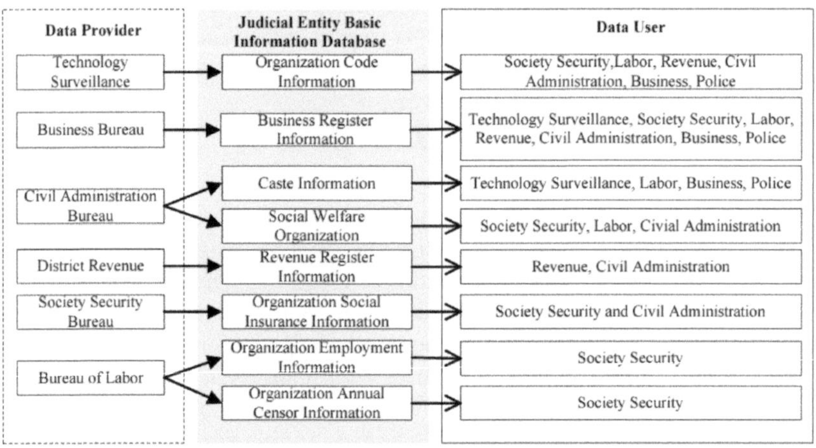

Figure 7. Relation of provider and user for judicial entity data.

ARCHITECTURE OF DATA CENTER BASED ON DATA WAREHOUSE TECHNOLOGY

The architecture of data center based on data warehouse is presented in Figure 8. Data center is composed of six main components: data share and exchange platform, kernel database, support application platform, application database, data center management platform, and data center security platform.

The very essence of the data warehouse is the flexible and unpredictable access of data. Thus, required is the ability to access data quickly and easily. If data is not efficiently indexed and users cannot access data rapidly, the data warehouse will not succeed. In addition, the data in the data warehouse needs to be able to be monitored at will. The cost of monitoring data cannot be so high and the complexity of monitoring data cannot be so hard that a monitoring program cannot be run whenever necessary. The data warehouse also needs to be able both to receive data from and pass data to the various departments of Nanhai city.

Data Share and Exchange Platform

Data share and exchange platform is made up of ETL (extraction, transformation and load) and data share agent. ETL is data provider for kernel data, which collects data from data source and load to kernel data. Data share agent deal with dispensing share data stored in kernel database into various departments that need data.

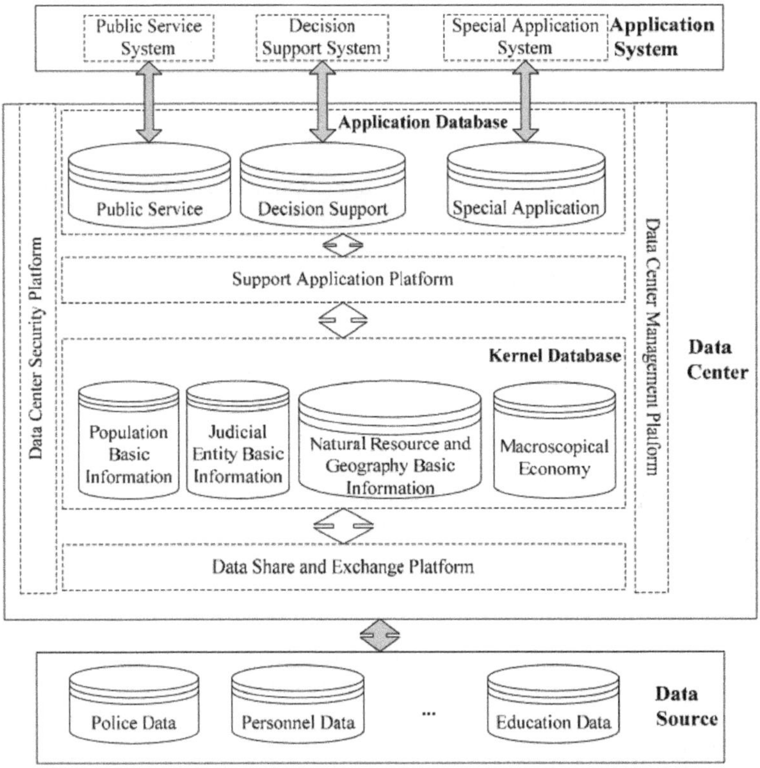

Figure 8. Architecture of Data Center.

Kernel Database

Kernel database of data center is composed of four parts: population basic information database, judicial entity basic information database, natural resource and geography basic information database, and macroscopical economy database, which is organized according to user requirements and is maintained by administrators of data center.

Support Application Platform

Support application platform is a secondary development tool possessed by data center, main function of which is establish special database by extracting data directly from kernel database according requirements of application.

Application Database

Application database may be treated as data mart, which is composed of three parts: public service database, decision support database and special application database. Data Special application database is provided by kernel database and source database according to application requirement. Application database is organized according to requirements of decision-making, which is maintained by both administrators of data center and department.

Data Center Management Platform

Its main function is to manage and control data center, including share management, exchange management, run management, log management, authorization management, backup management and recovery management.

Data Center Security Platform

To deal with alarming and unpredictable security threats, data center must consider security. Data center Security Platform is a base of other platform that monitors and protects data center.

KEY TECHNIQUES OF DATA CENTER

ETL Technique

The process of extracting data from data sources and bringing it into the kernel database is commonly called ETL, which stands for extraction, transformation, and loading. During Extraction, the desired data has to be identified and extracted from data sources. Very often, it is not possible to identify the specific subset of interest; therefore more data than necessary has to be extracted, since the identification of the relevant data will be done at a later point in time. The size of the extracted data varies from hundreds of kilobytes to hundreds of gigabytes, depending on the source system and the organization situation. Just as the size of the data extraction may vary widely, the frequency at which the data is extracted may also vary widely: the time span may vary between hours and minutes to near real-time. After extracting (and transporting) the data, the most challenging and time consuming parts of ETL follow: Transformation and Loading into the target system. This may include applying complex filters; validating the incoming data against information which already existing in target database tables; comparing new data to existing data in the data warehouse, to determine whether the new data needs to be inserted or updated; computing aggregations and other derived data based on the new data. Generally there are three kind approaches of ETL: transformation-then-load, load-then-transformation and transformation-while-load.

Data Storage Technique

Data storage techniques is very important and complicated for realizing goal of data center, to support future decision support system, star schema for the warehouse is adopted to build application databases. Every application database is composed of several fact tables and a set of dimensional tables, the fact table contains a list of all measures and points to the key value of the lowest level of each dimension. Each of these measurements is taken at the intersection of all dimensions. Dimensions are qualifiers that give meaning to measures.

They organize the data based on the what, when, and where components of a organization question. Dimensions are stored in dimension tables made up of dimensional elements and attributes. Each dimension is composed of related items or elements. Dimensions are hierarchies of related elements. Each element represents a different level of summarization.

Choosing the appropriate fact measures for the grain in the fact table depends on the organization and analysis purposes. For example, the star schema for the contract data is constructed as shown in Figure 9.

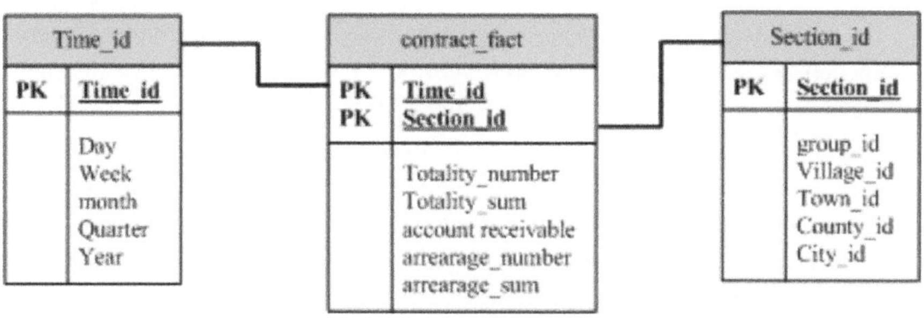

Figure 9. Star Schema of Contract Data.

Data Share and Exchange Technique

Data exchange is the problem of finding an instance of a target schema, given an instance of a source schema and a specification of the relationship between the source and the target. Such a target instance should correctly represent information from the source instance under the constraints imposed by the target schema, and should allow one to evaluate queries on the target instance in a way that is semantically consistent with the source data. XML stands for extensible markup language. XML was released in the late 90's and received a great amount of application. The XML standard was created by World Wide Web Consortium to provide an easy to use and standardized way to store self-describing data. The main benefit of XML is that you can take data from a platform, convert it into XML, and then share that XML with other platforms. Each of these receiving platforms can then convert the XML into a structure the platform uses normally and you have just communicated between two potentially very different platforms! So XML is adopted to realize data share and exchange. Data stored in the data source is converted into XML file, and then send it to data share and exchange platform, when receive XML file, data share and exchange platform again convert XML to structure data of kernel database, data stored in the kernel database is sent to application department in the same way, therefore, function of data share and exchange is realized easily.

CONCLUSION

In this chapter, definition, architecture, process of building and tools of data warehouse are introduced. Then Nanhai city E-government project is acted as example to illustrate the data warehouse based data center deign. Relation of provider and user for data in various departments of government is given in detail. On the base of data analysis, the architecture of data center based on data warehouse technology has been presented. In our proposed method, XML technology is used for data share and exchange. The proposed method has already been successfully used in development of data center system for Nanhai city.

REFERENCES

1. Teh Ying Wah, Ng Hooi Peng, and Ching Sue Hok. Building Data Warehouse. Special Issue of the International Journal of the Computer, the Internet and Management, Vol.15 No. SP4, November, 2007.
2. Donna Evansa, David C, Yenb. (2006). E-Government: Evolving relationship of citizens and government, domestic, and international development Government Information Quarterly 23, pp. 207–235.
3. State Information Construction Promotion Office (SICPO) (2001). Report on China's Internet Resources. July 2001. http://www.cei.gov.cn.
4. Lijuan Zhou, Chi Liu, Chunying Wang. (2006). The Design and Application of Data Warehouse during Modern Enterprises Environment. Data Mining, Intrusion Detection, Information Assurance, and Data Networks Security.
5. Xiaohua Hu, Nick Cercone. (2004). A Data Warehouse/Online Analytic Processing Framework for Web Usage Mining and Business Intelligence Reporting. International Journal of Intelligent Systems, Vol. 19, pp. 585–606.
6. Dr.Katherine Jones. (1998). An Introduction to Data Warehousing: What Are the Implications for the Network? International Journal of Network Management, Vol. 8, pp. 42–56.
7. Keqin Wang, Shurong Tong and et al. (2007). Review on Application of Data Mining in Product Design and Manufacturing, International Conference on Fuzzy Systems and Knowledge Discovery .
8. Alex A. Freitas, Jon Timmis. (2007). Revisiting the Foundations of Artificial

Immune Systems for Data Mining. IEEE Transactions on Evolutionary Computation, Vol.11, No.4, August.

9. http://www.sap.com/solutions/sapbusinessobjects/sme/reporting/crystalreportsserver/index.epx. http://www.microsoft.com/Sqlserver/2005/en/us/reporting-services.aspx. http://www.sas.com/technologies/dw/storage/mddb/index.html. http://en.wikipedia.org/wiki/Microsoft_SQL_Server. http://www.terry.uga.edu/~hwatson/DW_Architecture_Report.pdf .

10. Hu Xuanzi, Wang Kuanfu. Application of Data Warehouse Technology in Data Center Design. 2008 International Conference on Computational Intelligence and Security.

17
CHAPTER

DATA WAREHOUSE USE GEOGRAPHIC INFORMATION SYSTEM FOR ORNAMENTALS

Benjapuk Jongmuenwai, Parinya Chinjoho and Sangpetch Prachai

Keywords: Ornamentals, Data Warehouse (DW), Geographic Information System (GIS)

INTRODUCTION

In a 2003 IT spending survey, 45 % of American companies that participated indicated that their 2003 IT purchasing budgets had increased compared with their budgets in 2002. Among the respondents database applications ranked top in areas of technology being built or had been implemented, with 42 % indicating a recent implementation [9]. The fast growth of databases enables companies to capture and store a great deal of business operation data and other business-relate data.

The data is stored in the databases is either historical or operational, are considered corporate resources and an asset that must be manage and used effectively. The demands are in both internal and external information which are growing rapidly.

The rapidly growing are demand to analyze business information quickly led to an emergence in data warehousing [3]. Starting in the mid-to-late 1990s, data warehousing became one of the most important developments in the information systems field. It has been estimated that about 95 % of the Fortune 1000 companies either have a data warehouse in place or are planning to develop one [19]. Data warehousing are emerge from both business needs and technology advances. Since, the business environment has become more global, competitive, complex, and volatile, customer relationship management (CRM) and e-commerce initiatives are creating requirements for large,

Citation: Benjapuk Jongmuenwai, Parinya Chinjoho and Sangpetch Prachai, "Data Warehouse use Geographic Information System for Ornamentals," Proceedings of the International Multi-Conference of Engineers and Computer Scientists 2016 Vol I, IMECS 2016, March 16 - 18, 2016, Hong Kong. ISBN: 978-988-19253-8-1.

integrated data repositories and advanced analytical capabilities [8,16]. One of the reasons are data warehousing systems has been rapidly spreading over the last decade is due to their contribution to increasing the effectiveness and efficiency of decision-making processes within business and scientific domains [6]. The strategic are use of information from data warehousing can help to counter the negative effects of many of the challengers facing organizations. When data warehouse technologies are well position and properly implemented they can assist organizations by reduce business complexity, and discovering ways to leverage information for new sources of competitive advantage and business opportunities, and provide a high level of information readiness under conditions of uncertainty [12].

A data warehouse (or on a smaller-scale data mart) is a repository of data create to support decision making. Data are extract from source systems, cleaned/scrubbed, transformed, and placed in data stores [7]. The data warehouse, which normally includes both transaction and non-transactional data, is typically use as the foundation of a decision support system (DSS) that aims to meet the requirement for a business user community [11]. A data warehouse has data suppliers who are responsible for delivering data to the ultimate end users either through structured query language (SQL) queries or custom-built decision-support applications, including decision support system (DSS) and executive information systems (EIS). The data warehouse are derive, meaning integrate, subject-oriented, time-variant, and non-volatile [10]. By integrated, it means that a data warehouse is construct by integrate multiple heterogeneous sources and must put data from disparate sources into a consistent format, by subject-oriented, it means that a data warehouse are organize around some major subjects rather than concentrating on day-to-day operations and business transactions, by time-variant, it means that data are store to provide information from a historical perspective and a focus is given on change over time, may be at various points in time, by non-volatile, it means that a data warehouse are always a physically separate database storing data transformed from the application data find in the operational environment.

The data store are input data warehouse remain static [8, 11]. As for the statistics perspective, its emphasis is on validity because this perspective focuses on the mathematical soundness of data warehouse.

The propose are to create virtual glades of flowers using Kinect gestures. The user gestures are read [14]. Since the arrival of computer storage technology and higher level programming languages [10] organizations, especially larger organizations, have put enormous amount of investment in their information system infrastructures.

Therefore, this paper proposes data warehouse use geographic information system for ornamentals, under concept of storage data ornamental more than 100 record. The data warehouse will be propose in section 2. Section 3 describes procedure for data warehousing. Section 4 presents data mapping for implementation system and geographic information system (GIS) on website. Section 5 presents concept geographic information system. Finally, the conclusions and future work in section 6.

DATA WAREHOUSE

The data warehouse are new discipline much to do with the fact, that once one database (the transactional) are clear separate from the other (the historical/analytical), they are quite different kind in Table 1.

Table 1: Differences between transactional databases and data warehouse

	Transactional database	Data warehouse
Purpose	Daily operations. Support for the software applications.	Information retrieval, reports, data analysis.
Data characteristics	Data about the organization inner working, changing data, internal data, incomplete data.	Historical data, internal and external data, descriptive data
Data models	Relational, object-relational, normalized	Multidimensional, snowflake, partially denormalized.
Users	Hundreds or thousands, applications, operators, administrators	Dozens, managers, executives, analysts (farmers and explorers)
Access	SQL, Read and Write	SQL and specific OLAP operators (slice & dice, roll, pivot), read-only

The table 1. shows difference between transactional database and data warehouse are environmental the other. Thus, general user are use data warehouse for analysts data management over much in organization. Moreover, data warehouse help to for executives are reports from data models and multidimensional descriptive data.

Exploitation: OLAP Operators and Tools

A data model are comprises a set of data structures and a set of operators over these structures. In the previous section we are see that the data structures or data scheme in the dimensional model. The facts with their measures, and the dimensions with their hierarchies and attributes for each level. We are describe that a single "operator" define by just choosing a measure from the fact and a level for each dimension, forming a data cube, and then, selecting the values of one or more dimensions. The query tools are data warehouse under the multidimensional model usually are the graphical interface, which allow the user to select the data mart, to pick one or more measures for the facts (the aggregated projection), to choose the resolution in the dimension hierarchies and to express additional conditions.

With the multidimensional model and this hybrid data cube/table representation in mind it is easier to understand some additional operators that are more common in OLAP tools, called OLAP operators can be describes in 1-4:

1) Drill: de-aggregates the data following are paths of one or more dimensions.
2) Roll: aggregates the data following are paths of one or more dimensions.
3) Slice & dice: selects and projects the data into one of both sides of the report.
4) Pivot: changes one dimension from one side of the report to the other (rows by columns).

The design is data warehouse and OLAP tools are intend to avoid the recalculation of the aggregates each time one of the previous operators is apply. The idea are precalculate aggregations two several levels of the hierarchies and so making the traversal through dimension paths more efficient show in figure 1.

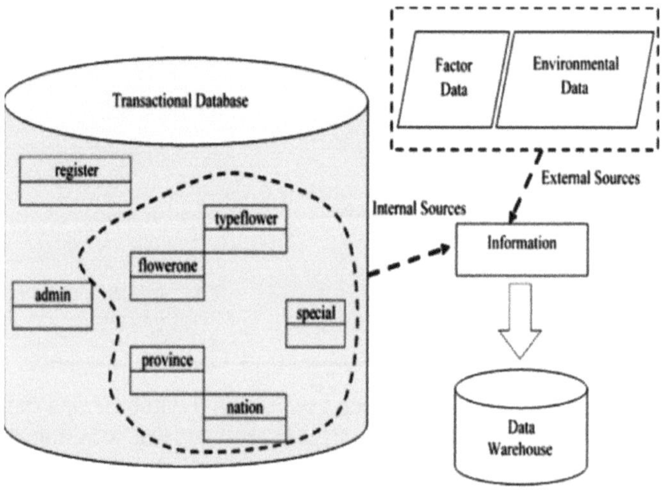

Figure 1. Show architecture for Data warehousing.

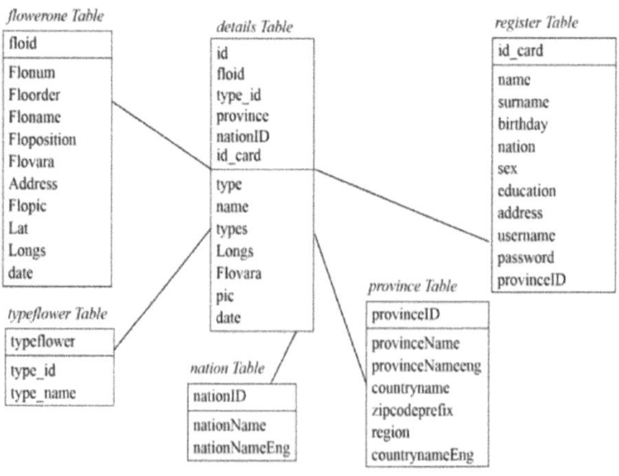

Figure 2. Simple Star Schema for DW.

Figure 1. We are show architecture for data warehousing. The active data warehouse is provide an integrate information repository to drive strategic and tactical decision support within an organization including of internal source and external source. The managing are evolution of a DW architecture exchange in transactional database. The basic issues are should be solve include:

1) DW are model and metadata capable of representing and storing the history of evolution that concerns not only data but also data structures.

2) DW are simple star schema of representing and storing the dataset in database. In the example, the ornamental are store data and store table several of six table show in figure 2.

Ornamental Dataset

The ornamental dataset uses in this provide by a major in Thailand. It's contains more than 100 records and more than 100 variables. The data are collect from January 2014 to December 2015. Each record has a class label to indicate its group ornamental status: either 'the north', 'the southern', 'the western', 'the north-eastern', 'the eastern' indicate data dictionary. Among these more than 100 records. For the purpose of ornamental classification, the 100 derive variables are choose to compute the model since they provide more precise information about group ornamental show figure 2.

In this section we illustrate how queries can be decompose into a number of smaller sub-queries that will act on fragments independently, with significant speedup. This subject is discussion in several works, which include our illustration is base on the query processing approach follow by the data warehouse architecture [4]. While, we also discuss other works on the next section such as querying metadata, version query, querying data warehouse in the other.

Figure 2 illustrates the basic architecture of DW for the share data warehouse, which can run the query is transform into high-level actions language by a query planner. We are describe basic query process functionality. For simplicity, start with the simplest possible example. Consider a single very large relation some 6 relation.

The number 3 step is specific actions are associate with the data warehouse that include:

1) The ADD_COLUMN event: it was add to data structure in a table. For example a table flowerone, details, typeflower, register, nation and province. In this case, the column is also added to a corresponding table in DW, according to a mapping that relates data structure between DW store and metadata dictionary.

2) The DROP_COLUMN event: it signalize that a column is drop from a data structure. The column retains it old values and new values are set to null. New_table causes that a new version of the table is create without the drop column.

3) The ALTER_COLUMN event: it is change to a data structure in a table into

multiple structures T_1, T_2, … , Tn, each of which stores the subset of rows from T. It modifies a new column or row is added to the table. This data merges the content of T_1, T_2, … , T_n before further processing.

While most SQL operations are ready in a way that may allow nodes to process data with exchange requirements, the join operator may occur in considerable data exchange overheads if rows to be join are not co-locate or equi-partition. Thus, we are the join must match rows from two data set with the same value for a specific attribute.

For instance, the following SQL query is search and categorical for ornamental that include:

1) Attribute of a given name and a type or an equivalent attribute are results submission in T1.

T1. Algorithm searching results:

```
Algorithm T1 :
A = flower, B = typeflower and R = type_id, flonum
SQL = "SELECT * from A r, B p where r.R = p.R";
If (R > 0)
{
  SQL .=" and r.R = " . $R;
Return;
if(R > 0)
{
  SQL .=" and R = " . $R;
Return;
If ($flovara != '')
{
  SQL .=" and flovara = '" . $flovara . "'";
Return;
If ($txt_n != '')
{
  SQL .=" and floname like '%" . $txt_n . "%'";
Return;
```

2) Query submission are including of: categorical structure of ornaments, we bring to group original, type theoretic constructions, such as the ornamental algebra and the algebraic ornament in categorical terms and uncover the build blocks out of which they are carve out. We are interpret the mathematical properties of ornaments into type theory such as the pullback of ornaments to discover meaningful software artefacts.

Being at the interface between type theory and category theory, this paper targets both communities. To the type theorist, we offer a more semantic account of ornaments and use website story map thus gained to introduce new type theoretic constructions. We present a type theory, i.e. programming language that offers an interesting for categorical ideas, story map. Our approach can be summarize as categorical structure programming. The ornaments are an instance of that graphic between a categorical concept and an analysis, type theory presentation, the universe of ornaments. To help bridge the gap between type theory and category theory, we have to provide the type theory with examples of the categorical ornamental with the computational intuition behind the type theoretic objects.

Categorical Map

In this section, we are definitions and results from category theory that will be use GIS. Therefore, we are well on the details. However, to help readers not familiar with these tools for analyze, we shall give many examples, thus provide an ornamental for these concepts.

1) Locally cartesian-close category.

There are locally cartesian-closed categories introduce. To give a categorical model of (extensional) dependent type theory. The key idea of that presentation is use of adjunctions to model types [20].

2) Definition (Locally cartesian-closed category): A locally cartesian-closed category are that a pullback complete and such that, data each base change function. The index map are remains change real time, because of but, following data ornamental and analysis, we can be rename it follow index function. We obtain the following definition:

$S: J \rightarrow SET$
$P: S_j \rightarrow SET$

Note that, to group for cluster, we are count quantify type variables, such as j in the definition of SET. S_j definition of P. The data of S, P, is call a container and is denoted $J \rightarrow SET, S_j \rightarrow SET$. The class can containers detail index of ornamental for category in figure 3.

Figure 3 DW for categorical map.

PROCEDURE FOR DATA WAREHOUSING

If you want to submit your file with one column for storage, please do the following:

Input: The data set A=A_1 , A_2 , A_3 , … , A_n}, *boundary* b

Querying Metadata

With the support of the DW a user can explicitly query metadata for the purpose of analyzing the change history of either the whole DW versions. The functionality of the language allows to execute two types of querying, namely:

1) A query searching for DW versions that include an indicated schema object or a dimension instance, and
2) A query retrieving the evolution history of an indicated schema object or a dimension instance. A query of the first type will be called a version query and a query of the second type will be called an object evolution query.

Version Query

In particular, a version query allows to search for DW versions that include:

1) An attribute of a given name and a type or an equivalent attribute (in the case of changing attribute names in DW versions) in a fact or a level table.
2) A table (either fact or level) of a given name or an equivalent table (in the case of changing table names in DW versions).
3) A table (either fact or level) that has a given exact or partial structure.
4) A dimension that has a given exact or partial structure.
5) A dimension instance that has a given exact or partial structure.

Querying Data Warehouses

In the area of querying temporal or multiversion data warehouses, to the best of our knowledge, only three contributions exist [15, 17, 18]. It allows to query either a DW version valid at a certain point in time or to query the latest DW version. It can provide consistent query results under changes to the structure of dimensions (adding a level) and dimension instances (adding a level instance, reclassifying a level instance). Additionally, OLAP allows to explicitly query metadata on DW changes. The support for handling missing fact or level attributes or domain changes between schema versions was not addressed in the publications.

The selection of DW versions is done based on a time interval provided by a user, Since queried DW versions may differ with respect to the structure of their dimension instances, in order to allow query result comparison, data coming from queried versions must be converted into the structure of a selected base version. Moreover, this a query language syntax in query processing the tables that difference with respect to their structures.

DATA MAPPING

Eder, J. et al. [1, 2]. The explore are possibilities impose by data transformations that require one-to-many mappings, i.e., transformations that produce several output tuples for each input tuple. This kind of operations is typically encountered in scenarios. Since relation algebra is not equipped with an operator that performs this kind of input-output mapping. Carreira et al. extend it by proposing a new operator called data mapper and explore its semantics and properties. In this discussion, we mainly focus on the work of a long version of a previous work [5]. The authors define the data mapper operator as a computable function mapping the space of values of an input schema to the space of values of an output schema. A second rule directs how a selection condition that uses attributes of the output of a data mapper can be translated to the attributes that generate them and thus be pushed through the mapper. A third rule deals with how projection can help avoid unnecessary computations of mappers that will be subsequently projected-out later. Finally, report some first results on their experimentation with implementing the data mappers in a real RDBMS. A more detail description of alternative implementations is given concern unions, recursive queries, table functions, stored procedures and pivoting operations as candidates for the implementation of the data mapper operator. The first four alternatives where use for experimentation in two different DBMSs and table functions appear to provide the highest throughput for data mappers [13].

GEOGRAPHIC INFORMATION SYSTEM (GIS)

The ornamental data model are introduces in GIS. This map are design to be use as a basemap by GIS professionals and as a reference map by anyone. The map includes administrative boundaries, cities, water features, physiographic features, parks, landmarks, highways, roads, railways, and airports overlay on land cover and shade relief imagery for add context. The map provides coverage for the world down to a scale of ~1:72k. Coverage is provide down to ~1:4k for the following areas: Australia and New Zealand, India, Europe, Canada, Mexico, the continental United States and Hawaii; South America and Central America; Africa, and most of the Middle East. Coverage down to ~1:1k and ~1:2k is available in select urban areas. This basemap is compile from a variety of best available sources from several data provider, including the U.S. Geological Survey (USGS), U.S. Environmental Protection Agency (EPA), U.S. National Park Service (NPS), Food and Agriculture Organization of the United Nations (FAO), Department of Natural Resources Canada (NRCAN), GeoBase, Agriculture and Agri-Food Canada, DeLorme, HERE, Esri, OpenStreetMap contributors, and the GIS User Community.

For more information on this map, including our terms of use, visit us online at url and show in Figure 4. (http://www.arcgis.com/home/webmap/viewer.html)

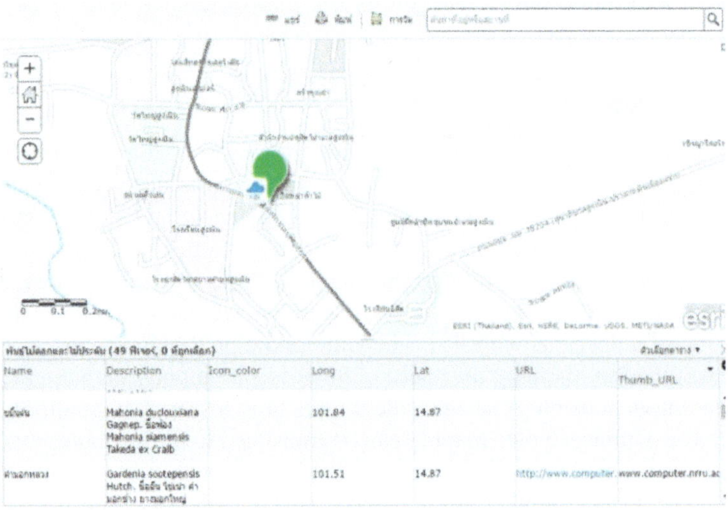

Figure 4. DW ornamental screen showing present of GIS.

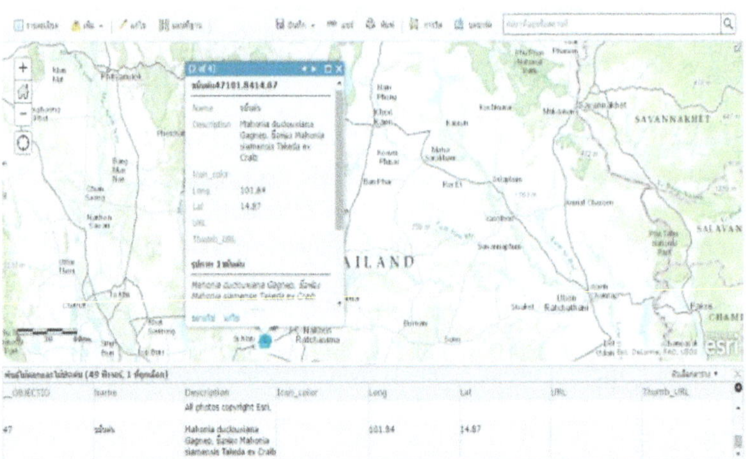

Figure 5. DW ornamental screen showing details of GIS.

The model defines a GIS dimension as composed of a set of graphs, each one describing a set geometries in a thematic layer. A GIS dimension is, as usual in databases, compose of a schema and instances. Table 2. Shows the instance of a GIS dimension: the bottom level of each hierarchy, denoted the Algebraic part, contains the infinite points in a layar, and could be described by means of linear algebraic equalities and in-equalities [5]. Below this part there is the Geometric part, which stores the identifiers of the geometric elements of the GIS, and is use to solve the geometric part of a query. Each point in the Algebraic part may correspond to one or more elements in the Geometric part (e.g., if more than one polylines intersect with each other). Thus, at the GIS dimension instance level. We are define rollup relations (denoted $r_L^{geo1 \to geo2}$). For instance, $r_{L_{city}}^{Point \to Pg}(x, y, pg_1)$ says that, in a layer L_{city} a point (x,y) corresponds to a polygon identify by pg_1 in the Geometric part.

Finally, there is the OLAP part for storing nonspatial data. This part contains the conventional OLAP structures, as define geometric part are associated to the OLAP part a function, (denoted $\propto_{L,D}^{\dim Level \to geo}$). For instance, $\propto_{L,Icon\_color}^{Name \to na}$) associates information about a name in the OLAP part (Icon_color) in a dimension Lat, Long to identifier of a polyline (n_a) in a layer denoted (L_{icon_color}), which represents detail in the GIS.

Figure 5. Shows detail of ornamental for GIS dimension instance for Lat and Long in the dimension schema from table II. We can see that an instance of a GIS dimension in the website.

Finally, while all GIS software components are open source: the database, postgres, and its GIS extension GIS url (http://www.arcgis.com/home/webmap/viewer.html)

Table 2: Category Instances

Category	Instance
OBJECTID	[{_OBJECTID}, ($OBJECTID_1$),($OBJECTID_2$), ($OBJECTID_n$)]
Name	[{Name}, ($Name_1$),($Name_2$) ,($Name_n$)]
Description	[{Description}, ($Description_1$),($Description_2$) , ($Description_n$)]
Icon_color	[{Icon_color}, ($Icon\_color_1$),($Icon\_color_2$), ($Icon\_color_n$)]
Long	[{Long}, ($Long_1$),($Long_2$),($Long_n$)]
Lat	[{Lat}, (Lat_1),(Lat_2) ,(Lat_n)]
URL	[{URL}, (URL_1),(URL_2),(URL_n)]
Thumb_URL	[{Thumb_URL}, ($Thumb\_URL_1$), ($Thumb\_URL_2$),($Thumb\_URL_n$)]

Example 1. Consider a fact table containing category instance in table II.

The GIS data model is basically compose of category instances, and the table of items. For example, our ornamental application above can include eight category schemas, OBJECTID, Name, Description, Icon_color, Long, Lat, URL and Thumb_ URL. Each category schema is compose of a set attributes that describe it. An element in a category is denote a category occur, and the set of all occur in all category in an application is a category instance. A set of category instances for our running example is show in Figure 4. Where, for example, the category name is one occurrences. A value of the attribute name represents the geometric extension of the corresponding category occur (e.g., in the first tuple, Long and Lat can be point (101.84, 14.87)). Adding a OBJECTID interval to a category occur, produces an item. All other attributes are store elsewhere.

CONCLUSION

Data warehouse is an effective tool that enables an organization or the other to manage data, and to transform them into strategic decision and show information. The data that organizations store are considered ornamental. Data controllers cannot do anything until they input into the data warehouse to Fig 4. DW ornamental screen showing present of GIS. Fig. 5. DW ornamental screen showing details of GIS corporate information into databases. Therefore, internal and web technology will become the interface for users, to allow users to open web browsers in their data warehouse worldwide on public and private networks, and eliminate the need to replicate data across diverse geographic locations. Thus strong data warehouse management sponsorship and an effective administration team may become a crucial factor to provide an organization with the information service.

Today's data warehouse is limited to storage of structure data in the form of records, field, and database. Unstructured data, such as multimedia maps, graphs, pictures, sound, and video files are demand increase in organizations. How to manage the storage and retrieval of unstructured data and how to search for specify data item set a real challenge for data warehouse administration and management. Alternative storage, especially the near-line storage, which is one of the two forms of alternative storage is considered to be one of the best for the future solution for managing the storage in data warehouse. This recent growth in website use and advances in e-business application push the data warehouse from the back office, where it is accessed by only a few businesses employees, to the front lines of the organization, where all users can use it. Additionally, building distribute warehouses, which are normally call data mart, will be a technical advance in data warehouses including an increasing ability to process, automatic information delivery, greater support of object extensions, very large database support, and user friendly web enable analysis applications. These are capabilities that should make data warehouses of the future more powerful and easy to use, which will further increase the importance of data warehouse technology for education or business.

REFERENCES

1. 1 Eder, J., and Koncilia, C., Changes of Dimension Data in Temporal Data Warehouses. Proceedings International Conference on Data Warehousing and Knowledge Discovery, Munich, Germany, 2001, pp. 284-293.
2. 2 Eder, J., Koncilia, C., and Morzy, T., The COMET Metamodel For Temporal Data Warehouses. Proceedings International Conference on Advanced Information Systems Engineering, Toronto, Canada, 2002, pp. 83-99.
3. 3 Finnegan, Murphy, and O'Riordan., Challenging the hierarchical perspective on information systems: Implications from external information analysis. Journal of

Information Technology, 1999, vol. 14(1), pp. 23-37.

4. 4 Furtado Pedro., A Survey of Parallel and Distributed Data Warehouses. 2011, pp. 148-169. Universidade Coimbra, Portudal.

5. 5 Gomez, Kuijpers, and Vaisman., A State-of-the-Art in Spatio-Temporal Data Warehousing, OLAP and Mining. 2011, pp. 200-236.

6. 6 Golfarelli, M., Lechtenborger, J., Rizzi, S., and Gossen, G. Schema versioning in data warehouses: Enabling cross-version querying via schema augmentation. Data & Knowledge Engineering, 2006, vol. 59, pp. 435-459.

7. 7 Gorla, N., Features to consider in a data warehousing system. Communications of the ACM, 2003, vol. 46(11), pp. 111-115.

8. 8 Han, J., and Kamber, M. (2006). Data mining: Concepts and techniques (2nd ed.). San Francisco, CA: Morgan Kaufmann Publisher.

9. 9 Information Technology Toolbox. (2004). "2003 IToolbox spending survey. Available: http://data-warehouse.ittoolbox.com/research.

10. 10 Inmon, W.H., (2002). Building the data warehouse (3rd ed.). New York, NY: John Wiley & Sons Inc.

11. 11 Khan, A. (2003). Data warehousing 101: Concepts and implementation. Electronic version, Online Bookstore: iUniverse.

12. 12 Love, B., Strategic DSS/data warehouse: A case study in failure. Journal of Data Warehousing, 1996, vol. 1(1), pp. 36-40.

13. 13 Moreno, F., Fileto, R., and Arango, F., Season queries on a temporal multidimensional model for OLAP, Mathematical and Computer Modelling, 2010, vol. 52(7-8), pp. 1103-1109.

14. 14 Roiger, R.J., and Geatz, M. W. (2003). Data mining: A tutorial-based primer. New York: Addison Wesley.

15. 15 Rizzi and Golfarelli., Temporal Data Warehousing: Approaches and Techniques. 2011 . pp. 1-18.

16. 16 TOUMI Lyazid, MOUSSAOUI Abdelouahab, and UGUR Ahmet. A linear programming approach for bitmap join indexes selection in data warehouse. ScienceDirect, 2015, vol. 52, pp. 169-177.

17. 17 Vaisman, A., and Mendelzon, A. (2001). A Temporal Query Language for OLAP: Implementation and a Case Study. Proceedings DBPL.

18. 18 Vassiliadis Panos., A Survey of Extract-Transform-Load Technology. 2011, pp. 171-199.

19. 19 Wixon, B.H., and Watson, H., An empirical investigation of the factors affecting data warehousing success. MIS Quarterly, 2001, vol. 25(1), pp. 17-41.

20. 20 Wixon, B.H., and Watson, H., Mathematical Proceedings of the Cambridge Phiosophical Society. (1984). Cambridge Philosophical Society, vol. 95, pp. 33-48.

18
CHAPTER

GOSSIP MANAGEMENT AT UNIVERSITIES USING BIG DATA WAREHOUSE MODEL INTEGRATED WITH A DECISION SUPPORT SYSTEM

Pelin Vardarlıer and Gökhan Silahtaroğlu

Keywords: Big Data, Data Collection, University Management, Gossip

INTRODUCTION

Modern business managements are benefitting from merits of digital era more and more. With the rapid improvement of computer devices, software tools and storage capacities, managers are much more comfortable to use these tools. Everyday another solution or idea emerges to assist modern managers when they are making their decisions. In this sense, Decision Support Systems (DSS) have been very helpful for years. Nevertheless, along with popularity of social networks and handy mobile devices, data stored in digital format have become enormous in size. Therefore, these days, valuable information hidden in this data has become much larger in volume than it ever was in the past. Data mining is to extract valuable information from large data sets, on which decision support systems are built. Thus, the importance of building data warehouses from Big Data and using it for management purposes is getting more and more crucial for competition, marketing, customer satisfaction and similar management issues. Managing a university is not only arranging classes, monitoring instructors and motivating them to work, teach and produce harder. Students are another important part of universities that should be taken into account for a better management. Their

Citation: Pelin Vardarlıer and Gökhan Silahtaroğlu, "Gossip Management at Universities Using Big Data Warehouse Model Integrated with a Decision Support System," Journal of Research in Business & Social Science 5 (1), 2016: 1-14. IJRBS ISSN: 2147-4478.

motivation and satisfaction is as important as that of instructors, research assistants and other office workers. That's why university administrators perform some surveys with students to learn how happy they are with campus facilities, teaching quality etc. However, this can be done only once or twice in an academic year. Although this is held to detect and solve or fix a problem, it is often too late to fix it, because the problem probably arose some time ago, and there is nothing to do for the person who suffered from it weeks, even months before it was detected. Yet, measures or precautions may be taken for future only. Therefore, it is obvious that university managers lack of a system that inform them about minor problems happening at school, misinformation among students, rumors and gossips. Using social media data integrated with other data available, a decision support system may be built to feed managers with information about minor problems that are happening somewhere in the university. Current technology, computer storage capacity, CPU speed, quality of algorithms and data available are altogether good enough to sort out this issue. In this study, a University Big Data Warehouse model which is enhanced with text mining and machine learning algorithms is presented.

In the first part of the paper we will give detailed information about Big Data, its key features, and challenges with Big Data and how to handle these challenges. In the second part, a literature review will be presented about how and to what extent Big Data and social media data are used for various management purposes. In the last part of the paper, you will find the proposed model and a sample study conducted within a prototype of the proposed system. Findings of the prototype study will also be discussed.

LITERATURE REVIEW

Big Data

Big Data is the collection of interrelated data gathered from different sources such as social media, transactional databases, maps, log files etc. Big Data is considered to be in the size of terabytes or petabytes. However, this is not the only feature of Big Data that makes it BIG. On the other hand, with this enormous size and being in different formats it has been a challenge to store, transfer and analyze Big Data. Big Data has five prominent characteristics or features. This is symbolized as 5 Vs of Big Data. As it is depicted in Fig 1. these characteristics are Variety, Velocity, Volume, Veracity and Value (Yu, 2013), (Zikopoulos, 2012).

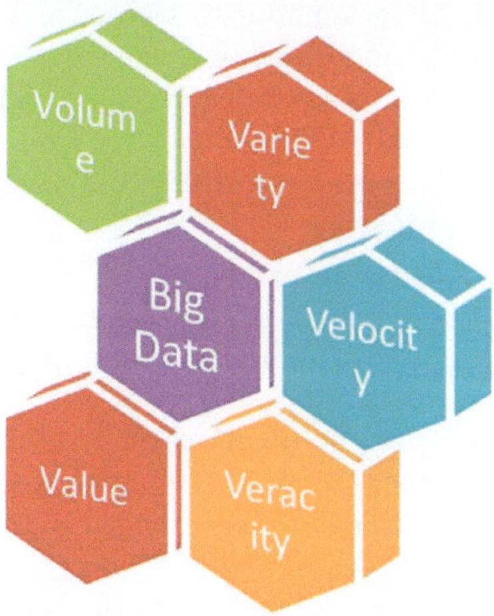

Figure 1: Features of Big Data.

Variety represents the data types that Big Data can be found in. As it is also stressed in the definition, Big Data may be generated in different formats and collected from various environments. For example, if it is map or geospatial data, it may be in the format of raster, vector or graph (Assuncao, Marcos D.et al, 2015) and if it is coming from social media it may be in the format of text and numbers residing in sentences or paragraphs. Variety feature of Big Data is considered to be high (Assuncao, Marcos D.et al, 2015). The second V for velocity refers to its being generated very fast and continuously. With the widespread and active usage of the Internet, users generate data every moment around the clock when it is thought globally. As companies and governments allow their customers and citizens to perform transactions online and when active social media usage is so popular, it goes without saying that data accumulation will speed up every day. This phenomenon will trigger the third V which stands for Volume. Perhaps it is the first thing to come to mind when Big Data term is first uttered. The adjective 'big' itself reminds us of high volume. Every day terabytes of interrelated data are generated and stored on disks. So, when we process Big Data we may be dealing with petabytes of data. Since Big Data is something in high volumes and coming from a variety of sources and formats, its quality is another important point. This is represented with Veracity. Although Big Data is thought to be authentic, it is very important that it ought to be valid and away from falsity. While millions of entries are stored in data disks each passing day, we cannot expect that all these are accurate and reliable data. Besides the provenance, integration of Big Data is another factor to determine the level of veracity. Even if the data are accurate and exact when they are put together or integrated for a Big Data Warehouse (BDW), their accuracy, reliability and exactness may be harmed because of disorganization. So, although all other Vs are thought to be high, when it comes to Veracity, it is doubted to be high and considered as low. The fifth V is Value. As it is seen, it will be a hard work to find, integrate, store and process this much data. It will need a great deal of effort. So, is that really worth it? Will you or your business be able to extract valuable enough information to satisfy the team and the cost sacrificed? It is not always possible to predict or forecast whether the data you will grab and tackle may yield valuable information that can be turned into benefits or not. Eventually, data selection and integration will play a crucial role for a future value to be gained. As the first V (Variety) suggests, data come from different sources. As it is depicted in Fig 2, some of the sources are as follows:

- Social media, such as Facebook, Twitter, LinkedIn, Pinterest, Google Plus+, Tumblr, Instagram, VK, Flicker etc include text, images and video files which are all stored and organized in free styles and formats.
- Corporate databases may be the most easily accessible data for businesses. They are stored and organized within Database Management Systems (DBMS) mostly with entity relational, object oriented or hierarchical data model (Ramakrishnan, R. and Gehrke J., 2003). All data are stored in properly labeled tables and connected to each other with certain ID numbers which are called primary or secondary keys.
- Another source for Big Data is databases managed and run by (mostly) state institutes. Criminal records, law system files and even health care system data are some of them. These data are stored and systematized or structured in DBMS like enterprise databases (Silberschatz. et al., 2010).
- Third party databases which are open to public usage are another important source. There are numerous web sites which store and display data such as, weather forecast, traffic information, finance, geospatial data (Lee, J. & Kang , M., 2015) and even DNA sequencing. Most of them may be considered as data with high veracity.
- Big Data across other organizations is merely another corporate database like Enterprise Data Warehouse (EDW) of a company or Big Data Warehouse which belongs to another institution.

Figure 2: Sources for Big Data.

Although Big Data is considered to be as valuable as gold or petroleum, it is also as difficult as the others to be dealt with. Challenges to tackle Big Data may be categorized under four subtitles: Capturing, Storage, Integration and Processing.

Dealing with Big Data requires a big and well organized information system. As we all know, the very first thing an information system performs is to capture data (Hardcastle E., 2011). A regular Big Data Warehouse (BDW) will require a space of terabytes or petabytes, so it is not hard to imagine how difficult to capture it. That amount of data is mostly disk resident that cannot be transferred from one platform to another easily. In addition to this, the data do not have to be in only one, single place, platform or media. When the data reside in the transactional data base which belongs to a company, things are much easier. However, if it is in another company's or institution's DBMS, things will be more complicated in terms of accessing data. On the other hand, the data we are interested in may be at social media platforms or Big Data borrowed from other organizations. Then, difficulty level and type will change. This does not have to be because of technical issues. Problems may arise from ethical or confidential issues as well. After accessing data, we will face another question: how and where to store this huge amount of data. This is not only for space requirements. It is also for the structure of the system where data will reside. This is because, except DBMS , most of the data to compose BDW will be unstructured data (Chen, M. , 2014). Recently, some solutions have been developed to overcome this problem. Solutions are based on cloud technology as well as local databases.

Hadoop Distributed File System (HDFS) is a technology to overcome issues like capturing, storing and deployment (Chen, M., 2014). Hadoop is a framework that uses clusters of computers. It is an open source MapReduce implementation. HDFS partitions data sets and carries them on different nodes. MapReduce is a programming model to process large amount of data which reside on clusters of computers (Chen et al., 2012), (Guo & Fox, 2012). The task Hadoop performs is to partition and replicate data chunks across multiple nodes and to provide APIs to be used with MapReduce applications (Guo & Fox, 2012).

HBase is another solution that can be used on top of Hadoop and HDFS (Bhupathiraju & Ravuri, 2014). It is and open source non-relational database model.

PIG Latin is a scripting language which enables Hadoop users to write MapReduce applications. It runs in YARN (MapReduce) and access any dataset stored in HDFS (Huang et al, 2012). As Hadoop and HDFS can be used in local drivers or dedicated servers there are plenty of cloud services which support HDFS and MapReduce processes. Google File System, Amazon Simple Storage Service, Nirvanix Cloud Storage, Open Stack Swift and Windows Azure Binary Large Object are some of them (Assuncao, Marcos D.et al, 2015).

There are also data warehouse software platforms developed for managing and querying large data sets which reside in Hadoop. One them is HIVE (Song et al, 2015). HIVE has a SQL like language called QL or HIVE QL. Although it is built under Hadoop project now it is a standalone project itself. SQL MapReduce is another platform to enable users to write MapReduce functions in programming languages such as Java, C#, Python, C++, and R (Gu et al, 2014), (Yuan et al, 2010), (Plimpton & Devine, 2011).

Empirical Review

Extracting information is the main focus in Big Data process. In literature there are plenty of tools and algorithms to analyze datasets and generate informative reports. Data analysis may be held in three different ways. It may be descriptive, predictive and prescriptive (Linda et al, 2015), (Zhang et al, 2001). Descriptive analysis answers the question of "What happened?". For a descriptive analysis or information extraction, besides statistics, data mining algorithms are also used. K-means and derivatives of K-Means such as Spherical K-Means (Agarwal & Singh, 2012), Bisecting K-Means (Kashef & Kamel, 2009), (Savaresi & Boley, 2001), K-Means ++,(Agarwal & Singh,2012) also Suffix Tree Clustering (Han et al, 2006), (Largeron-Leténo, 2003) and Fuzzy Clustering [Son, 2015] algorithms are used for structured and text data. These algorithms are centroid based algorithms. On the other hand algorithms like DBSCAN, DENCLUDE,OPTICS and DBCURE-MR operate on the principle of density to segment data (Younghoon et al, 2014). All of them are widely used algorithms for a descriptive analysis. Another way of data analysis is Predictive Big Data analysis which deals with future. It tells what will happen and when it will happen. For predictive Big Data analysis, decision tree algorithms like C4.5 (Quinlan, J., 1993) , J48 (Bhargava, 2013), CART (Breiman et al., 1984), or Artificial Neural Network algorithms (Fausett A., 1994) are mostly used. All algorithms and techniques make predictions using the data available. The third type of Big Data analysis is prescriptive. Although Prescriptive Big Data analysis tells about future like predictive analysis do, it mostly answers questions like "why will it happen?" and it also gives answers to questions like how to prevent it happening. Furthermore this analysis may suggest possible and feasible options to exploit some future events. Algorithms from different disciplines like machine learning, computer vision, signal processing are used for prescriptive analysis (Bose et al., 2001) , (Vallmuur, 2015).

Integration is the fourth challenge to tackle. Since data are collected from a variety of sources and in different formats, it demands a big and reasonable endeavor to integrate or put them together. Integrating data of two or more different businesses stored in different systems is relatively easier, because in DBMS data are stored in a logical order. There are unique primary and foreign keys to identify each record, entity or relation. Data redundancy is not allowed in transactional databases. However, if it is a geospatial data or social network data containing images and text, there will be no predetermined attributes, tables or IDs to help you put them together as in DBMS. Matching two or more data entries or records in different sources is one challenge as organizing and integrating them is another. Often, there is no data model and meta data for the Internet data which makes most of Big Data.

Big Data has recently been used by many scholars from universities and also by researchers and technicians in different sectors. Tourism is one of them. Using web data, Fuchs et.al. presented a knowledge infra structure to be used for mountain tourism (Fuchs, 2014). They used business intelligence approach within the framework of Destination

Management Information System (DEMIS) to understand and assess customer behavior and experience before and after travelling. They used web navigation, booking and feedback data within DEMIS. Their proposal to use Big Data and business intelligence tools together will enable managers to receive real time information on tourists' on-site behavior and destinations. The Big Data which is made up of electronic word-of-mouth (Luo and Zhong, 2015) in social networks have been used by some other researchers to understand tourist behaviours and promote or manage tourism activities efficiently in Istanbul (Altunel and Erkut, 2015), Honk Kong(Vu, 2015), Finland (Mynttinen, 2015) and so on.

For marketing, there are plenty of studies. Using clickstream data, it is possible to extract online customers' age, gender and any other behavioral patterns (Silahtaroglu, 2015a). It is sort of web farming that researchers can harvest valuable information for managers to be used for marketing (Silahtaroglu and Dönertasli, 2015b). Xu et.al. studied the effects of using Big Data analysis to promote new products in the market. The study which has been held from a knowledge fusion perspective suggests that Big Data analytics play a prominent role on new product success (Xu, 2015). Another study shows that Big Data has the potential to impact nearly every area of marketing, and it is a new competitive advantage tool to be used by firms, therefore companies which will not build and employ a Big Data warehouse will face challenges in competition in the market (Erevelles, 2015).

Big Data residing on the Internet and social networks have been used at times of government crises for communication. The research have examined 300 local government officials from municipalities across the United States and samples of the crises like wildfires in California, the 2009 crash of U.S. Airways flight 1549, the 2010 Haiti earthquake, and Hurricane Sandy have been used, Graham (2015). Twitter and Facebook data have been used to analyze the role of user generated data during the school crisis on September 30, 2014 during active shooter incidents in a high school, in the USA, Mazer et al. (2015). When there is a crisis, thoughts, gossips, rumors, information and even misinformation started to be texted among people. The study presented a model that schools may manage social media during and after such crises to help control the situation. A similar model has also been proposed by Yates and Paquette after the Haitian Earthquake in 2010. They have showed how social media supports disaster and emergency response mechanisms from an organizational level, Yates and Paquette (2011). Two different research and study shows that a proper data warehouse of Big Data may be used for tobacco usage Link et al. (2015) and anti-smoking campaigns Chung (2015).

Nguyen et al., discussing the effect of web content, social networks and Big Data on brand innovation, stresses that customer needs can be retrieved as information via data mining and business intelligence tools, Nguyen et al. (2015). Researchers also emphasize that if social media content is transformed into a data warehouse and analyzed, it will provide valuable information for competition and may be used for strategic behavior by business managements. As it is also stressed in other studies Luo et al. (2015), Kim et al. (2015), Big Data analysis is an asset for firm value. Big Data analysis has been used to discover whether there is a relationship between social media usage and academic performance of students as well. A research held in Saudi Arabia, Alwagait (2014) and another one in the US and Europe, Ozer (2014) are two of the recent studies. In addition a more specific study has been conducted by Zhang et al. Exploiting social media content with the help of CiteSpace II, they showed that the evolution of social networks develop Collaborative Learning (CL) and eventually, Big Data accumulated in social networks may be used by instructors and university managements if it is handled properly Zhang (2015).

RESEARCH AND METHODOLOGY

Proposed Model and Analysis

Big Data mostly come from social networks and web content. Young people and university students are probably the ones who use social networks most frequently. University students add a lot of data to social networks, so it is clear that they play an important role in developing Big Data. Since we know that there is very valuable and useful information hidden in Big Data why not using it for university management for various purposes such as class allocations, facility organizations, rumor and gossip control, problem detection? In this study, we propose a data warehouse a model which enables to sort out some management issues via machine learning algorithms.

The model requires a dedicated server to keep the University BDW and perform the data retrieving, cleaning and analysis processes seamlessly. The university Big Data Warehouse is to consist of seven data sources. We propose them as follows:

- Social Network Data: This may be taken from one or more social networks such as, Facebook, Twitter, Pinterest, Instagram etc.
- University Student Database: This should include university automation system data like grades, attendance and so on.
- Learning Management System (LMS): announcements by instructors, tasks, assignments, lecture notes and comments may be included.
- University official mail server data: this may or may not include staff emails.
- Third party Data: Traffic information and weather information are some of them.
- Web content: Depending on the objective of the management one or more news portals may be added to be analyzed along with student and enterprise database.
- Office Automation System (OAS).

We have realized a prototype of the system with 300 students who are active Twitter users. We have built a database of those 300 students with the following data: Gender, year, GPA, school or department. A summary of this dataset is given in Table 1. 165 of volunteers were girls. Average GPA of students is 2.41. 50 students are freshmen and 40 of them are girls. 63 are sophomores and 31 of sophomores are girls, 32 are boys. 125 of all students were junior students and 72 were girls. Finally, we had 62 senior students; 22 girls and 40 boys.

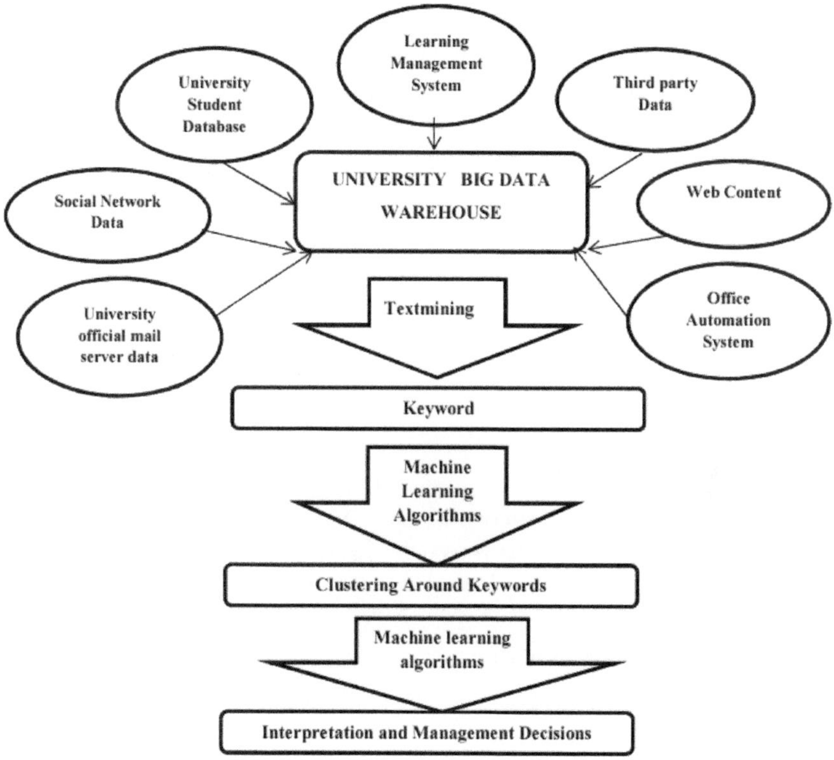

Figure 3: Overall Model proposed.

EMPIRICAL DATA AND ANALYSIS

We have also used Application Program Interface (API) tools to grab the tweets of those volunteers. Moreover, they forwarded their messages related to school to an email address so that they could be stored in a separate database. All volunteers were motivated to use their Twitter and mail accounts actively to talk about subjects related to university.

Table 1: Summary of Student İnformation Dataset

	Average/ Distribution	Female	Male
GENDER		165	135
YEAR	1(50);2(63);3(125);4(62)	1(40);2(31);3(72);4(22)	1(10);2(32);3(53);4(40)
GPA	2.41 (Average)	2.54	2.27

So, we had three datasets; one in database format, one in Excel format, Twitter text data and one email data in text format. We filtered the Twitter data with some key words and also with most frequently used words in a certain period of time. The keywords we used are the name of the university and the word "university" in a number of spelling formats. When we used the name of the university to collect keywords appearing, we were not limited with the tweets of 300 students. In addition, we have collected keywords within various time periods as much as Twitter allowed. This dataset has been united with excel data which holds students information like gender, GPA etc. Secondly, we did the same filtering with email data and united the three data sets as shown in Fig 4 below.

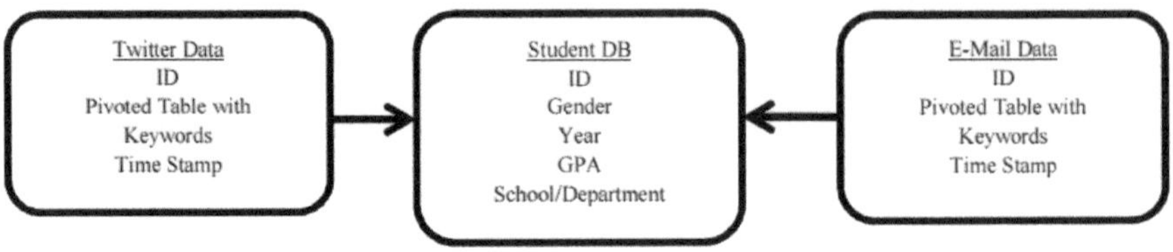

Figure 4: Pilot Big Data Warehouse.

We used Artificial Neural Networks and DBSCAN algorithms to analyze and cluster the data around most frequently used words, keywords and timestamp. The algorithm created clusters around a keyword in the middle.

RESULTS AND DISCUSSION

The analysis indicates that if some important words or phrases have been chosen by the model correctly, they may give valuable information about the happenings at school. The phrases automation system, the name of an instructor, holiday, lunch and elevator has been chosen as topics by the system. Each of these words or phrases makes up a cluster. The topic words are the cluster centers. Fig 5 represents one of the clusters. Results are informative enough to be used by university management. Here in Table 2, we present the most striking and usable keywords and summary of results in various time periods.

Table 2 Findings of the study

Duration	Keyword	School	Gender	GPA	Year	Total (Users)
3 days	Automation System	No Majority	No Majority	2.2	1(30);2(20);3(15);4(2)	67
1 day	Instructor Mrs X.	Architecture	Majority Female	1.81	1(0);2(0);3(45);4(5)	50
5 days	Midterms	No Majority	No Majority	1.99	1(30);2(38);3(79);4(24)	171
3 days	Half Day (holiday)	Engineering, Business	No Majority	2.1	1(43);2(28);3(16);4(2)	89
10 days	Elevator					
25 Days	Lunch	GENERAL	KEYWORD			

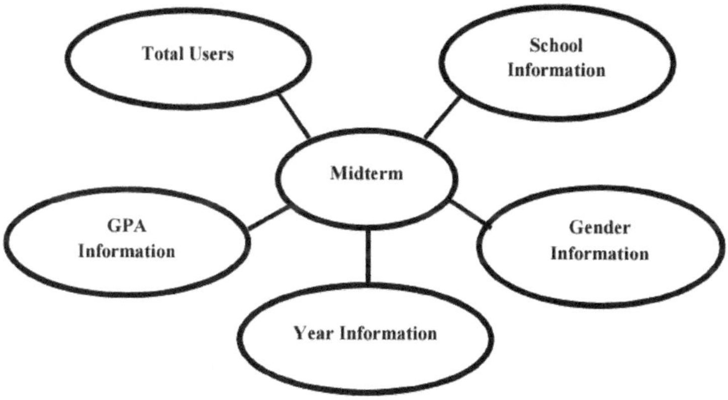

Figure 5: A prototype of clusters.

The pilot analysis shows that student automation system was mentioned by 67 students for 3 days. In fact, there was a problem with the student automation system during those dates. So, if the system had been used by the university management at that time, it could have been learned by the management easily and they would have had a chance to intervene with it. Here, we see that our decision support model enhanced with Big Data worked well. In the second row of Table 2, we see that 50 students talked about an instructor, some Mrs. X. Actually we did not check if there was a problem or not, yet it is obvious that there was an issue with that instructor. It may have been a problem or a piece of homework or assignment or any other gossip. During the midterm week, 171 students mentioned midterm and that is quite normal. Just before a Turkish national holiday, 89 students probably wanted to learn if there would be any classes on that day which is a half day off. We see that only engineering and business students were talking about this. We may guess that they were not informed about half day holiday classes. Last two rows have been taken from general keyword clustering which is done around the name of the university. We see that for 10 days *elevator* and 25 days *lunch* were hot topic among students. One can easily guess that there may have been a problem with the elevators and lunch at school.

CONCLUSION

Big Data has been used by practitioners and scholars and academics. In this study, we suggest a novel University Big Data Warehouse (UBDW) for universities to be used by university managements. The model consists of multiple data sources. These are social media data source which may be grabbed from social networks such as Twitter, Facebook, Pinterest, Instagram etc.; students' database source which includes gender, class, department, GPA etc.; students' school mail data source, learning management system (LMS) data source which includes lecture notes, comments on lecture notes, announcements by instructors etc.; students' automation system data which includes enrollment and registration data, grades, students mails to instructors and groups also surveys about classes and staff; office automation system data used by staff, third party databases and finally other web content.

Apart from this we built a prototype of the proposed system and tested it with 300 volunteer students. Students agreed to use their twitter and mail accounts actively for 65 days. They forwarded their mails which are related to school to an email address. We created a dataset with students' gender, year, GPA and school or department data. All these data were converted into a prototype Big Data warehouse after being transformed, filtered and cleaned. We applied some clustering process around most frequently used words and university's own name. When we used the university' name as keyword we were not limited to the tweets of those 300 students, but we have collected and finally clustered all tweets between two certain dates. For clustering we used DBSCAN and Artificial Neural Networks algorithms. Our model generated twenty five clusters with a keyword in the center. However, we filtered and used only six of them which may be used by university management. Our model and study showed that during these 65 days of study, phrases *students' automation system, Instructor some Mrs. X, midterms, half day classes, elevator* and *lunch* have been discussed and gossiped by students. Our study also gives information about the students who talked about these subjects. The information supplied by the system or model are as follows: Majority of the gender of the students, average GPA of students who are talking on a certain issue, school or department of the students and how many years they have been attending the university.

When we examined and thought about the cluster center keywords we see that our model is informative enough to feed university management with information about issues that needs to be dealt with on the spot. Although our model may be used for different management purposes and tactical and strategical decision making processes, our prototype worked well for problem, gossip and rumor management. We believe that with the development of technology, faster, more informative and smarter systems will be built for the use of managers both at universities and other sectors.

REFERENCE

1. Agarwal, S., Yadav, S., & Singh, K. (2012, March). Notice of Violation of IEEE Publication Principles K-means versus k-means++ clustering technique. InEngineering and Systems (SCES), 2012 Students Conference on (pp. 1-6). IEEE.
2. Altunel, M. C., & Erkut, B. (2015). Cultural tourism in Istanbul: The mediation effect of tourist experience and satisfaction on the relationship between involvement and recommendation intention. Journal of Destination Marketing & Management, 4(4), 213-221.
3. Alwagait, E., Shahzad, B., & Alim, S. (2014). Impact of social media usage on students academic performance in Saudi Arabia. Computers in Human Behavior.
4. Assunção, M. D., Calheiros, R. N., Bianchi, S., Netto, M. A., & Buyya, R. (2015). Big Data computing and clouds: Trends and future directions. Journal of Parallel and Distributed Computing, 79, 3-15.

5. Bhupathiraju, V., & Ravuri, R. P. (2014, March). The dawn of Big Data-Hbase. In IT in Business, Industry and Government (CSIBIG), 2014 Conference on(pp. 1-4). IEEE.
6. Bose, I., & Mahapatra, R. K. (2001). Business data mining—a machine learning perspective. Information & management, 39(3), 211-225.
7. Breiman, L., Friedman, J. H., Olshen, R., & Stone, C. J. (1984). Classification and Regression Trees. Wadsworth & Brooks/Cole Advanced Books & Software. Pacific California.
8. Chen, M., Mao, S., Zhang, Y., & Leung, V. C. (2014). Big Data: related technologies, challenges and future prospects. Springer.
9. Chen, Y., Alspaugh, S., Borthakur, D., & Katz, R. (2012, April). Energy efficiency for large-scale mapreduce workloads with significant interactive analysis. In Proceedings of the 7th ACM european conference on Computer Systems (pp. 43-56). ACM.
10. Chung, N., Lee, S., & Han, H. (2015). Understanding communication types on travel information sharing in social media: A transactive memory systems perspective. Telematics and Informatics, 32(4), 564-575.
11. Erevelles, S., Fukawa, N., & Swayne, L. (2016). Big Data consumer analytics and the transformation of marketing. Journal of Business Research, 69(2), 897-904.
12. Fausett, Laurene. Fundamentals of neural networks: architectures, algorithms, and applications. Prentice-Hall, Inc., 1994.
13. Fuchs, M., Höpken, W., & Lexhagen, M. (2014). Big Data analytics for knowledge generation in tourism destinations–A case from Sweden. Journal of Destination Marketing & Management, 3(4), 198-209.
14. Graham, M. W., Avery, E. J., & Park, S. (2015). The role of social media in local government crisis communications. Public Relations Review.
15. Gu, R., Yang, X., Yan, J., Sun, Y., Wang, B., Yuan, C., & Huang, Y. (2014). SHadoop: Improving MapReduce performance by optimizing job execution mechanism in Hadoop clusters. Journal of Parallel and Distributed Computing,74(3), 2166-2179.
16. Guo, Z., & Fox, G. (2012, May). Improving mapreduce performance in heterogeneous network environments and resource utilization. In Proceedings of the 2012 12th IEEE/ACM International Symposium on Cluster, Cloud and Grid Computing (Ccgrid 2012) (pp. 714-716). IEEE Computer Society.
17. Hardcastle Elizabeth, (2011). Business Information Systems, Elizabeth Hardcastle & Ventus Publishing ApS.
18. Huang, J., Ouyang, X., Jose, J., Wasi-ur-Rahman, M., Wang, H., Luo, M., ... & Panda, D. K. (2012, May). High-performance design of hbase with rdma over infiniband. In Parallel & Distributed Processing Symposium (IPDPS), 2012 IEEE 26th International (pp. 774-785). IEEE.
19. il Han, S., Lee, S. G., Kim, K. H., Choi, C. J., Kim, Y. H., & Hwang, K. S. (2006). CLAGen: A tool for clustering and annotating gene sequences using a suffix tree

algorithm. BioSystems, 84(3), 175-182.

20. Kashef, R., & Kamel, M. S. (2009). Enhanced bisecting k-means clustering using intermediate cooperation. Pattern Recognition, 42(11), 2557-2569.
21. Kim, S., Koh, Y., Cha, J., & Lee, S. (2015). Effects of social media on firm value for US restaurant companies. International Journal of Hospitality Management, 49, 40-46.
22. Kim, Y., Shim, K., Kim, M. S., & Lee, J. S. (2014). DBCURE-MR: an efficient density-based clustering algorithm for large data using MapReduce. Information Systems, 42, 15-35.
23. Largeron-Leténo, C. (2003). Prediction suffix trees for supervised classification of sequences. Pattern Recognition Letters, 24(16), 3153-3164.
24. Lee, J. G., & Kang, M. (2015). Geospatial Big Data: Challenges and Opportunities. Big Data Research, 2(2), 74-81.
25. Link, A. R., Cawkwell, P. B., Shelley, D. R., & Sherman, S. E. (2015). An Exploration of Online Behaviors and Social Media Use Among Hookah and Electronic-Cigarette Users. Addictive Behaviors Reports.
26. Luo, N., Zhang, M., & Liu, W. (2015). The effects of value co-creation practices on building harmonious brand community and achieving brand loyalty on social media in China. Computers in Human Behavior, 48, 492-499.
27. Luo, Q., & Zhong, D. (2015). Using social network analysis to explain communication characteristics of travel-related electronic word-of-mouth on social networking sites. Tourism Management, 46, 274-282.
28. Mazer J.P et al. 2015." A cross-cultural qualitative examination of social-networking sites and academic performance", Computers in Human Behavior, 53, 238-248.
29. Miner, L., Bolding, P., Hilbe, J., Goldstein, M., Hill, T., Nisbet, R., ... & Miner, G. (2015). The Nature of Insight from Data and Implications for Automated Decisioning: Predictive and Prescriptive Models, Decisions, and Actions,Practical Predictive Analytics and Decisioning Systems for Medicine, Chapter 22, Pages 1008-1018.
30. Mynttinen, S., Logrén, J., Särkkä-Tirkkonen, M., & Rautiainen, T. (2015). Perceptions of food and its locality among Russian tourists in the South Savo region of Finland. Tourism Management, 48, 455-466.
31. Neeraj, D. B., Girja, S., Ritu, D. B., & Manisha, M. (2013). Decision Tree Analysis on J48 Algorithm for Data Mining. International Journal of Advanced Research in Computer Science and Software Engineering (JARCSSE), 3(6).
32. Nguyen, B., Yu, X., Melewar, T. C., & Chen, J. (2015). Brand innovation and social media: Knowledge acquisition from social media, market orientation, and the moderating role of social media strategic capability. Industrial Marketing Management.
33. Ozer, I., Karpinski, A. C., & Kirschner, P. A. (2014). A cross-cultural qualitative examination of social-networking sites and academic performance. Procedia-

Social and Behavioral Sciences, 112, 873-881.

34. Plimpton, S. J., & Devine, K. D. (2011). MapReduce in MPI for large-scale graph algorithms. Parallel Computing, 37(9), 610-632.
35. Quinlan, J. R. (1993). C4. 5: Programming for machine learning. Morgan Kauffmann.
36. Ramakrishnan, R., & Gehrke, J. (2003). Database management systems, 3rd Edition,McGrwaw-Hill.
37. Savaresi, S. M., & Boley, D. L. (2001, April). On the performance of bisecting K-means and PDDP. In SDM (pp. 1-14).
38. Silahtaroglu G. (2015a) "Predicting Gender of Online Customer Using Artificial Neural Networks", 2nd International Conference on Management and Information Technology, pp. 45 – 50, New York, USA.
39. Silahtaroglu G., Donertasli H., (2015b), "Analysis and Prediction of E-Customers' Behavior by Mining Clickstream Data", Proceedings of 2015 IEEE International Conference on Big Data (Big Data), pp. 1466 – 1472, San Jose, USA.
40. Silberschatz, A. et al.(2010). Database System Concepts, McGrwaw-Hill.
41. Son, L. H. (2015). A novel kernel fuzzy clustering algorithm for geo-demographic analysis. Information Sciences: an International Journal, 317(C), 202-223.
42. Song, J., Guo, C., Wang, Z., Zhang, Y., Yu, G., & Pierson, J. M. (2015). HaoLap: a Hadoop based OLAP system for Big Data. Journal of Systems and Software, 102, 167-181.
43. Vallmuur, K. (2015). Machine learning approaches to analysing textual injury surveillance data: A systematic review. Accident Analysis & Prevention, 79, 41-49.
44. Vu, H. Q., Li, G., Law, R., & Ye, B. H. (2015). Exploring the travel behaviors of inbound tourists to Hong Kong using geotagged photos. Tourism Management,46, 222-232.
45. Xu, Z., Frankwick, G. L., & Ramirez, E. (2015). Effects of Big Data analytics and traditional marketing analytics on new product success: A knowledge fusion perspective. Journal of Business Research.
46. Yates, D., & Paquette, S. (2011). Emergency knowledge management and social media technologies: A case study of the 2010 Haitian earthquake.International Journal of Information Management, 31(1), 6-13.
47. Yuan, Y., Wu, Y., Feng, X., Li, J., Yang, G., & Zheng, W. (2010). VDB-MR: MapReduce-based distributed data integration using virtual database. Future Generation Computer Systems, 26(8), 1418-1425.
48. Zhang, L., Price, R., Aweeka, F., Bellibas, S. E., & Sheiner, L. B. (2001). Making the most of sparse clinical data by using a predictive-model-based analysis, illustrated with a stavudine pharmacokinetic study. European journal of pharmaceutical sciences, 12(4), 377-385.
49. Zhang, X., Wang, W., de Pablos, P. O., Tang, J., & Yan, X. (2015). Mapping

development of social media research through different disciplines: Collaborative learning in management and computer science. Computers in Human Behavior.

50. Zikopoulos, P., & Eaton, C. (2012). Understanding Big Data: Analytics for enterprise class hadoop and streaming data. McGraw-Hill Osborne Media.

INDEX